THE DISAPPEARED

THE DISAPPEARED

**The stories of 35 historical disappearances
from the *Mary Celeste* to Jimmy Hoffa**

Ian Crofton

Quercus

CONTENTS

INTRODUCTION

They are all gone into the world of light,
And I alone sit lingering here.
Henry Vaughan (1622–95)

Like tens of thousands of others, I was entranced as a child by Rosemary Sutcliff's historical novel, *The Eagle of the Ninth*. This told the story of the Legio IX Hispana – the Ninth Legion – which in AD 117 ventured north of Hadrian's Wall to pacify the wild tribes of Caledonia, never to be seen again. Disappointingly, although the Ninth Legion did drop out of the historical record some time in the 2nd century AD, scholars have now found references to it that post-date the Caledonian expedition. Historians don't know whether the legion was disbanded or destroyed – and if it was destroyed, they can only speculate where and when: perhaps in the Hebrew revolt of the 130s, or during the upheavals on the Danube three decades later.

Whatever the fate of the Ninth, whole armies *have* disappeared. Herodotus tells us that an army of the Persian Emperor Cambyses was buried by a sandstorm in Egypt; some historians have doubted whether this could really have happened – but clearly something out of the ordinary occurred two and half millennia ago in the Western Desert. Herodotus is our only source for this story, but there are many contemporary or near-contemporary accounts that attest to the annihilation of three Roman legions in the Teutoburger Forest of northwest Germany, over a century before the Ninth left the safety of Hadrian's Wall for the wilderness to the north. Since then, there have been other stories of mass disappearances in war – such as the 'Vanished Battalion' of the Norfolk Regiment, said to have been absorbed by a strange, luminous cloud at Gallipoli in 1915. This turned out to have been a tall tale, woven many years later; the men had indeed 'disappeared', but rather than being swept up heavenward, they had penetrated beyond the Turkish front line, where they had all been wiped out: a bloody but prosaic end.

Although in this book I deal with events that have some degree of mystery about them, I have eschewed the credulous speculations of pseudo-history and pseudo-science: hence no Atlantis, no Philadelphia Experiment, no Bermuda Triangle, no alien abductions – and no 'Vanished Battalion'. Similarly, with the exception of Lord Lucan and Jimmy Hoffa, I have steered clear of the sordid, sad little 'true crime' tales so beloved of the tabloid press. Not that the book avoids 'murder most foul', from the Princes in the Tower and Count Königsmarck (the man who slept with the wife of the future King George I) to the victims of Hitler, Stalin and Argentina's Dirty War; not to mention those blown to oblivion in the killing fields of Flanders. These last must stand for all those hundreds of thousands declared 'missing in action' in the wars of the last hundred years.

Some of the disappeared are more heroes than victims – albeit, in some cases, heroes with feet of clay. Generations have been thrilled by the stories of explorers who went into the unknown and were never seen again: John Cabot, who sailed towards the setting sun; Sir John Franklin, dead in the Arctic ice; Ludwig Leichhardt, consumed by the burning interior of Australia; Mallory and Irvine, lost 'between heaven and earth' near the summit of Everest; and Colonel Fawcett, who disappeared – perhaps deliberately? – into the jungles of Amazonia. Then there is that gallant trio of pioneer fliers, Amelia Earhart, Amy Johnson and Antoine de Saint-Exupéry, who perished doing what they loved, but whose bodies have never been found.

In many of the above cases the probable fate of the disappeared is reasonably clear. Other cases remain puzzling – although possible explanations abound. What happened to the Lost Colony of Roanoke Island, to the British diplomat Benjamin Bathurst, to the crew of the *Mary Celeste*, to the lighthouse keepers of the Flannan Isles, to the eponymous inventor of the diesel engine, who disappeared in the night from a cross-Channel ferry? The one thing we can be sure of is that we will never be sure.

Around all these men and women mythologies have arisen. Perhaps it is human nature to feel unsatisfied if the story of one's hero or heroine has an unexplained or unglamorous ending. No one likes an unfinished life; it must be enlarged, rounded out, connected to the sweep of history rather than accident or human error. The closer one gets to the present, it seems, the more a cloud of conspiracy theories and dubious sightings obscures whatever the truth might be. The case of Amelia Earhart offers a paradigm in this regard. Those who want a 'finished' life tend to find what they are looking for.

There is no doubt that nothing enlarges a man's or a woman's reputation more than a mystery concerning their fate. Many have suggested that Agatha Christie, with book sales in mind, engineered her own temporary disappearance for this very reason. If Raoul Wallenberg had avoided the black hole of the Gulag he might very well have resumed the disappointing, embittered life of a none-too-successful businessman – the postwar fate of Oskar Schindler, another man who risked everything to save his fellow human beings, but who, instead of disappearing, had to get on with the dreariness of everyday life in an unheroic world.

But those who have disappeared – whatever their fate, however horrid their end – they are all in some way transfigured in our imaginations by the mystery of their absence. In many cases, it is this very circumstance that has lent them fame. And now, in Vaughan's words, 'They are all gone into the world of light.'

Ian Crofton
London 2008

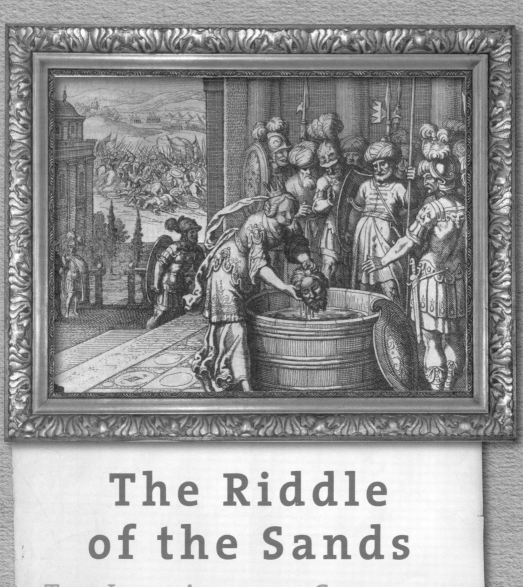

The Riddle of the Sands

THE LOST ARMY OF CAMBYSES

(523 BC)

'As they were at their midday meal, a wind arose from the south, strong and deadly, bringing with it vast columns of whirling sand, which entirely covered up the troops and caused them wholly to disappear …' These few words, from the ancient Greek historian Herodotus, are all we know of the Persian army supposedly overwhelmed two and a half millennia ago by a sandstorm in Egypt's Western Desert, never to be seen again.

The 50,000-strong army of the Emperor Cambyses had been on its way to the Siwa Oasis, an island of greenery, shade and fresh water between the Qattara Depression and the Great Sand Sea, in the midst of the inferno of the Western Desert. Nearly 2500 years later, on 13 September 1940, Major Ralph Bagnold of the British army established the first operational base of the Long Range Desert Group at Siwa. That same day Italian forces began their invasion of Egypt from Libya.

Bagnold had brought his men and trucks 150 miles across the Sand Sea, hitherto supposed impassable. 'We could not travel at midday at all but lay under our trucks and gasped,' he wrote. At night the men froze in temperatures below zero. Bagnold was not unused to such conditions, having explored the Western Desert in the 1930s, but … 'Never in our peacetime travels had we imagined that war could ever reach the enormous empty solitudes of the inner desert, walled off by sheer distance, lack of water and impassable seas of sand dunes.' And then, of course, there were what the Egyptians call ghiblis – the sandstorms that could blow up out of nowhere, turning day to night …

VAUNTING AMBITION

In 525 BC the Persian emperor Cambyses II, son of Cyrus the Great, conqueror of Media, Lydia, Ionia, Babylonia, Syria and Palestine, sought to extend his father's empire by leading a mighty army into Egypt. Cyrus himself had cherished this ambition, but died in 529 before he could achieve it. It was said that Cambyses invaded Egypt to pay back a slight: he had requested a daughter of Pharaoh Amasis (Ahmose II) to take as a wife, and was displeased when he was palmed off with a lady of lower status. Another tale tells how he had, as a boy, sworn to his mother that he would ravage Egypt in revenge for some insult that had been offered to her honour. These accounts, and much else of what has come down to us about Cambyses, are from Herodotus, who, as a Greek, had no love for the Persians, and portrayed their rulers – Cambyses in particular – as cruel and debauched tyrants.

Cambyses, before entering Egypt, had laid his plans carefully, first making an alliance with the Arab chieftains of the desert that lay between Palestine and the Nile. In accordance with this treaty, the Arabs kept his men supplied with water as they crossed the arid wastes of Sinai.

Reaching the city of Pelusium at the eastern edge of the Nile Delta, the Persians dealt a decisive blow against Psamtek III, son of the late Pharaoh Amasis. Psamtek had been counting on the support of his Greek mercenary allies under Phanes of Halicarnassus, but the mercenaries changed sides at the last moment.

THE COST OF HUBRIS

After Pelusium, Egypt was in Cambyses' hands. He took the name Mesuti-Ra, thus presenting himself as the offspring of Ra, the Egyptian sun god and lord of creation. Psamtek was captured and dispatched in chains back to Susa, the Persian capital. According to Herodotus, it was at this point that things began to go wrong for Cambyses – apparently as a consequence of the outrages and sacrileges he perpetrated in Egypt. He not only desecrated the mummy of the dead pharaoh, Amasis, but, in a jealous rage, drew his dagger and stabbed the Apis bull, a reincarnation of the god Osiris much revered by the Egyptians. (They believed the Apis bull to be born of a virgin mother who bears no other calf, receiving the bull-god Apis through a flash of lightning from heaven.) Shortly after, the bull-calf died of its wound, and was buried with due ceremonial in the vaults of the Serapeum at Sakkara.

On the Frailty of Persian Skulls

When the Greek historian Herodotus visited the site of the Battle of Pelusium a century later, he found the remains of the dead still scattered about, the bones bleached in the sun. He noted that if one threw a pebble at a Persian skull it would make a hole, whereas the Egyptian skulls remained intact, even if one struck them with a rock. He suggested that this difference might arise from the Egyptian practice of shaving the head from infancy, whereas the Persians swaddled the heads of their babes in folds of cloth.

After this abomination, says Herodotus (although the chronology is not absolutely clear), Cambyses was punished with madness and ill fortune, killing his brother and sister and leading a disastrous military expedition up the Nile to Ethiopia. But his poorly supplied army ran out of food in the Nubian Desert, the men being obliged to feed on the flesh of their dead companions. In the end they were forced to turn back, humiliated.

But a worse fate was to befall the army Cambyses sent in 523 to the Siwa Oasis, site of the Oracle of Amun. Herodotus says Cambyses believed the priests of the Oracle were inciting resistance to his rule. They certainly appear to have played an influential role in recognizing the legitimacy of the rulers of Egypt: two centuries later Alexander the Great was to make a similar journey to Siwa, following a flock of birds across the desert, to gain the blessing of the priests.

INTO THE INFERNO

The Siwa Oasis lies 350 miles from Cairo, in the heart of the Western Desert – a vast, lifeless area of sand and rock that stretches from Libya eastward to the Nile. It is one of the hottest places on earth – the highest temperature ever recorded, 136 °F (57 °C), occurred at Al' Aziziyah, Libya, in 1922. According to the Greeks, it was in the Western Desert that snake-headed Medusa turned men to stone, until the hero Perseus slew her with a curved sword forged from adamantine. It is said the drops of blood from her severed head grew into serpents – with which Libya now abounds.

The full account in Book III of Herodotus' *Histories* of the disappearance of the Persian army goes as follows:

The men sent to attack the Ammonians [the inhabitants of Siwa] started from Thebes, having guides with them, and may be clearly traced as far as the city Oasis [Kharga Oasis], which is inhabited by Samians, said to be of the tribe Aeschrionia. The place is distant from Thebes seven days' journey across the sand, and is called in our tongue 'the Island of the Blessed'. Thus far the army is known to have made its way; but thenceforth nothing is to be heard of them, except what the Ammonians, and those who get their knowledge from them, report. It is certain they neither reached the Ammonians, nor even came back to Egypt. Further than this, the Ammonians relate as follows:– That the Persians set forth from Oasis across the sand, and had reached about half way between that place and themselves when, as they were at their midday meal, a wind arose from the south, strong and deadly, bringing with it vast columns of whirling sand, which entirely covered up the troops and caused them wholly to disappear. Thus, according to the Ammonians, did it fare with this army.

(FROM THE 1858–60 TRANSLATION BY GEORGE RAWLINSON)

For Herodotus, such an eventuality would have had a certain poetic justice – never mind if it were true or not.

Would it be possible for such a large army to be wiped out in this way? Egyptologists have generally been sceptical about the whole story. There may not have been as many as 50,000 men involved – sizes of armies involved in battles were regularly exaggerated by chroniclers up until the early modern period. But, even so, it seems incredible that an army of at least several thousand men could be wiped out by a sandstorm. Or is it so unbelievable?

THE SKY IS SHUT OUT

The great Egyptian explorer of the 1920s, Ahmed Hassanein, who made the first crossing of the Western Desert from north to south, left a vivid description of a sandstorm:

> *It is as though the surface were underlaid with steam-pipes, with thousands of orifices through which tiny jets of steam are puffing out. The sand leaps in little spurts and whirls. Inch by inch the disturbance rises as the wind increases its force. It seems as though the whole surface of the desert were rising in obedience to some upthrusting force beneath. Larger pebbles strike against the shins, the knees, the thighs. The sand-grains climb the body till it strikes the face and goes over the head. The sky is shut out, all but the nearest objects fade from view, the universe is filled.*

Such storms can last hours, even days. Armies advancing or retreating across the Western Desert during the Second World War, seeing a dark wall of windblown sand approaching from the horizon, were brought to a standstill. Fighting was abandoned, and men took what shelter they could. As the storm overwhelmed the columns, visibility was reduced to zero, and soldiers found their noses and ears and eyes and mouths – and even more intimate orifices – uncomfortably stuffed with sand. These armies were prepared for such conditions, and could sit out a storm without running out of food or water. But the Persian army heading for Siwa, if it was as ill-equipped as the one Cambyses sent into Nubia, and if it was without guides who knew the terrain, might well have become hopelessly lost in such a storm. Without adequate water supplies, they could easily have perished of thirst, until the sands covered all traces of their passing.

It seems as though the whole surface of the desert were rising ...

AHMED HASSANEIN, EXPLORER OF THE WESTERN DESERT IN THE 1920s, DESCRIBES A SANDSTORM

Since 1792, when William George Brown became the first European to reach Siwa since ancient times, various fruitless attempts have been made to find evidence of the lost army in the vast ocean of sand. Certainly bones and rusted weaponry have turned up, but these have proved to be relics of the fighting in 1941–3 between the British Eighth Army and Rommel's Afrika Korps.

In the year 2000, a team of geologists from Cairo's Helwan University prospecting for petroleum just 30 miles from Siwa found themselves walking through sand dunes scattered with arrow heads, daggers, fragments of cloth – and bones bleached white in the sun. Archaeologists have yet to examine the site in detail, so it not known whether Cambyses' lost army has at last been found.

THE END OF CAMBYSES

As for Cambyses, the ill fortune he brought upon himself by his sacrileges continued. Hearing of the disasters in Egypt, a group of nobles back in Persia mounted an insurrection in favour of Cambyses' younger brother, Bardiya. Hearing of the revolt Cambyses hurried back home. But as he leapt on his horse in the Syrian town of Ecbatana he accidentally stabbed himself in the thigh with his own dagger – supposedly in the same place that he had fatally wounded the Apis bull.

After the accident Cambyses recalled an old prophecy that he would die in Ecbatana. He had assumed the prophecy referred to the Persian Ecbatana, the summer capital, and that he would die peacefully in old age. But, plunged into despair as he was by his misfortunes, he was now convinced that it was in the Syrian Ecbatana that he was prophesied to die. So, as the wound became gangrenous and his blood gradually filled with poison, he simply lay down and awaited his end.

Give Me Back My Legions

Disaster in the Teutoburger Wald

(AD 9)

In AD 9, in the reign of Augustus Caesar, three Roman legions and their camp followers – perhaps as many as 20,000 men, women and children – marched into the dark swampy forests of the Teutoburger Wald in northwest Germany, under the command of Publius Quintilius Varus. Very few of them were ever seen alive again, and those who did escape told of a terrible slaughter at the hands of the Germanic tribes, whom the Romans had believed they had pacified. It was one of the gravest and most humiliating defeats in Roman history.

A few years later, in AD 15, Germanicus, the nephew of the Emperor Tiberius, led a large army into Germany, intent on re-establishing Roman domination. During the course of the campaign, the army entered the Teutoburger Wald to see what trace they could find of the missing legions. The Roman historian Tacitus, writing many decades after the event, describes the scene of horror that met their eyes:

> *In the centre of the field were the whitening bones of men, as they had fled, or stood their ground, strewn everywhere or piled in heaps. Near, lay fragments of weapons and limbs of horses, and also human heads, prominently nailed to trunks of trees. In the adjacent groves were the barbarous altars, on which they had immolated tribunes and first-rank centurions.*

Tacitus tells us that the Roman legionaries, 'in grief and anger, began to bury the bones of the three legions, not a soldier knowing whether he was interring the relics of a relative or a stranger, but looking on all as kinsfolk and of their own blood'.

THE ROMANS IN GERMANY

Sixty years previously, Julius Caesar had completed the conquest of Gaul – what is now modern France. Since then, Gaul had become peaceful, Romanized and wealthy – a tempting target for the wandering, warlike Germanic tribes who dwelt to the east, between the Rhine and the Danube. These two rivers then formed the frontiers of the Roman Empire in mainland Europe. But around 15 BC the Emperor Augustus decided that for the security of the *pax romana*, he must pacify the Germanic tribes and create a new frontier at the River Elbe, far to the east.

Near, lay fragments of weapons and limbs of horses, and also human heads, prominently nailed to trunks of trees.

TACITUS DESCRIBES THE DISCOVERY OF THE REMAINS OF THE LOST LEGIONS.

To this end, Roman armies campaigned in Germany for twenty years, gradually gaining ground. 'The barbarians,' wrote the historian Dio Cassius some two centuries later, 'were adapting themselves to Roman ways, were becoming accustomed to hold markets, and were meeting in peaceful assemblages. They had not, however, forgotten their ancestral habits, their native manners, their old life of independence, or the power derived from arms.'

In AD 6 Augustus appointed a new commander in Germany, Publius Quintilius Varus. It seems that it was to his kinship to Augustus rather than to his military capabilities that Varus owed his new position. Another Roman historian, Marcus Velleius Paterculus, writing around AD 30, has this to say about the man:

Varus Quintilius, descended from a famous rather than a high-born family, was a man of mild character and of a quiet disposition, somewhat slow in mind as he was in body, and more accustomed to the leisure of the camp than to actual service in war. That he was no despiser of money is demonstrated by his governorship of Syria: he entered the rich province a poor man, but left it a rich man and the province poor. When placed in charge of the army in Germany, he entertained the notion that the Germans were a people who were men only in limbs and voice, and that they, who could not be subdued by the sword, could be soothed by the law. With this purpose in mind he entered the heart of Germany as though he were going among a people enjoying the blessings of peace, and sitting on his tribunal he wasted the time of a summer campaign in holding court and observing the proper details of legal procedure.

It seems Varus was overly complacent, ratcheting up the taxes levied on the tribespeople and, according to Dio Cassius, 'issuing orders to them as if they were actually slaves of the Romans', while at the same time failing to keep the legions under his command in constant readiness for action. Paterculus says that Varus 'came to look upon himself as a city praetor administering justice in the forum, and not a general in command of an army in the heart of Germany'.

THE REVOLT OF ARMINIUS

The German tribes were by no means pacified, and in the person of Arminius, the son of the chief of the Cherusci, they found someone around whom they could rally. Paterculus describes Arminius – who had served in the Roman army, and achieved equestrian rank as a Roman citizen – as being 'of noble birth, brave in action and alert in mind, possessing an intelligence quite beyond the ordinary barbarian'. Arminius, according to Paterculus, 'made use of the negligence of the general as an opportunity for treachery, sagaciously seeing that no one could be more quickly overpowered than the man who feared nothing, and that the most common beginning of disaster was a sense of security'.

It appears that Arminius also had a personal motive: he had wanted to marry the daughter of his uncle Segestes, one of Varus's favourites, but had been refused, and the couple had eloped instead – although Tacitus maintains that Arminius, whom he regards as guilty of treachery, had abducted the young woman.

Arminius set his trap. He fabricated reports of a minor revolt, and, even though Segestes warned Varus what was afoot, the Roman commander set off with three legions – the XVII, XVIII and XIX – to restore order. Arminius, still pretending loyalty to Rome, offered to guide Varus and his legions through the unfamiliar, though supposedly friendly, territory of his own tribe, the Cherusci.

He entertained the notion that the Germans ... who could not be subdued by the sword, could be soothed by the law.

MARCUS VELLEIUS PATERCULUS ON THE ROMAN COMMANDER IN GERMANY, PUBLIUS QUINTILIUS VARUS; *ROMAN HISTORY* (C.AD 30), BOOK II

ANNIHILATION IN THE FOREST

The Teutoburger Wald is a region of hills between the modern cities of Detmold and Osnabrück , and the area is still thickly forested. When Varus and his legions entered it, it was early autumn. Not expecting trouble, the Romans were not marching in combat formation, and did not send scouts ahead of the main column – which stretched perhaps nine miles along the narrow, muddy forest tracks. In these conditions, when the column was hit by ambushes at various points, it was impossible for the Romans to deploy their superior tactics. Heavy rain and strong winds only made things worse. By this time, Arminius had already faded away to lead the rebels. Intermittent fighting went on for two or three days, as the Romans tried to break away from their attackers – but in vain. They eventually found themselves trapped at the foot of a hill called the Kalkriese, and here the Germanic tribesmen moved in for the final slaughter. Varus and other senior officers did what the Romans considered the honourable thing in the face of defeat: they fell on their swords. Most of the other Roman soldiers were killed or, according to Tacitus, sacrificed in pagan ceremonies – though a few were ransomed, and some were taken as slaves.

Paterculus records the shock of a disciplined Roman army being overwhelmed by barbarians:

> *An army unexcelled in bravery, the first of Roman armies in discipline, in energy, and in experience in the field, through the negligence of its general, the perfidy of the enemy, and the unkindness of fortune was surrounded, nor was as much opportunity as they had wished given to the soldiers either of fighting or of extricating themselves, except against heavy odds … Hemmed in by forests and marshes and ambuscades, it was exterminated almost to a man by the very enemy whom it had always slaughtered like cattle, whose life or death had depended solely upon the wrath or the pity of the Romans.*

When news filtered back to Rome, Augustus feared that panic might break out, and put in hand various emergency measures to keep order both in Rome and around the empire. The emperor himself, according to Suetonius in his *Lives of the Twelve Caesars*, 'was so greatly affected that for several months in succession he cut neither his beard nor his hair, and sometimes he would dash his head against a door, crying: "Quintilius Varus, give me back my legions!"' It was a devastating humiliation for Roman arms – and no legions were ever again given the fateful numbers XVII, XVIII or XIX.

The *Hermannsschlacht*

It was Martin Luther in the 16th century who first called Arminius 'Hermann', emphasizing his German identity, and since then the Battle of the Teutoburger Wald has often been referred to in Germany as the *Hermannsschlacht* ('Hermann's battle'). Hermann's role as a German national hero was given a great boost in 1808 by Heinrich von Kleist's play *Die Hermannschlacht*, written when Napoleon was attempting to impose French domination in Germany. Initially, in the post-Napoleonic era, Hermann was the hero of German liberals, who called for unity and freedom for the then fragmented country. In 1838 they began to construct a massive statue to Hermann in the Teutoburger Wald, but ran out of funds, and it was not until after Germany had been united under the conservative regime of Bismarck and Kaiser Wilhelm I in 1871 that money became available to complete the monument, which came to represent their brand of right-wing, militaristic nationalism. The monument stands over 170 feet high, and on the sword that Hermann holds aloft is the following inscription:

Deutschlands Einigkeit meine Stärke – meine Stärke Deutschlands Macht.

('Germany's unity my strength – my strength Germany's might.')

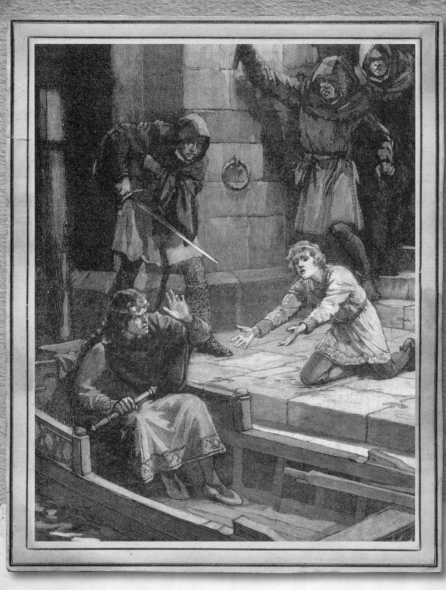

The Prisoner of Rouen

Arthur, Duke of Brittany

(1203)

King John was not a good man,
He had his little ways,
And sometimes no one spoke to him
For days and days and days.

These lines from A.A. Milne encapsulate the received view of the medieval English monarch, the wicked man who tried to usurp his heroic brother Richard the Lionheart, the king who imposed oppressive taxes on his subjects, and lost great territories in France. Above all, John was the man said to have been responsible for the disappearance and presumed murder of his nephew, the young Prince Arthur.

Arthur was born in the city of Nantes, on the River Loire, on 29 March 1187. His father, Geoffrey, Duke of Brittany, had died in August of the previous year. Geoffrey was the third of King Henry II's four legitimate sons, the others being Henry (who died before his father), Richard and John. At this time the kings of England – descended as they were from Duke William of Normandy, better known as William the Conqueror – held vast lands in France. Henry II had acquired even more territory in France by his marriage to Eleanor of Aquitaine, and found himself ruling more of the country than the French king.

The foul corruption of a sweet child's death.

THE EARL OF SALISBURY REACTS TO THE NEWS OF
ARTHUR'S DEMISE IN SHAKESPEARE'S *KING JOHN*, IV.II

Henry and Eleanor's sons were often at daggers drawn, both between themselves and with their father. When Richard succeeded Henry to the throne of England in 1189, John and he patched up their quarrel, but their amity was short lived. The following year, when Richard was away on Crusade, he nominated the infant Arthur as his heir. John was incensed. He returned to England, breaking an oath he had made to Richard that he would not do so while Richard was abroad, and set about trying to seize the throne. His plans came to nothing when Richard returned in 1194. In that same year Arthur's mother Constance had her son proclaimed Duke of Brittany, in a bid to establish greater independence for her fiefdom. Arthur was only seven years old.

A PAWN IN THE GAME OF PRINCES

By the time of his death in 1199, Richard seems to have forgiven his younger brother, as he named him as his heir and successor. But the French nobility refused to recognize John as their overlord, preferring young Arthur. Eventually, in 1200, an agreement was reached whereby John recognized the French king, Philip Augustus, as overlord in his French territories, while Arthur in turn acknowledged John as his overlord.

This arrangement did not last. John's second marriage, to the heiress of Angoulême, angered one of his vassals, Hugh de Lusignan, to whom she had been betrothed. Hugh and his followers came out in rebellion, and appealed to King Philip. After John failed to appear at the French court to account for his actions, Philip declared all his lands in France forfeit, giving Normandy and Anjou to Arthur.

John was now at war with Philip and Arthur. John captured the latter – no more than a pawn in this game of princes – at the siege of Mirabeau in August 1202. At first Arthur was imprisoned at Falaise Castle under the custody of Hubert de Burgh. Early in the following year he was transferred to the castle at Rouen, where he was held by William de Braose. After April 1203, no more was heard of him.

SHAKESPEARE'S VERSION

William Shakespeare, in his play *King John*, has John giving Hubert de Burgh a heavy hint as to what he should do with his young charge:

> **King John**: *Good Hubert, Hubert, Hubert, throw thine eye*
> *On yon young boy: I'll tell thee what, my friend,*
> *He is a very serpent in my way;*
> *And whereso'er this foot of mine doth tread,*
> *He lies before me: dost thou understand me?*
> *Thou art his keeper …*
> **Hubert**: *And I'll keep him so,*
> *That he shall not offend your majesty.*
> **King John**: *Death.*
> **Hubert**: *My lord?*
> **King John**: *A grave.*
> **Hubert**: *He shall not live.*
> **King John**: *Enough.*
> *I could be merry now. Hubert, I love thee;*
> *Well, I'll not say what I intend for thee …*

Hubert subsequently receives orders to kill the young prince by burning out both his eyes with hot irons, but is overcome with pity and promises to spare the lad, sending him secretly to England. Hubert informs John that Arthur is dead, and it is given out that he has died of natural causes – though no one believes this. John's conscience is pricked (partly because his barons are incensed at the news), but the king blames Hubert's 'abhorr'd aspect' for putting the idea into his head. At this point Hubert confesses that Arthur is still alive. Immediately afterwards we see Arthur attempting to escape by jumping off a castle wall, but the leap proves fatal.

> *The wall is high, and yet will I leap down:*
> *Good ground, be pitiful and hurt me not!*
> *There's few or none do know me: if they did,*
> *This ship-boy's semblance hath disguised me quite.*
> *I am afraid; and yet I'll venture it.*
> *If I get down, and do not break my limbs,*
> *I'll find a thousand shifts to get away:*
> *As good to die and go, as die and stay.* [Leaps down]
> *O me! My uncle's spirit is in these stones.*
> *Heaven take my soul, and England keep my bones.* [Dies]

Shakespeare's account of Arthur's death is, of course, complete fiction.

THE MANY FATES OF THE BOY-PRINCE

It is possible that Hubert de Burgh did have some knowledge of Arthur's death, as he later stated that Arthur had been castrated while in his custody by John's agents, and had died of shock. However, he later withdrew this claim.

The unknown Welsh monk who wrote the *Margam Annals* in the early 13th century describes Arthur's death thus:

> *After King John had captured Arthur and kept him alive in prison for some time, at length, in the castle of Rouen, after dinner on the Thursday before Easter, when he was drunk and possessed by the devil, he slew him with his own hand, and tying a heavy stone to the body cast it into the Seine. It was discovered by a fisherman in his net, and being dragged to the bank and recognized, was taken for secret burial, in fear of the tyrant, to the priory of Bec called Notre Dame de Pres.*

It is unlikely that John personally slew the young prince, but it *is* likely that he was responsible. Arthur's jailer at Rouen, William de Braose, was awarded new titles and lands in the Welsh Marches shortly after Arthur's disappearance, and his wife Matilda later directly accused King John of the crime. For her pains, she and her son were imprisoned in Windsor Castle, where they were starved to death. De Braose managed to escape to France.

Foul as it is, Hell is defiled by the fouler presence of John.

MATTHEW PARIS (*c.*1200–59)

As for John, his crime did him little good. By 1204 he had lost both Anjou and Normandy, the best part of his French lands, and his lack of military prowess had earned him the disparaging nickname 'Softsword'. Posterity has not judged him kindly. The chronicler Matthew Paris (*c.*1200–59), for example, was of the opinion that 'Foul as it is, Hell is defiled by the fouler presence of John.' John's reputation as England's wickedest king (on a par with Richard III, also blamed for the death of young princes) went unmodified for centuries – as can be seen from the following judgement in John Richard Green's *Short History of the English People* (1890), damning John as the damnedest of his dynasty:

> *In his inner soul John was the worst outcome of the Angevins. He united into one mass of wickedness, their insolence, their selfishness, their unbridled lust, their cruelty and tyranny, their shamelessness, their superstition, their cynical indifference to honour or truth.*

Today, historians are kinder to King John, praising his skills as an administrator and diplomat, and pointing out that his reign gave birth to that great charter of liberties, the Magna Carta. But the death of Prince Arthur still remains a terrible and ineradicable blemish on his name.

When the Waters Failed to Part

The Children's Crusade

(1212)

In 1095 Pope Urban II preached a sermon that changed the course of history. Speaking in Clermont, France, he called on the princes of Christendom to aid the eastern emperor in his struggles against the Turks, then gnawing at the fringes of the Byzantine Empire. The response was greater than Urban could have dreamed of, for the following year the counts and dukes of France, Germany and southern Italy took up the Cross and led huge armies into Palestine. Their aim was the 'liberation' of the holy city of Jerusalem, which had been in Muslim hands since the 7th century.

The First Crusade was followed by several others, involving not only the knights and nobles of Western Europe, but also kings and even emperors. By the early 13th century, however, the Crusaders had abandoned their lofty ideals, and were almost entirely absorbed by secular politics and material interest. The armies of the Fourth Crusade of 1200–4 went nowhere near the Holy Land, and instead diverted their efforts to sack the Christian city of Constantinople, capital of the Byzantine Empire, at the urging of its trade rival, Venice.

'WHAT THEIR END WAS IS UNKNOWN'

It was in reaction to this sort of worldly cynicism that unarmed messianic movements emerged among the poor of Western Europe, intent to reclaim their place in the working out of God's purpose. In 1198 a popular ascetic and miracle-worker called Fulk of Neuilly, insisting on the virtues of poverty, summoned crowds of his followers to follow him in a pilgrimage to liberate the Holy Land. They got no further than the coast of Spain, where, according to one source, they 'perished miserably'.

The next such movement was the so-called Children's Crusade of 1212. According to the near contemporary *Chronica Regiae Coloniensis*, 'In this year there took place an extraordinary thing, a cause of much wonder, for nothing like it is known down the ages.' The chronicle continues:

> *Around the time of Easter and Pentecost, without the spur of a preacher or sermon, and prompted by who knows what spirit, many thousands of boys, ranging in age from six years to grown youths, left the ploughs or carts they were driving and the flocks they were tending, and, against the urgings of their families and friends, expressed the sudden wish to take up the Cross. Groups of twenty or fifty or a hundred raised banners and set off for Jerusalem. … Everyone thought them foolish and imprudent in their attempt. They responded that they were equal to the Divine will and that, however God wished to dispose of them, they would accept it willingly and in a spirit of humility. Thus they slowly progressed on their journey. Some stopped at Metz, others at Piacenza, while others reached as far as Rome. Still others found their way to Marseilles, but whether they crossed to the Holy Land or what their end was is unknown. One thing is certain: of the many thousands who set off, only very few returned.*

This account only gives the bare bones of what were, in fact, two separate, but similar, stories. And the 'boys' – or at least many of them – may not have been boys at all, as the Latin word *pueri* was used disparagingly by contemporaries to refer to dispossessed peasants, as well as children.

THE SHEPHERDS AND THE INNOCENTS

Because the Children's Crusade so rapidly became mythologized as an exemplar of the fate of innocence in a naughty world, it is difficult to distinguish fact from fiction in detailing the main elements of the narratives. However, it is clear that there were actually two separate movements, one beginning in France, the other in Germany, although in later versions these were conflated.

The account in the *Chronica Regiae Coloniensis* presumably refers to the German crusade. This originated in the Rhineland, and was inspired by a shepherd called Nicholas, who persuaded his several thousand followers that they – unarmed innocents, poor in material goods but strong in faith – could succeed where the armoured knights of the temporal powers had failed. Nicholas promised his band that once they reached the Mediterranean the waters would part, allowing them to march dry-shod to Jerusalem. The expedition comprised, according to the legend, both boys and girls, some from the nobility, as well as 'a number of disreputable vagabonds and prostitutes'. The pilgrims crossed the Alps, where they faced great hardships and lost many of their number. Some reached the Mediterranean at Genoa, others at Ancona, but in neither port did the promised miracle take place. Some made for home, while others moved down the coast. A few found ships to take them to Palestine, but we know nothing of their subsequent fate.

> *One thing is certain: of the many thousands who set off, only very few returned.*
> CHRONICA REGIAE COLONIENSIS (1213)

Nicholas himself, and some of his followers, ended up in Rome, where Pope Innocent III persuaded them that their piety was outweighed by their folly, and that they should return home. But only a few out of the thousands who had set out found their way back to the Rhineland. Nicholas does not seem to have been among them. Nevertheless, aggrieved parents insisted that Nicholas's father should bear the sins of the son, and he was arrested and hanged.

The same year as the Rhineland crusade, a French shepherd boy called Stephen de Cloyes claimed he had a letter from Jesus addressed to the king of France. Followed by thousands of young people – including some priests – he travelled to Saint-Denis, where the king ordered them to return to their homes. Some did, but others made their way south, to Marseille. Here again the waters failed to part, but two local merchants, Hugh the Iron and William the Pig, offered to hire ships for the pilgrims to take them to Palestine. Nothing was heard of their fate for nearly two decades.

NEWS FROM NOWHERE: THE PRIEST'S TALE

In 1230, according to one version of the story, a priest appeared in France who claimed to have been among those who had embarked with such high hopes from Marseille nearly twenty years previously. In the priest's version of events, the pilgrims never reached their intended destination. Two of the seven ships were wrecked in a storm on the island of San Pietro, off the southwest coast of Sardinia, and all aboard perished. The surviving ships were shortly thereafter intercepted by a Saracen fleet – as previously arranged by the merchants of Marseille, who had all along planned to sell the pilgrims into slavery.

The wretched innocents were taken to Bejaia (Bougie) on the Barbary Coast, in what is now Algeria, where some remained, but many were shipped on to Egypt, where the prices paid for pale-skinned slaves were higher. Most were bought by the governor, al-Adil, and worked on his estates, although some were taken on to Baghdad, where 18 were put to death for refusing to convert to Islam. The priest and a few others who could read and write were purchased by al-Kamil, son of the governor of Egypt, who wished to learn more of European languages and letters. They were kept in comfortable conditions in Cairo, until eventually al-Kamil agreed that the priest could return to France. The priest reported that some 700 of the slaves still lived in Egypt. A later version of the story provides an element of justice: some years later Hugh the Iron and William the Pig, the scheming merchants of Marseille, attempted to kidnap the Emperor Frederick and sell him to the Saracens. Luckily their plot was foiled, and they were hanged.

The Vagabond Poet

François Villon

(1463?)

François Villon was a wastrel, a drunk, a thief and a murderer. He was also the finest French poet of the Middle Ages, and his lyrics, some of the most poignant ever written, are steeped in the blood and joy and sorrow of what it means to be human. In straightforward yet highly crafted verse, Villon writes, without sentimentality or artifice, of dissipation, disillusionment, regret, suffering, the bitterness of love, and, above all, the fear of death.

Throughout his riotous life, spent in and out of prison, Villon consorted with pimps and prostitutes, rogues and renegades, boozers and bawds. He only narrowly escaped the gallows – instead, on 5 January 1463, his sentence of death was commuted to banishment from Paris. From this point we know no more of Villon, who simply slips out of history. No one knows how or where or when he died.

A RACKETY LIFE

Much of the little we know about François Villon comes from police records. He was born in 1431, when the Hundred Years' War against the English still had another twenty years to run. His home was Paris, a city he called a 'Great Carnival', but one that was then mired in filth and poverty. His real name may have been François Montcorbier or François Des Loges; the French antiquary Claude Fauchet (1530–1602) asserted that *villon* was a slang word for 'cheat' or 'rascal'. This may or may not be the case, although in *A Dictionarie of the French and English Tongue* (1611), Randle Cotgrave defines *villon* as a 'cousener, conycatcher, cunning and wittie rogue; a nimble knave; a pleasant theefe; (for such was one François Villon, whose death a halter [noose] suited to his life)'.

Villon's father died when he was young, and although his mother lived until at least 1461, he appears to have been adopted by the chaplain of Saint-Benoît-le-Bétourné in the Latin Quarter of Paris, one Guillaume de Villon, who may have been his uncle.

Villon was educated at the university in Paris, where he studied theology. He was awarded a master's degree in 1452. But his behaviour did not reflect his subject of study, and he, like many other impoverished students unattached to an ecclesiastical community or college, led a debauched, reckless, rackety life on the margins of society. It seems he was suspended at one point for his involvement in removing a piece of stonework called the *pet-au-diable* ('Devil's fart'). Subsequently he appears to have mixed with an outcast group called *les coquillards* – a desperate bunch of robbers, murderers and deserters. At some point he began to write poetry.

Nothing is heard of Villon for a few years, until, on 5 June 1455, he killed a priest. There had been a scuffle, and it was said that the priest, Philippe Sermaise, had been the first to draw his dagger in an attempt to relieve Villon of his purse. Villon, who ran through the priest with his sword, was sentenced to banishment, but he was pardoned in January 1456, when witnesses petitioning King Charles VII claimed that Sermaise had forgiven Villon before he died. Having blood on his hands, Villon was barred from academia, and turned to scraping a living by singing his ballades and chansons to lowlifes and *voyous* ('hooligans') in the inns of Paris's Latin Quarter, such as Le Grand Godet, Le Barillet and La Pomme de Pin.

It wasn't long before Villon was once again in trouble, after he and some of his criminal associates burgled the chapel of the Collège de Navarre. When his role in the crime became known to the authorities, Villon was once more forced to leave Paris. It was around this time that he wrote what he called *Le Lais* ('the legacy'), but which is now known as *Le Petit Testament*. In this poem he satirically bequeaths his few possessions to friends and acquaintances – some loose change to local money-lenders, clippings from his hair to his barber, his sword (in pawn) to the clerk of criminal justice.

OÙ SONT LES NEIGES D'ANTAN?

Over the next few years, Villon is known of in different locations – possibly Angers, certainly Blois, Bourges and Meung-sur-Loire – in and out of prison for brawling and thieving. Freed in an amnesty in 1461, Villon wrote *Le Grand Testament*, his longest and perhaps greatest work, in which he looks back regretfully over his life, a life of wasted talent and opportunities, a life marred by sickness and imprisonment, a life dissipated in taverns and brothels, with only old age and death to look forward to.

Do not harden your hearts against us …

VILLON'S APPEAL TO POSTERITY IN HIS 'BALLAD OF THE HANGED MEN'

Villon was back in Paris in 1462, where he was once more imprisoned for robbery. The following year he had his closest brush with death: following a street brawl he was sentenced to be *pendu et etranglé* ('hanged and strangled'). It was while awaiting for the sentence to be carried out that Villon wrote his *'Ballade des pendus'* ('Ballad of the Hanged Men'):

> *Frères humains qui après nous vivez,*
> *N'ayez les coeurs contre nous endurcis,*
> *Car, si pitié de nous pauvres avez,*
> *Dieu en aura plus tôt de vous mercis …*
> *Mais priez Dieu que tous nous veuille absoudre!*

> ('Brother humans who live after us,
> do not harden your hearts against us,
> for if you take pity on us poor ones,
> God will more likely show mercy to you.
> But pray God that he wishes to absolve us all.')

As it happened, when he appealed to the Parlement, they did indeed show some pity, and on 5 January 1463 commuted his sentence to ten years' banishment from Paris. That is the last we know of this tragicomic, self-destructive clown, what the French would call *un bon follastre*. Was he killed in another brawl? Did he die drunk in a piss-filled gutter, or succumb to jail fever in some foetid prison? We shall never know, nor know what works he might have produced had he lived. The wasted, wonderful, impossible life of this *poète maudit* (as Rimbaud called him) – and the transience of youth and beauty in any age – is poignantly evoked in his most famous line:

> *Mais où sont les neiges d'antan?*
> ('But where are the snows of yesteryear?')

The Princes in the Tower

King Edward V and Richard, Duke of York (1483)

The precise fate of the royal children identified as the Princes in the Tower is one of the great unknowns of English history. The mystery lies not so much in what happened to them – they were almost certainly murdered – but rather in the conundrum of who ordered their deaths. The blame is usually laid at the feet of their uncle, King Richard III – but it is by no means certain that he was the villain of the piece, and there are others who have come under suspicion.

The 15th century in England was a turbulent time, one of violent dynastic struggles known as the Wars of the Roses, from the red and white roses worn respectively by the rival houses of Lancaster and York. In 1455 Richard, Duke of York, had risen against the feeble and mentally unstable Henry VI, of the House of Lancaster. York himself was captured and executed in 1460, but his son carried on the struggle, and in 1461 was declared king as Edward IV. The Lancastrians had by no means thrown in the towel, however, and in 1470 Henry VI's supporters put him back on the throne, while Edward fled to the Low Countries. Edward's wife, Elizabeth Woodville, remained in England, seeking sanctuary from her enemies in Westminster Abbey. It was here that she was delivered of a boy-child, Edward, on 4 November 1470. On his father's restoration in June of the following year, the infant Edward was created Prince of Wales. His younger brother, Richard, born two years later, became Duke of York in 1474.

A COUP D'ÉTAT

On the night of 22/23 May 1471, the deposed Henry VI was murdered, probably on the orders of Edward IV. This put an end for the moment to the Lancastrian threat. The remaining years of Edward IV's reign saw a return of stability and prosperity, and the young Prince of Wales grew up secure in the knowledge that in due course he would succeed to the throne.

But on 9 April 1483 fate intervened: Edward IV, at the age of only 40, succumbed to pneumonia and died. Prince Edward, then aged 12, was in Ludlow, in the Welsh Marches, when he heard the news. He set out for London, accompanied by Lord Rivers, his mother's brother. On the way the party was intercepted by his uncle, Richard, Duke of Gloucester, whom the dying Edward IV had appointed as protector of his young heir. Richard accused Rivers and others in the Woodville clan of trying to usurp his position as protector, and two months later Rivers, together with Lord Hastings, Richard Grey and Thomas Vaughan, were put to death.

CONFINEMENT IN THE TOWER

Richard lodged young Edward – now notionally King Edward V, but never crowned – in the Tower of London, where he was joined in June by his younger brother, Richard of York. Meanwhile, Richard of Gloucester claimed that his late brother Edward IV had been contracted to marry Lady Eleanor Butler before he married Elizabeth Woodville, making the latter marriage invalid and the two young princes bastards. On 25 June Parliament, seeing which way the wind was blowing, endorsed Richard's claim, declaring his nephews illegitimate. This made Richard next in line to the throne, and on 6 July he was crowned king, as Richard III. The young princes were never seen in public again – and by the end of the year it was widely rumoured that they were dead.

> ### 'I do not like the Tower, of any place.'
> So says young Edward in Shakespeare's *Richard III* (III.i) when informed by his uncle, the future Richard III, that he is to reside in the Tower of London – known simply as 'the Tower'. Edward's younger brother, Richard of York, is equally filled with foreboding, complaining 'I shall not sleep in quiet at the Tower.' He is afraid of the 'angry ghost' of his uncle, the Duke of Clarence, executed in the Tower for plotting against his brother Edward IV.

These rumours had already begun to circulate in July, as recorded by Dominic Mancini, an Italian cleric who spent several months in England in 1483, possibly spying for the French. His report, *De Occupatione Regni Anglie per Riccardum Tercium* ('The occupation of the throne of England by Richard III'), discovered in the Municipal Library in Lille in 1934, includes the following account:

[Edward V] and his brother were withdrawn into the inner apartments of the Tower proper, and day by day began to be seen more rarely behind the bars and windows, till at length they ceased to appear altogether. A Strasbourg doctor, the last of his attendants whose services the King enjoyed, reported that the young King, like a victim prepared for sacrifice, sought remission of his sins by daily confession and penance, because he believed that death was facing him.

The doctor referred to was John Argentine, possibly Mancini's source, and one of the last people who had seen the princes alive. Mancini concludes: 'Whether, however, he [Edward] has been done away with, and by what manner of death, so far I have not at all discovered.' It is possible that the rumour of the princes' deaths was started by Richard's enemies, who, joined by his erstwhile ally, the Duke of Buckingham, mounted an abortive rising in October 1483. Buckingham was captured and executed.

THE TUDOR VERSION

The reign of Richard III came to an end as bloodily as it had begun. On 22 August 1485 he was cut down at the Battle of Bosworth Field, and his body 'despoiled to the skin, besprung with mire and filth'. The man who had led the rebellion against him, Henry Tudor, Duke of Richmond, took the throne as Henry VII.

History is always written by the victors, and the history written under the Tudors is no exception. Chroniclers such as Sir Thomas More and Polydore Vergil, anxious to bolster the legitimacy of the reigning dynasty, did all they could to blacken the name of the man the Tudors had overthrown. Richard III was turned into a bogeyman to scare the children, a malevolent and deformed creature steeped in blood.

A rumour was spread that the sons of K[ing] Edward had died a violent death

THE CONTEMPORARY *CROYLAND CHRONICLE* RECORDS THE COMMON SUSPICION THAT THE PRINCES HAD BEEN MURDERED

There is barely any contemporary evidence of the fate of the princes once they had entered the Tower. Yet the Tudor chroniclers had no doubt as to what had happened. Here, for example, is Polydore Vergil's account, from his *Anglica Historia*, originally commissioned by Henry VII around 1505. It is a wonderfully colourful narrative, but almost entirely based on surmise:

Richard ... lived in continual fear, for the expelling whereof by any kind of mean he determined by death to dispatch his nephews, because so long as they lived he could never be out of hazard; wherefore he sent warrant to Robert Brackenbury, lieutenant of the Tower of London, to procure their death with all diligence, by some mean convenient ... But the lieutenant of the Tower at London after he had received the king's horrible commission was astonished with the cruelty of the fact, and fearing lest if he should obey the same might at one time other turn to his own harm, did therefore defer the doing thereof ... when King Richard understood the lieutenant to make delay ... he anon committed the charge of hastening that slaughter unto another, that is to say James Tyrrell, who, being forced to do the king's commandment, rode sorrowfully to London, and, to the

> *... within a while, smothered and stifled, their breath failing, they gave up to God their innocent souls into the joys of heaven ...*
>
> SIR THOMAS MORE,
> *THE HISTORY OF RICHARD III* (WRITTEN 1513–18)

worst example that hath been almost ever heard of, murdered those babes of the issue royal. This end had Prince Edward and Richard his brother; but with what kind of death these silly [innocent] children were executed it is not certainly known.

There is no evidence of such a warrant being sent to Brackenbury, and the assertion that James Tyrrell was the hired hand who did the deed is based entirely on a confession said by the Tudor chroniclers to have been extracted from him under torture in 1502. Tyrrell – who implicated two other men, Forrest and Dighton, in the murder – was apparently unable to say where the boys he killed were buried. He was beheaded on 6 May 1502.

In his *History of King Richard III* (written 1513–18), Sir Thomas More adds more colour and detail to the scene, but without any evidential support for his vivid imaginings:

Then, all the others being removed from them, this Miles Forrest and John Dighton, about midnight ... came into the chamber and suddenly lapped them up among the clothes, so bewrapped them and entangled them, keeping down by force the feather bed and pillows hard unto their mouths, that within a while, smothered and stifled, their breath failing, they gave up to God their innocent souls into the joys of heaven, leaving to the tormentors their bodies dead in the bed ... Sir James [Tyrrell] ... caused those murderers to bury them at the stair foot, meetly deep in the ground, under a great heap of stones. Then rode Sir James in great haste to King Richard, and showed him all the manner of the murder, who give him great thanks and, as some say, there made him a knight. But he allowed not, as I have heard, the burying in so vile a corner, saying he would have them buried in a better place, because they were a King's sons. Lo the honourable courage of a King!

SHAKESPEARE SPINS THE TALE

Shakespeare's *Richard III*, written *c.*1591, follows the Tudor line and elevates the eponymous anti-hero into a combination of arch-Machiavel and the Vice figure from the old morality plays. In Shakespeare's drama Richard first attempts to persuade his ally, the Duke of Buckingham (rather than Brackenbury), to arrange the deaths of the princes. Buckingham equivocates:

Give me some little breath, some pause, dear lord,
Before I positively speak in this.

Furiously gnawing his lip, Richard turns to a page, inquiring of him:

Know'st thou not any whom corrupting gold
Will tempt unto a close exploit with death?

The page, apparently a boy with good underworld connections, suggests a 'discontented gentleman / Whose humble means match not his haughty spirit'. This is Tyrrell who turns out to be a villain with a tender heart, albeit one who sees the contract through, with the aid of two associates:

> *The tyrannous and bloody act is done,*
> *The most arch deed of piteous massacre*
> *That ever yet this land was guilty of.*
> *Dighton and Forrest, who I did suborn*
> *To do this piece of ruthless butchery,*
> *Albeit they were fleshed villains, bloody dogs,*
> *Melted with tenderness and mild compassion,*
> *Wept like to children in their deaths' sad story.*
> *'O, thus,' quoth Dighton, 'lay the gentle babes.'*
> *'Thus, thus,' quoth Forrest, 'girdling one another*
> *Within their alabaster innocent arms.*
> *Their lips were four red roses on a stalk,*
> *And in their summer beauty kissed each other.*
> *A book of prayers on their pillow lay,*
> *Which once,' quoth Forrest, 'almost changed my mind;*
> *But, O! The devil' – there the villain stopped;*
> *When Dighton thus told on – 'We smothered*
> *The most replenished sweet work of nature*
> *That from the prime creation e'er she framed.'*
> *Hence both are gone with conscience and remorse:*
> *They could not speak; and so I left them both,*
> *To bear this tidings to the bloody king.*

The 'bloody king' is pleased, adjuring Tyrrell to 'think how I may do thee good / And be inheritor of thy desire'.

ALTERNATIVE SUSPECTS

Some historians have suggested that the man responsible for the deaths of the princes was not Richard, but Henry Stafford, 2nd Duke of Buckingham. It had been Buckingham who had encouraged Richard's *coup d'état*, but Buckingham himself was of royal descent with a claim that was stronger than Henry Tudor's, on whose behalf he unsuccessfully revolted against Richard in October 1483. Buckingham might have suspected that the allegations of the princes' illegitimacy would not long hold water, so if he himself was to make a bid for the throne, he needed them dead. On the other hand he might have had them killed to please Richard when he was still loyal to him. However, if Richard knew that Buckingham was guilty, it is surprising that he did not broadcast the fact after Buckingham's beheading on 2 November.

Suspicion has also fallen on Henry Tudor, Duke of Richmond – later Henry VII. The young princes would certainly have been major obstacles in the way of his own claim, which he strengthened on 18 January 1486 by marrying the princes' elder sister, Elizabeth of York. Later that year, Henry issued not one but two pardons to Sir James Tyrrell, and it is possible that Buckingham, as he changed sides, arranged the murders on Henry's behalf. However, historians generally conclude that Henry had little opportunity to do away with the princes until after his accession in 1485 – and against this we must put the only hard evidence that survives of what might have become of the princes.

THE SKELETONS IN THE CHEST

In 1674 some workmen demolishing a staircase in the Tower of London came across a wooden chest, which, when they opened it, revealed two small skeletons. The location matched the place where Thomas More had said the two princes were originally buried, although he said they had subsequently been reburied elsewhere. It was assumed at the time that these were the mortal remains of Edward V and Richard, Duke of York, and, on the orders of King Charles II, some of the bones were gathered into an urn and buried in Westminster Abbey. Nearly three centuries later, in 1933, the remains were scientifically examined, and, although many parts of the skeletons were missing, the experts concluded from the stage of bone development and from the teeth that they belonged to two children, aged ten and twelve – the ages that the princes would have been in the autumn of 1483.

If these were indeed the remains of the princes, then the evidence of the age of the victims at the time of death seems to let Henry off the hook, and this, along with all the other circumstances, would suggest that Richard still remains the prime suspect. But if he did hope to benefit from their deaths by removing the figureheads from any possible rebellion, he badly miscalculated. The widespread belief at the time that he had had the boys put to death caused almost universal repugnance, and by the time Henry Tudor landed at Milford Haven in August 1485 with 3000 French mercenaries, Richard's support in the country had all but faded away.

On 30 October 1485 the archbishop of Canterbury placed the crown of England – which after the Battle of Bosworth Field had been found hanging in a hawthorn tree – on the head of Henry Tudor. As the contemporary *Great Chronicle of London* observed of Richard's fatal error:

Had he ... suffered the little children to have prospered according to his allegiance and fealty, he would have been honourably lauded over all, whereas now his fame is darkened.

Impersonators of the Princes

Although Thomas More in his *History of Richard III* gives a graphic description of the murder of the princes, he nevertheless admits that their 'death and final infortune hath natheless so far come in question that some yet remain in doubt whether they were in his [Richard III's] days destroyed or no'.

Rumours that the princes were still alive first emerged in 1486, providing opportunities to the enemies of Henry VII. In Oxford an unscrupulous young priest called Richard Symons fancied he saw a resemblance to the late Edward IV in one Lambert Simnel, the ten-year-old son of a joiner, and decided to pass him off as one of the princes. The following year he dropped this claim and instead put forward Simnel as the Yorkist claimant, Edward, Earl of Warwick. Simnel became the figurehead of a Yorkist rebellion against Henry VII, but the rebels were defeated and Simnel captured, subsequently being put to work in the royal kitchens.

Four years later, another impersonator emerged. This was Perkin Warbeck, a handsome youth who was groomed by Margaret of Burgundy to play the part of her nephew Richard, the younger of the Princes in the Tower. Warbeck obtained the backing of various European powers in a number of attempts to take the throne from Henry VII, but he had little support in England. He was captured in 1497, imprisoned in the Tower of London, and executed for treason in 1499 after a failed escape bid.

west coast, from where fishermen had long braved the cold, grey waters of the North Atlantic in search of cod, perhaps sailing as far as the Grand Banks – and even, some have suggested, reaching Newfoundland and Labrador. In Bristol Cabot would find men experienced in these hostile seas, and also, he hoped, merchants interested in sponsoring his expedition.

Cabot also needed royal authority. On 5 March 1496 King Henry VII of England issued letters patent authorizing Cabot and his sons to sail 'to all parts, countries and seas of the East, of the West, and of the North' and to 'discover and find whatsoever isles, countries, regions or provinces of heathens and infidels, in whatsoever part of the world they be, which before this time were unknown to all Christians'. It is clear from this that Henry did not want to tread on Spanish or Portuguese toes (in line with his generally pacific foreign policy), but that he was as eager as his Continental rivals to build up an overseas trading empire. Cabot and his heirs would hold a monopoly of trade with all new-found lands, this trade to be channelled through the port of Bristol.

ACROSS THE ATLANTIC

Cabot's first attempt to cross the Atlantic, in 1496, was short-lived. He set out from Bristol with one ship, but was forced to turn back by bad weather, lack of food and a discontented crew.

In May 1497 he set sail again, in a small ship called the *Matthew*, with a crew of 18. They first crossed to Ireland, where Dursey Head in Kerry was the last land they were to see for 35 days. On 24 June, St John's Day, they made landfall. The new land was wooded, and there were signs of habitation, but they saw no people. It may have been Newfoundland, or Labrador, or Cape Breton Island, or even Maine. Cabot raised the flags of both England and Venice, and proceeded to sail along the coastline for another 30 days, giving names to the various features he found: Cape Discovery, Island of St John, St George's Cape, the Trinity Islands, England's Cape. It is unclear whether these features belong to the Gulf of St Lawrence, Newfoundland, Labrador, Nova Scotia or even, it has been suggested, the west coast of Greenland. Some authorities believe the likeliest scenario was that Cabot made landfall in Maine or southern Nova Scotia and sailed as far as Cape Race in southeastern Newfoundland.

John Day, an English merchant in Spain, describes Cabot's first landfall, in a letter written in December 1497–January 1498 to the 'Lord Grand Admiral', presumed to be Christopher Columbus:

> *Your Lordship will know that he landed at only one spot of the mainland, near the place where land was first sighted … and they found tall trees of the kind masts are made, and other smaller trees, and the country is very rich in grass. In that particular spot, as I told your Lordship, they found a trail that went inland, they saw a site where a fire had been made, they saw manure of animals which they thought to be farm animals, and they saw a stick half a yard long pierced at both ends, carved and painted with brazil [the red dye derived from brazil wood], and by such signs they believe the land to be inhabited. Since he was with just a few people, he did not dare advance inland beyond the shooting distance of a crossbow, and after taking in fresh water he returned to his ship.*

Cabot was greeted with great enthusiasm on his return to England. He himself was convinced he had 'discovered … the country of the Grand Khan'. The land he found was rich in brazil wood and silk, and the seas abounded with codfish. Cabot himself was called 'the Great Admiral', according to Lorenzo Pasqualigo, a Venetian in England at the time, 'and vast honour is paid to him, and he goes dressed in silk, and these English run after him like mad'.

''TIS NOT TOO LATE TO SEEK A NEWER WORLD'

To those raised on the eastern shores of the Atlantic, the west, that unknown place across the sea where the sun sets, has always been a place of both mystery and promise. In the past it was believed to be the location of Hy-Brasil, the Islands of the Blest, the Happy Isles, those lands where youth and beauty endure for ever. It is into this visionary otherworld that Tennyson's Ulysses sets sail on one last voyage, beyond the Pillars of Hercules:

> *Come, my friends,*
> *'Tis not too late to seek a newer world.*
> *Push off, and sitting well in order smite*
> *The sounding furrows; for my purpose holds*
> *To sail beyond the sunset, and the baths*
> *Of all the western stars, until I die.*
> *It may be that the gulfs will wash us down:*
> *It may be that we shall touch the Happy Isles,*
> *And see the great Achilles, whom we knew.*

Whether Cabot's motives were so purely heroic is doubtful. Fame and riches might have been more what he had in mind, but any man prepared to brave the unknown, for whatever reason, has a claim on our admiration. In December 1497 Cabot explained his plans for a further voyage to the king. While the men of Bristol enthused about the rich fisheries, Cabot 'has his mind set upon even greater things,' according to Raimondo de Soncino in a letter to the Duke of Milan, 'because he proposes to keep along the coast from the place at which he touched, more and more towards the east [i.e. the Far East, to be reached by sailing westward], until he reaches an island which he calls Cipango [Japan], situated in the equinoctial region, where he believes all the spices of the world to have their origin, as well as the jewels'.

Cabot received new letters patent from the king on 3 February 1498. In early May five ships, carrying merchandise and provisioned for one year, set sail from Bristol. One was forced to turn back after being damaged in a storm. The others pressed on, determined, in the words of Tennyson's Ulysses, 'To strive, to seek, to find, and not to yield.'

Nothing more was heard of Cabot or his crew. According to the *Anglica Historia* of the Tudor historian Polydore Vergil: 'In the event he is believed to have found the new lands nowhere but on the very bottom of the ocean, to which he is thought to have descended together with his boat … since after that voyage he was never seen again anywhere.'

However, there are indirect and by no means definitive suggestions from Spanish sources around this time of an incursion into their area of influence in the Americas by English ships from the northeast. Whether Cabot's expedition fell victim to scurvy or storms or mutiny or attacks from Native Americans we shall probably never know. The ultimate fate of 'the Great Admiral' and his men is likely to remain a mystery.

Amerigo or Ameryk?

America is generally thought to have been named after the Florentine merchant adventurer Amerigo Vespucci, said to have sailed there in 1497. He didn't – although he did make subsequent voyages to the New World between 1499 and 1502. It was Martin Waldseemüller in his *Cosmographiae Introductio* (1507) who first proposed that the new continent should be 'given the name of its discoverer, Amerigo, wise man of genius'.

There is, however, an alternative (sadly less plausible) theory, which suggests that it was John Cabot who named America, after Richard Ameryk, sheriff of Bristol and one of the merchants who was said to have funded his first voyage.

The Lost Colony

The Vanished Settlers

of Roanoke Island

(1587)

In 1584 Queen Elizabeth I of England granted her dashing favourite, Sir Walter Raleigh, a patent 'for the inhabiting and planting of our people in America'. A consummate courtier, Raleigh named the land 'Virginia' in honour of Elizabeth, the Virgin Queen. The area then known as Virginia extended far beyond the present state, taking in the whole of the eastern seaboard from North Carolina to the mouth of the St Lawrence River. The intention was both to profit from the riches of the New World, and to establish a base from which English privateers could raid the great treasure fleets of Spain.

That same year, Raleigh sent out an exploratory expedition led by Phillip Amadas and Arthur Barlowe, who reported that the Outer Banks of North Carolina would provide an ideal location. The following year a fleet of seven ships commanded by Sir Richard Grenville set sail from England and established a colony at the north end of Roanoke Island. However, this was abandoned the following year. Unabashed, in 1587 Raleigh sent out another group of colonists – and it was this group of over a hundred men, women and children who established what was to become known as the Lost Colony.

JOHN WHITE, THOMAS HARRIOT AND THE *BRIEF AND TRUE REPORT*

The leader of the 1587 expedition was John White, a gentleman-artist and friend of Raleigh. White had first come into contact with the people of the New World in 1578 when Martin Frobisher returned from his quest to find the Northwest Passage – the fabled sea route that it was suspected would lead to the Pacific and the riches of Asia. Back in Bristol, White drew the two Inuit that Frobisher had brought back with him as trophies of his quest; Frobisher had also brought 1000 tons of what he believed to be gold ore, but which turned out to be worthless lumps of rock.

White made his first voyage to Virginia on the expedition of 1585–6, with a brief that one may surmise, from the results, was similar to that given to another artist in around 1582:

> Draw to life all strange birds beasts fish plants herbs trees and fruits and bring home of each sort as near you may ... Also draw the figures and shapes of men and women in their apparel as also of their manner of weapons in every place as you shall find them differing.

His beautiful drawings of the local Algonquians and their complex and sophisticated culture were included in the *Brief and True Report of the New Found Land of Virginia*, published in 1588 by the mathematician Thomas Harriot, who had accompanied White to the mainland villages of Pomeiooc, Aquascogoc and Secotan. Their intention was to put a positive spin on the wealth of the new territory, and the friendliness and civility of the people, in order to encourage future colonists.

Many that after gold and silver was not so soon found, as it was by them looked for, had little or no care of any other thing but to pamper their bellies

THOMAS HARRIOT COMPLAINS ABOUT SOME OF THE FIRST GROUP OF COLONISTS ON ROANOKE ISLAND, IN HIS *BRIEF AND TRUE REPORT OF THE NEW FOUND LAND OF VIRGINIA* (1588)

In the *Brief and True Report* Harriot hints that there were a number of malcontents on the expedition, who, on returning home, had circulated 'many envious, malicious, and slanderous reports', apparently disappointed that they had not discovered hoards of gold and silver; such persons, according to Harriot, 'had little or no care of any other thing but to pamper their bellies':

> *Of our company that returned some for their misdemeanour and ill dealing in the country, have been there worthily punished; who by reason of their bad natures, have maliciously not only spoken ill of their Governors; but for their sakes slandered the country itself … Some also were of a nice bringing up, only in cities or towns, or such as never (as I may say) had seen the world before. Because there were not to be found any English cities, nor such fair houses, nor at their own wish any of their old accustomed dainty food, nor any soft beds of down or feathers: the country was to them miserable, & their reports thereof according.*

Despite Harriot's efforts to put a gloss on the affair, the 1585–6 expedition had been fraught with difficulties. On arrival, one of the ships had hit a shoal on the Outer Banks, and most of the food supplies were spoiled. The would-be colonists burnt a village and killed its chief in retaliation for the theft of a silver cup, and encounters with the Native Americans thereafter tended to be marked by violence.

Grenville had promised to return with a relief fleet in April 1586, but it did not turn up until June. By this time, the colonists had been evacuated by Sir Francis Drake, on his way back from attacking the Spanish in the Caribbean. Fifteen men were left behind to maintain the English claim in Virginia.

THE CITY OF RALEIGH

White and Harriot's public relations exercise seems to have worked. With Raleigh's patronage, White persuaded perhaps 120 men, women and children to join him in setting up a new colony in Virginia. It was to be called the 'City of Raleigh', and White was to be the governor. They set sail in 1587.

Their first task was to pick up the 15 men left on Roanoke Island the previous year, and then the idea was to establish a colony further to the north, in the area of Chesapeake Bay. But when they landed on Roanoke on 22 July 1587, all they found was a single skeleton. The Croatans, the only local tribe still on good terms with the English, told White that the garrison had been attacked, although nine had survived and escaped by boat.

The new colonists ended up staying on Roanoke, and on 18 August White's daughter Eleanor Dare gave birth to the first English child born in the New World, a baby girl christened Virginia. White tried to re-establish friendly relations with the other tribes in the region, but to no avail, and it was not long before one of the colonists, George Howe, was found murdered in the area of Albemarle Sound. Fear seems to have overcome the colonists, and White was persuaded to return to England to fetch reinforcements and fresh supplies.

RESCUE PLANS THWARTED

It was now late in the year, the time of equinoctial storms, and White's ship struggled to make it back to England. Once there, he could find no captain prepared to brave the return journey across the Atlantic in winter. Then the war with Spain intervened, as all large seaworthy ships were commandeered to face the threat of the Spanish Armada, then being assembled in preparation for the invasion of England.

Eventually White managed to hire two smaller ships, whose captains only agreed to the voyage if they could indulge in some freelance privateering en route. This proved unsuccessful, and in fact the two ships were themselves captured and looted. Having lost the supplies intended for the colonists, White had no alternative but to return to England.

With the Spanish war continuing, it was another two years before White could mount another attempt to return to Roanoke. Eventually, in 1590, he set sail with two more privateers, the *Admiral* and the *Moonlight*. On 18 August 1590 – Virginia Dare's third birthday – he returned to the site of the settlement on Roanoke Island. Neither his granddaughter, nor his daughter, nor any of the other settlers were there.

THE GRAVEYARD OF THE ATLANTIC

White left a vivid narrative of his return to Roanoke, published by Richard Hakluyt in Book III (1600) of his *Principal Navigations, Voyages, Traffics and Discoveries of the English Nation*.

> *The 15 of August towards Evening we came to an anchor at Hatorask [Hatteras Island, just south or Roanoke Island] … in five fathom water, three leagues from the shore. At our first coming to anchor on this shore we saw a great smoke rise in the Isle Roanoak near the place where I left our Colony in the year 1587, which smoke put us in good hope that some of the Colony were there expecting my return out of England.*

White and his men had considerable difficulty in the rough seas in making a successful landfall on Roanoke – this is the area now known as the 'Graveyard of the Atlantic'. The waters being shallow, they had to row some distance in the ships' boats, and when, on 16 August, they were halfway between the ships and the coast of Hatteras Island they saw another plume of smoke, and set off in that direction. But exhaustion set in, and, having collected fresh water, they returned to the ships.

Disaster struck the next day. White set off with Captain Cooke of the *Admiral*. Their ship's boat almost sank after a large wave broke over it, half filling it with water. However, after some difficulty, they reached shore. The boat from the *Moonlight*, fared less well:

At our first coming to anchor on this shore we saw a great smoke rise in the Isle Roanoak near the place where I left our Colony in the year 1587, which smoke put us in good hope that some of the Colony were there expecting my return out of England. GOVERNOR JOHN WHITE RECALLS HIS RETURN TO ROANOKE ISLAND IN 1590. HIS HOPES WERE SOON DASHED.

Captain Spicer came to the entrance of the breach with his mast standing up, and was half passed over, but by the rash and indiscreet steerage of Ralph Skinner, his master's mate, a very dangerous Sea brake into their boat and overset them quite; the men kept the boat, some in it, and some hanging on it, but the next sea set the boat on ground, where it beat so, that some of them were forced to let go their hold, hoping to wade ashore, but the Sea still beat them down, so that they could neither stand nor swim, and the boat twice or thrice was turned the keel upward; whereon Captain Spicer and Skinner hung until they sunk, & seen no more. But four that could swim a little kept themselves in deeper water and were saved by Captain Cooke's means, who so soon as he saw their oversetting, stripped himself, and four other that could swim very well, & with all haste possible rowed unto them, & saved four. They were 11 in all, & 7 of the chiefest were drowned … This mischance did so much discomfort the sailors, that they were all of one mind not to go any further to seek the planters [settlers].

White and Captain Cooke managed to persuade the men to continue, and after they had put the boats back in order, they set off from the Hatteras shore for Roanoke. Night overtook them before they could land, but in the 'exceeding dark' …

we espied towards the North end of the Island the light of a great fire through the woods, to the which we presently rowed: when we came right over against it, we let fall our Grapnel near the shore, & sounded with a trumpet a Call, & afterwards many familiar English tunes of Songs, and called to them friendly; but we had no answer …

RETURN TO ROANOKE

After three long years, at daybreak on 18 August 1590, White set foot once more on Roanoke Island. But what he had seen the previous night seems to have been nothing but a wildfire, for they 'found the grass & sundry rotten trees burning about the place'. They then made their way round the northern point of the island.

A Favourable View

Thomas Harriot, who had been on the 1585–6 expedition to Virginia, brought back favourable reports in order to encourage future settlers from England. In the following passage from his *Brief and True Report of the New Found Land of Virginia* (1588) he considers the friendliness of the Native Americans: 'And by how much they upon due consideration shall find our manner of knowledges and crafts to exceed theirs in perfection, and speed for doing or execution, by so much the more is it probable that they should desire our friendships & love, and have the greater respect for pleasing and obeying us. Whereby may be hoped if means of good government be used, that they may in short time be brought to civility, and the embracing of true religion.'

In all this way we saw in the sand the print of the Savages' feet of 2 or 3 sorts trodden at night, and as we entered up the sandy bank upon a tree, in the very brow thereof were curiously carved these fair Roman letters C R O …

White had left instructions that if the colonists moved their settlement for any reason, they were to carve the name of the place they were going to. And if they were in distress or under attack, they were to carve a cross. White and his companions could find no cross.

And having well considered of this, we passed toward the place where they were left in sundry houses, but we found the houses taken down, and the place very strongly enclosed with a high palisado of great trees, with cortynes and flankers very Fort-like, and one of the chief trees or posts at the right side of the entrance had the bark taken off, and 5 foot from the ground in fair Capital letters was graven CROATOAN without any cross or sign of distress …

White found that three of his chests that he had buried had been dug up, and 'about the place many of my things spoiled and broken, and my books torn from the covers, the frames of some of my pictures and Maps rotten and spoiled with rain, and my armour almost eaten through with rust …' White presumed that hostile 'savages' had watched the settlers depart, and then moved in to pick up anything they judged to be of value. White continues: 'although it much grieved me to see such spoil of my goods, yet on the other side I greatly joyed that I had safely found a certain token of their safe being at Croatoan [Croatoan Island, the home of the friendly Croatan tribe]'.

AT THE MERCY OF THE ELEMENTS

In a gathering storm, White and the others only just made it back to the ships after 'much danger and labour', and as the seas and the wind rose through the night they 'doubted our Cables and Anchors would scarcely hold'. In the morning it was agreed to set sail for Croatoan, but the seas were wild and they lost all but one anchor, and only by luck avoided being grounded. They were in dire straits: 'the weather grew to be fouler and fouler; our victuals scarce, and our cask and fresh water lost'. White proposed that they sail south to the Caribbean to resupply and indulge in some profitable privateering, before returning in the spring. To White's relief, 'the captain and the whole company in the *Admiral* (with my earnest petitions) thereunto agreed'.

However, the master of the *Moonlight* 'alleged that their weak and leaky ship was not able to continue', and set sail for England. The *Admiral* set a course for Trinidad, but after two days another storm blew up, and the wind shifted to the west and northwest, blowing so strongly that they could carry no sail but the forecourse, the lowest foresail. They had no choice but to run before the wind back across the Atlantic to the Azores, where they took on fresh water and other supplies. On 23 October they sighted the island of Ushant off the coast of Brittany, and the following day, 'we came in safety, God be thanked, to an anchor in Plymouth'.

> ## A Hostile View
>
> Captain John Smith, who became head of the first permanent Virginia colony, established in 1607, had a low opinion of the Native Americans. In his *Map of Virginia with a Description of the Country, the Commodities, People, Government and Religion* (1612) he gives his views: 'They are inconstant in every thing but what fear constrains them to keep. Crafty, timorous, quick of apprehension and very ingenious. Some are of disposition fearful, some bold, most cautious, all Savage. Generally covetous of copper, beads and suchlike trash. They are soon moved to anger, and so malicious that they seldom forget an injury ...'

WHAT HAPPENED TO THE COLONISTS?

All kinds of theories have been put forward as to the fate of the Lost Colonists. Most of these involve the settlers becoming integrated into a friendly tribe – most likely the Croatans of Croatoan Island – or being enslaved by a hostile one. There is currently a DNA project underway to see whether any descendants of the Lost Colonists can be found among local Native Americans.

Chief Powhattan apparently told Captain John Smith, leader of the Jamestown colony established in Virginia in 1607, that he had massacred the Roanoke colonists because they were living with the Chesepian, a tribe he considered hostile. However, doubts have been cast on this scenario. It is also possible that the colonists perished at sea trying to get to the mainland or even return to England – White had left them a number of smaller vessels when he left them in 1587.

Archaeological excavations carried out in 1998 at the site of the Croatan capital, 50 miles from the Roanoke settlement, unearthed a gold signet ring, a flintlock musket and two farthings, all English and dating from the 16th century. The lion on the signet ring has been identified as the crest of the Kendall family: there was a 'Master Kendall' involved in the earlier, 1585–6 settlement on Roanoke Island.

Another piece of evidence came to light in 1998, which may prove critical. Climatologists and archaeologists examining tree rings from 800-year-old cypresses from the area established that the period 1587–9 was the driest in the whole sequence. Such a drought would have been devastating for the colonists, preventing them from growing crops. It is possible they simply died of starvation, having first abandoned the settlement in the hope of finding food elsewhere, or came into conflict with the local people (or between themselves) over scarce food resources, and perished as a result.

The Man Who Cuckolded King George

Count Phillip Christoph von Königsmarck

(1694)

In 1714, at the age of 54, the uninspiring Georg Ludwig, Elector of Hanover and Duke of Brunswick-Lüneburg, became King George I of Great Britain and Ireland. Dull and parochial, he was interested in little other than horseflesh, food and the female sex. He had no fondness for his new kingdom, his only claim to succeed the heirless Queen Anne being via his grandmother Elizabeth, a daughter of King James I. But he was a Protestant, unlike the four dozen Catholics with a better claim to the throne – but they had all been barred from the succession on the grounds of their religion.

When on 18 September 1714 George landed at Greenwich in a thick fog to claim his new kingdom, he brought with him a score of cooks, a washerwoman, an official mistress and three illegitimate daughters. But of the woman he had married in 1682, Sophia Dorothea of Celle, there was no sign. For the previous twenty years she had been confined to the castle at Ahlden in Lower Saxony. George had discovered her affair with a dashing young Swedish officer, Count Phillip Christoph von Königsmarck, and as a consequence divorced her, and kept her at Ahlden for the rest of her life. As for Königsmarck, no one knows quite what happened to him.

AN UNSUITABLE MATCH

Sophia Dorothea was the only child of Georg Wilhelm, Duke of Brunswick-Lüneburg, and his mistress Eleanor, Countess of Williamsburg, whom he subsequently married. Sophia Dorothea's portraits show her possessed of a prettily plump face with eyes like a heifer and skin like cream: the impression is of a young woman with an amiable disposition and not the swiftest of intellects. Sophia Dorothea was, however, passionate in nature and easily roused to anger.

As was the custom of the time, when she came of marriageable age Sophia Dorothea was touted around the courts of Europe as a prospective bride. The future King of Denmark was talked of, as was the Duke of Wolfenbüttel, to whom she was actually engaged. But then George of Hanover's mother, the formidable and cultured Electress Sophia, persuaded Sophia Dorothea's father that she should marry her son. Sophia Dorothea was told that the engagement with Wolfenbüttel was off. 'I will not marry the pig snout,' she shouted, and smashed a miniature portrait of George against the wall. When she first met the 'pig snout' (George's nickname in Hanover), she fainted.

I will not marry the pig snout!

SOPHIA DOROTHEA OF CELLE,
ON BEING TOLD SHE WAS TO MARRY
THE FUTURE GEORGE I OF ENGLAND

The ill-matched pair were married in 1682. He was 22, she just 16. It was the dowry that made the match particularly attractive to the Electress Sophia: 'One hundred thousand thalers a year is a goodly sum to pocket,' she wrote, 'without speaking of a pretty wife, who will find a match in my son George Louis, the most pigheaded, stubborn boy who ever lived, and who has round his brains such a thick crust that I defy any man or woman ever to discover what is in them.'

George liked Sophia Dorothea no more than she liked him – that is, not at all. Their mutual loathing resulted in some almighty public rows. Although he managed to father two children on his young wife, his attentions became increasingly and publicly focused on his mistress, Melusine von der Schulenburg, although he never passed up any opportunity to inflict casual cruelties on his neglected wife.

L'AFFAIRE KÖNIGSMARCK

Sophia Dorothea had first met Königsmarck in 1681, when he was 16 and she a year younger. His portrait shows a fleshy, full-lipped, somewhat sensual face and carefully coiffed head of hair. They had flirted, innocently, but nothing came of it. They met again one fateful morning in 1689 when

Karl Philipp, one of George's younger brothers (who all adored Sophia Dorothea), brought Königsmarck to see her, with the intention of cheering her up.

In those days, it was quite permissible for married aristocratic ladies to have male admirers, within formal constraints. Their husbands were more openly permitted to have mistresses, the principal one being given the rank of *maîtresse en titre*. But while husbands could father any number of bastards, their wives were expected not only to remain chaste, but to appear to remain chaste. Any suggestion that their offspring might have been fathered by another man would spell chaos to the orderly inheritance of titles, lands and property.

Königsmarck, by now a young officer in the army of Hanover, was everything that George was not, being both passionate and poetic – all in all the gallant cavalier. His lifestyle was extravagant: he kept 29 servants (when even the most important men in Hanover kept on average 20), and gambled his way into considerable debt. In 1690 he was sent away on campaign, and it was from this date that his correspondence with Sophia Dorothea begins. Their letters – written while Königsmarck was away from Hanover, attending to his military duties – make it clear that from March 1692 the affair became physical.

Both Sophia Dorothea and Königsmarck were impulsive characters, and did little to keep their affair secret. Both were warned by their friends to be more careful, but to no avail. Königsmarck was furiously jealous of George, could not bear the thought of him *montant à cheval* (to adapt Königsmarck's euphemism) with Sophia Dorothea, while agreeing it might be prudent for her to maintain conjugal relations with her husband. It seems they planned to elope together, the only barrier being a lack of cash. What they may or may or not have realized was that they were both being watched.

THINGS COME TO A HEAD

Things came to a head in the summer of 1694. On 5 July Königsmarck, then in Hanover, was due to join his regiment on the Rhine. Sophia Dorothea had been staying with her parents in Celle (as she often did, to be away from the hateful George), but in late June rushed back to Hanover and shut herself up in her rooms, pleading illness.

On the night of 1 July Königsmarck was observed to enter the Leineschloss palace and to approach Sophia Dorothea's apartments. It is uncertain whether he ever reached them. Reports circulated among the courts of Europe that he had been assassinated by four Hanoverian courtiers, and his body, weighted with stones, thrown into the River Leine – or concealed under some floorboards in the Leineschloss, or walled up in some hidden niche.

Some suggested he had been kidnapped and spirited out of the country, others that he had chosen exile over death. Eleonore von dem Knesebeck, one of Sophia Dorothea's ladies-in-waiting who was imprisoned in the castle at Scharzfels for 'having helped to alienate her mistress's affection from George', said after her escape that she had heard Königsmarck singing in a neighbouring cell.

Supporters of the assassination theory – which is the most likely – point out that Montalban, one of the courtiers suspected of responsibility, shortly afterwards received the massive sum of 150,000 thalers from George's father, Ernst August.

The version of the story that has George himself killing Königsmarck after catching him *in flagrante* with his wife must be discounted on the basis that George was in Berlin at the time. Another dramatic account points the finger at Klara, Countess of Platen, the official mistress of Ernst August, but who also took many younger men as lovers. According to this story (probably originating with the disaffected Eleonore von dem Knesebeck), among these lovers was the young Königsmarck. La Platen, so the story continues, was so consumed by jealousy when the count left her for Sophia Dorothea that she arranged his murder. In a colourful touch, she was said to have stamped on his face as he lay dying. This is the stuff of romance, rather than history, although Countess Platen may well have been a party to Ernst August's plan to get rid of Königsmarck.

RAMIFICATIONS OF THE AFFAIR

The letters between Königsmarck and Sophia Dorothea that were intercepted or found concealed in her apartments show just how much Sophia Dorothea loathed and despised her husband. She wishes at one point for his death in battle, and elsewhere compares his performance in bed unfavourably with that of the dashing young count. Even the lumpish George must have felt the sting, and when Sophia Dorothea refused to cohabit with him, she gave him the grounds he needed for divorce.

After the divorce, which went through on 28 December 1694, Sophia Dorothea was well provided for, but restricted to the castle at Ahlen. She had not known, when agreeing to the divorce, that she was to be deprived of access to her children – a particularly vindictive cruelty on the part of George. For many years she became the focus of intrigue among the enemies of Hanover in Germany, and the opponents of Hanoverian rule in Britain – it is said she was visited by three Scottish Jacobites in 1718, presumably looking for some propaganda coup against George. But nothing appears to have come of these machinations, and the 'Princess of Ahlden' remained a prisoner – albeit surrounded by luxury and her own small court – for a total of 32 years, until her death on 13 November 1726. All her pleas for a recognition that she had been unjustly treated had fallen on deaf ears. As for her feelings for her lost lover, she does not appear to have pined for him for the rest of her days: when Königsmarck's relatives offered in 1724 to sell her back her letters to him, the high price demanded seems to have overcome any lingering sentiment on her part, and she declined the offer.

George the Turnip

In Britain King George I was personally unpopular, partly because of his unwillingness to speak English, and partly because he showed very little interest in his new kingdom, preferring to spend time in Hanover. His plan to turn over St James's Park in London – an elegant royal park open to the public – to the cultivation of root vegetables earned him the nickname 'Turnip-Hoer'.

This was not George's only association with turnips. In allusion to his wife's adultery, he himself was frequently depicted as a turnip – a symbol of cuckoldry. The Reverend William Stratford gives the following account of rustic celebrations on George's coronation day:

> Our bumpkins in the country are very waggish and very insolent. Some honest justices met to keep the Coronation day at Wattleton, and towards the evening when their worships were mellow they would have a bonfire. Some bumpkins upon this got a huge turnip and stuck three candles just over Chetwynd's house ... They came and told their worships that to honour King George's Coronation day a blazing star appeared above Mr Chetwynd's house. Their worships were wise enough to take horse and go and see this wonder, and found, to their no little disappointment, their star to end in a turnip.

Despite such taunts, George does not seem to have been unduly put out by the Königsmarck affair. According to J.H. Plumb, the great historian of the Hanoverian period, the mysterious fate of the count 'added a touch of the sinister to George's character and certainly enhanced his attraction in the eyes of many women of his Court'. George shared his life not only with 'La Schulenburg', his *maîtresse en titre* (whom he made Duchess of Kendal), but also with 'La Kielmansegge' (Sophia von Kielmansegge, Countess of Darlington), while taking his pleasure with any number of attractive young ladies – the plumper and duller the better.

Le Comte
Slips Off *La Carte*

Jean François de Galaup,
Comte de La Pérouse

(1788)

It was to be a grand voyage of exploration and scientific inquiry, a credit to the rational, humane values of the French Enlightenment. The crews aboard the frigates *Astrolabe* and *Boussole* as they sailed out of Brest on 1 August 1785 included ten men of science: an astronomer, a geologist, a botanist, a physicist, three naturalists and three illustrators. Even the two chaplains had had a scientific education. In command of the expedition was Jean François de Galaup, Comte de La Pérouse, the celebrated French naval captain. An admirer and emulator of the English explorer Captain James Cook, La Pérouse intended to sail into the Pacific to find the bits that Cook had missed.

There was one young man, a 16-year-old Corsican with an interest in mathematics and geography, whose spirits were not as high that day, his application to join the expedition having been rejected. If he had sailed with La Pérouse it is unlikely he would ever have been heard of again. As it was he abandoned the idea of a career in the navy, and took up a commission in the artillery instead. His name was Napoléon Bonaparte.

AROUND THE PACIFIC

La Pérouse was always destined for the sea, having enrolled as a cadet at the naval academy in Brest at the age of 15. Shortly afterwards he saw action against the British in the Seven Years' War. By the time France joined America in its struggle for independence from Britain, La Pérouse had achieved the rank of commodore, and in 1782 captured two British forts on the coast of Hudson Bay. He demonstrated his humanity by leaving the settlers sufficient arms and provisions to see them through the following winter. In 1783, with the advent of peace, he overcame his family's objections and married Louise-Eléonore Broudou, a creole from Mauritius.

But the sea was his real mistress, and within two years he was off on his great expedition. The *Boussole* and the *Astrolabe* entered the Pacific via Cape Horn, and by April 1786 had reached Easter Island, the easternmost outpost of Polynesia. From there they sailed northwest to Hawaii – where La Pérouse became the first European to set foot on the island of Maui – and then headed north to Alaska, with the intention of looking for the Northwest Passage. La Pérouse appears to have abandoned this project, as from Alaska he sailed down the coast of British Columbia to Monterey in California, where he expressed criticism of the Spaniards' treatment of the Native American people.

From Monterey the expedition then crossed the Pacific again, taking only 100 days to reach Macao. In 1787 La Pérouse directed his attention to the far northeastern coasts of Asia, visiting Korea and sailing through the strait between Sakhalin and Hokkaido (now called La Pérouse Strait). He found the people of Sakhalin *très sympathiques*:

French Frigate Shoals and La Pérouse Pinnacle

French Frigate Shoals lie some 600 miles to the northwest of Honolulu. The name – originally *Basse des Frégates Françaises* – was coined by La Pérouse to commemorate a narrow escape on the night of 6 November 1786. The sailors of the *Boussole* and the *Astrolabe* thought they were in clear, deep water in the middle of the Pacific Ocean. Then suddenly lookouts spotted waves breaking only 300 yards ahead. The ships were smartly turned about, and catastrophe avoided. In the morning La Pérouse returned to chart the area, and found the great rock that now bears his name: La Pérouse Pinnacle. Under the light of the moon the guano-spattered pinnacle so resembles a fully rigged sailing ship that the sight of it has lured more than one vessel to destruction on the surrounding reefs.

It went against our preconceived ideas to find among a hunting and fishing people, who neither cultivated the earth nor raised domestic animals, manners which were in general more gentle and grave – and who perhaps had greater intelligence – than that to be found in any European nation.

The expedition wintered in Kamchatka, from where La Pérouse dispatched his valuable journals back to France, and received orders to investigate the new British settlement in Australia. En route, the commander of the *Astrolabe* and 11 of his men were killed by natives in Samoa. At Botany Bay, which he reached via Tonga and Norfolk Island, La Pérouse found the British welcoming, although, desperately short of food themselves, they could not resupply him. In fact, they were in the process of abandoning Botany Bay for Port Jackson. They did, however, offer to send back his papers to France via the next British ship returning to Europe. La Pérouse set sail from Botany Bay (whose northern shore is now named after him) on 10 March 1788, having announced that he expected to be back in France by June the following year.

Any news of La Pérouse?

LOUIS XVI ASKS AFTER THE
MISSING EXPLORER PRIOR TO HIS
EXECUTION IN 1793.

THE WRECKS OF VANIKORO

June of 1789 came, and then 14 July and the storming of the Bastille, but no word came from the South Seas. It is said that Louis XVI went to the guillotine inquiring 'Any news of La Pérouse?' As the years passed and La Pérouse still did not return, the revolutionary government in France decided to send out a search expedition. On 25 September 1791 Admiral d'Entrecasteaux set sail from Brest, aiming to follow La Pérouse's intended route northeast from Australia. In May 1793 he reached the Santa Cruz Islands, between Vanuatu and the Solomons. What appeared to be smoke signals were spotted on the island of Vanikoro, but the sailors could not get ashore through the dangerous reefs.

By now, Britain and France were again at war, but as far as La Pérouse was concerned there was a truce. The initiative came from Sir Joseph Banks, who had been the expedition naturalist when Captain Cook sailed round the world in 1768–71, and who was now the highly respected president of the Royal Society. Banks secured a promise from the British government that no harm would come to La Pérouse or his small ships from any vessel of the Royal Navy. He also sought out any captain heading for the South Seas and offered them money to search for the lost Frenchman.

More years passed without news. Then in 1826 an Irish captain called Peter Dillon, visiting the island of Tikopia in the Santa Cruz group, bought some European swords from the natives, who said they had come from nearby Vanikoro, where long ago two European ships had been wrecked. The swords were later identified as belonging to La Pérouse's expedition. In 1828 the French explorer Jules Dumont d'Urville sighted wreckage on the reefs surrounding Vanikoro, and learnt from the inhabitants that some thirty sailors had been massacred by the islanders, although others, who were well armed, had managed to escape. Some time later the survivors had built a boat out of the remains of the *Astrolabe*, and had sailed off to the west. Nothing was known about their fate. Two men, a 'chief' and his servant, had remained on Vanikoro, but had died in 1823, five years before Dumont d'Urville's visit. If this was indeed La Pérouse – known for his good relations with native peoples – he had perhaps lived out his days peaceably, in something close to a tropical paradise.

One of Our Diplomats is Missing

Benjamin Bathurst

(1809)

On 25 November 1809, while travelling back to England, the British envoy to Vienna, Benjamin Bathurst, stopped to dine at a coaching inn in the German town of Perleberg. It was the height of the Napoleonic Wars, and Bathurst was in an agitated state, fearing for his life at the hands of French agents. At some point in the evening he went out to inspect his coach before continuing his journey, and was never seen again.

Immediately a number of rumours circulated: he was murdered by his valet; he had been put to death by the French in the fortress of Magdeburg; he had died when his ship went down crossing the Baltic to Sweden; in fear and desperation he had taken his own life. The British government offered a substantial reward for information, as did Bathurst's family and Prince Frederick of Prussia. The military, civil and police authorities all conducted inquiries, as did Bathurst's wife, brother-in-law and sister. But no conclusive answer was ever found.

He stood outside the inn watching his portmanteau, which had been taken within, being replaced on the carriage, stepped round to the heads of the horses – and was never seen again …

THE ACCOUNT OF BATHURST'S DISAPPEARANCE GIVEN IN *HISTORICAL ODDITIES* (1889) BY THE REVEREND SABINE BARING-GOULD – BETTER KNOWN AS THE AUTHOR OF THE HYMN 'ONWARD CHRISTIAN SOLDIERS'.

THE BATHURST CLAN

Benjamin Bathurst, born in 1784, was the scion of a notable aristocratic family. His father was Henry Bathurst (*c.*1744–1837), Bishop of Norwich, 'the only liberal bishop' in the House of Lords, and a supporter of Catholic Emancipation. The bishop, according to *The Gentleman's Magazine* in 1853, reviewing a memoir of him by his daughter, was 'the third child of a second marriage, his father having had twenty-two children by the former wife, and adding fourteen by the second'. Among Benjamin Bathurst's innumerable uncles was the politician Allen, 1st Earl Bathurst (1684–1775) – the 'Lord Bathurst' to whom the poet Alexander Pope wrote Epistle III of his *Moral Essays*. The 1st Earl's son Henry (1714–94), the 2nd Earl, was lord chancellor, and *his* son, also Henry (1762–1834), the 3rd Earl, was a prominent figure in the governments of Pitt the Younger, the Duke of Portland, Spencer Perceval, and Lord Liverpool.

After a conventional upper-class education at Winchester and Oxford, Benjamin Bathurst was eased into a diplomatic career thanks to the influence of his illustrious relative, the 3rd Earl, and in 1804 was posted in a minor capacity to the embassy in Vienna. The following year he married Phillida, the daughter of Sir John Call, by whom he had three children. In the same year as his marriage, he was appointed secretary to the legation at Stockholm, where he remained for three years. Apparently he regarded this as something of a dead-end, and suffered both disappointment and ill health as a consequence.

Things looked up after Bathurst's return to England. George Canning, the foreign secretary, was seeking the support of Earl Bathurst, then president of the Board of Trade, in his efforts to topple his bitter enemy, the minister for war, Lord Castlereagh. To this end, in March 1809, he tossed young Benjamin a titbit – the position of envoy-extraordinary to Austria.

AN IMPORTANT MISSION

Bathurst was only given a few days' notice, and his brief was to persuade the Austrians to join Britain in its war against Napoleon. This had

> ### A Tragic Family
>
> Two of Benjamin Bathurst's three children also met unfortunate ends. His son died after falling from his horse while racing in Rome, while one of his daughters was drowned in the River Tiber. The other daughter maintained the Italian connection by choosing as her second husband a Signor Pistocchi.

been on the cards since late 1808, when the Austrian court began to be dominated by the vociferous war party, anxious to avenge the punitive Peace of Pressburg imposed by the French in 1805 after the debacle at Austerlitz. It is unlikely that Canning would have dispatched so young and inexperienced a diplomat if the Austrians had not seemed set on war already – or perhaps, given the lack of readiness of the Austrian army, Canning judged that the Austrians were unlikely to prove effective allies and so attached little importance to the mission.

The Austrians declared war on Napoleon in April 1809. In May, under threat of bombardment, Vienna surrendered to the French, the court (and with them Bathurst) having previously fled to Komorn (Komárom) in Hungary. The final defeat came in July, at the Battle of Wagram, following which the Austrians were forced to agree to an armistice. By the Treaty of Schönbrunn, signed in October, Austria was obliged to break off diplomatic relations with Britain.

FLIGHT FROM BUDA

At the time of the Treaty of Schönbrunn Bathurst was in Buda, the great Magyar fortress on the western bank of the Danube, now part of modern Budapest. He had, apparently, become convinced that Napoleon had conceived a particular enmity towards him personally, owing to his role in encouraging the Austrians to go to war.

According to his family, Bathurst had originally planned to make his way home by a southerly route, via the port of Trieste and the Adriatic to Malta, but by the terms of the treaty the Austrian provinces in that direction (Frioul, Carniola, Carinthia), together with Trieste and most of Illyria, were ceded to the French, making the route, in Bathurst's view, much too dangerous. Instead, he determined to travel by the northern route, through Germany to Berlin, capital of Prussia, and thence to the port of Hamburg. The German states were then ostensibly either neutral or allied to France, but there was an upsurge of nationalistic, anti-Napoleonic feeling throughout Germany, and presumably Bathurst was relying on this to see him safely home.

Bathurst appears to have been genuinely fearful for his life, although by the diplomatic conventions of the time an envoy in his situation should have had no cause for undue alarm. He assumed the identity of a German merchant called Koch, but his lack of fluency in German, his fine clothes and his carriage and four made him more conspicuous than he might have intended. Travelling with his valet and private secretary, and carrying pistols at all times, he passed through Berlin without making contact with the British consul, and on the afternoon of 25 November arrived at the town of Perleberg on the western border of the Kingdom of Prussia, halfway between Berlin and Hamburg.

Bathurst appears to have been aware that there were French troops in the vicinity, and asked Captain Klitzing, the military governor of the town, for two soldiers to act as bodyguards. A lady who saw him that day later reported on his agitated state, and noted that he trembled so much he could not drink without spilling his tea.

He dined early at the White Swan inn, then retired to his room where he spent time writing, and also burnt some papers. He dismissed his bodyguards at about 7 or 8 p.m., and some time later went out into the courtyard to supervise the preparation of his coach for the onward journey, which he intended to undertake at night in the hope of evading Napoleon's agents. At 9 p.m., the appointed time of departure, his servants looked for him, but he could not be found anywhere. It was pitch dark outside, and hitherto no one had been paying much attention to his whereabouts.

> ## A Red Herring?
>
> On 23 January 1810 a Hamburg newspaper printed the following report from London:
>
> *Sir Bathurst, Ambassador Extraordinary of England to the Court of Austria, concerning whom a German newspaper, under date of 10 December, stated that he had committed suicide in a fit of insanity, is well in mind and body. His friends have received a letter from him dated 13 December, which, therefore, must have been written after the date of his supposed death.*
>
> When inquiries were made, Bathurst's friends denied ever having received such a letter.

A VICTIM OF THE FRENCH?

The Prussian authorities organized a thorough search, even dragging the River Stepnitz. The only trace of Bathurst that ever came to light was a pair of his trousers, found on 16 December by two old women gathering firewood outside the town. The trousers appeared to have been left only a day or two previously in a place where they would be sure to be found. In one of the legs there were two bullet holes – but no sign of blood – and in a pocket was an unfinished letter from Bathurst to his wife, scratched in pencil. In this he said he feared he would never see England again, and blamed his plight on the Comte d'Entraigues – an exiled French nobleman who later turned out to be a double agent working on behalf of Napoleon. Suspicion immediately fell on the French secret service, who were presumed to be after letters Bathurst was carrying from the Austrian government to his masters in London; it was perhaps these papers that he burnt on the evening of his disappearance. *The Times* of London, in a leader of 23 January 1810, pointed the finger at Napoleon. The French would have none of it. Already, on 12 December 1809, *Le Moniteur* of Paris had carried a piece from its Berlin correspondent stating:

It is only the English diplomatic service which contains crazy people.

LE MONITEUR NEWSPAPER GIVES THE FRENCH VIEW OF THE AFFAIR, 29 JANUARY 1810.

Sir Bathurst on his way from Berlin showed signs of insanity, and destroyed himself in the neighbourhood of Perleberg.

On 29 January 1810, in response to the tirade in *The Times*, a leader in *Le Moniteur* opined:

From information we have received from Berlin, we believe that Mr Bathurst had gone off his head. It is the manner of the British Cabinet to commit diplomatic commissions to persons whom the whole nation knows are half fools. It is only the English diplomatic service which contains crazy people.

Napoleon himself went out of his way to assure Bathurst's wife that he had had no hand in the affair, and supplied her with a passport to visit the Continent. In 1810 she and her brother spent four months trying to find out what had happened to the missing envoy. Initially she believed her husband – apparently not in the best of mental health – had taken his own life, unable to put up with the strain of such a hazardous journey. Later, she was persuaded that the French were to blame. The British government, however, never themselves pointed the finger at Napoleon, perhaps also aware of Bathurst's embarrassing mental instability.

LOCAL SUSPECTS

There is another possibility. One of his servants later described how Bathurst had somewhat carelessly, among the crowds at the inn, pulled out his pocket watch, 'and likewise his purse, containing a considerable sum of money'. It is possible therefore that he was simply the victim of a violent robbery. On 27 November Bathurst's sable greatcoat lined with violet velvet was found in the outhouse owned by the Schmidt family, and suspicion fell on an ostler at the inn called Auguste Schmidt. According to this theory, Bathurst's bullet-riddled trousers had been planted to throw suspicion on the French. However, no firm evidence was produced against Schmidt, and it is possible that Bathurst had left the coat at the inn.

Over the years, the remains of a number of men who had met violent ends turned up around Perleberg. In 1852 a skeleton with an axe blow on the back of the skull was found in the cellar of a house that had at one time belonged to a man called Martens. In 1809 Martens was working as a servant at the White Swan inn. However, when the skull was shown to Bathurst's sister, Mrs Tryphena Thistlethwayte, she declared that it lacked her brother's high forehead and Roman nose. Only an expert can reconstruct a face from a skull, so her opinion can hardly be taken as conclusive – especially as she had not seen her brother for over four decades.

There is one last theory, one that was believed in Perleberg at the time – although there is no evidence for it. This states that Bathurst's 'disappearance' was deliberately engineered to throw his French pursuers off the scent. What actually happened, according to this theory, was that Captain Klitzing secretly accompanied Bathurst to the Prussian frontier, and so to safety. But why Bathurst never contacted his wife or anyone else back in England remains a mystery – unless he was still totally consumed by his belief that Napoleon was out to get him, and assumed another identity and another life.

'He Walked Around the Horses'

The case of Benjamin Bathurst has inspired a number of writers of fiction. In H. Beam Piper's short story 'He Walked Around the Horses' (1948), narrated via fictional letters and reports, Bathurst and his papers slip into a parallel universe, one in which the French Revolution never happened. The last letter in the story ends:

I was baffled ... by one name, frequently mentioned in those fantastic papers. This was the English general, Wellington. I haven't the least idea who this person might be.

I have the honour, Your Excellency, et cetera, et cetera, et cetera,

Sir Arthur Wellesley

20,000 POUNDS
STERLING
(100,000 Dollars)
REWARD!

TO BE GIVEN BY

HER BRITANNIC MAJESTY'S GOVERNMENT

to such private Ship, or distributed among such private Ships,
or to any exploring party or parties, of any Country, as may, in
the judgment of the **BOARD OF ADMIRALTY**, have ren-
dered efficient assistance to

SIR JOHN FRANKLIN,

HIS SHIPS, OR THEIR CREWS,

and may have contributed directly to extricate them from the Ice.

H. G. WARD,
Secretary to the Admiralty.

LONDON, *March 23, 1849.*

The attention of **WHALERS**, or of any other Ships or
parties disposed to aid in this service, is particularly directed to
SMITH'S SOUND and **JONES'S SOUND**, in **BAFFIN'S
BAY**, to **REGENT'S INLET** and the **GULF of BOOTHIA**,
as well as to any of the Inlets or Channels leading out of **BAR-
ROW'S STRAIT**, particularly **WELLINGTON STRAIT**,
or the Sea beyond, either Northward or Southward.

VESSELS entering through **BEHRING'S STRAITS**
would necessarily direct their search North and South of **MEL-
VILLE ISLAND.**

NOTE.—Persons desirous of obtaining information relative to the Missing Expedi-
tion, are referred to EDMUND A. GRATTAN, Esq., Her Britannic Majesty's Consul,
BOSTON, MASSACHUSETTS; or ANTHONY BARCLAY, Esq., Her Britannic
Majesty's Consul, NEW YORK.

Icebound in
the Arctic

FRANKLIN'S LAST EXPEDITION

(1845–51?)

On 19 May 1845 Sir John Franklin set sail from Greenhithe in England with two well-equipped ships, the *Terror* and the *Erebus*, crewed by 23 officers and 110 men. Their aim was to find a way through the Northwest Passage, a much sought route that was imagined to exist around the frozen northern edges of the North American continent. On 26 July Captain Dannett, of the whaler *Prince of Wales*, encountered Franklin's ships at more than 75° north, off the west coast of Greenland. No European ever saw either Franklin or any of his men alive again.

It was by no means the first attempt to find a way through the maze of islands and ice-choked channels of the Canadian Arctic. In 1497 John Cabot had endeavoured to find a route to the Far East by sailing west, and many other attempts followed. The pace quickened in the early decades of the 19th century, as John Barrow, the visionary second secretary to the British Admiralty, sent out a series of naval expeditions to fill in various blanks on the map. One of the biggest blanks lay between Baffin Bay, to the west of Greenland, an area long familiar with whalers, and the mouth of the Coppermine River, 1500 miles east of the Bering Strait, which had been reached in 1771 by Samuel Hearne. It was somewhere in this blank that Barrow was convinced, as many had been convinced before him, there would be found a Northwest Passage to Asia.

AN HONOURABLE AND USEFUL EMPLOYMENT

John Franklin, born in Spilsby, Lincolnshire, in 1786, was one of 12 children of Willingham Franklin, a dealer in fine fabrics. His father intended him for the Church, but Franklin – although he remained a pious sort throughout his life, loath even to write a letter on the Sabbath – had conceived a passion for the sea. Perhaps in the hope of putting him off, Willingham Franklin secured a passage for his son on a merchantman bound for Lisbon, but this only served to fire the boy up. At the age of 14 the young Franklin joined the Royal Navy vessel *Polyphemus*, and six months later found himself present at the Battle of Copenhagen, where Nelson famously turned his blind eye. Franklin's next posting was aboard HMS *Investigator*, under his uncle Matthew Flinders, with whom he made the first circumnavigation of Australia; during the course of this epic voyage they were stranded on a sandbank for six weeks. Back in Europe, Franklin saw action at Trafalgar in 1805, and then at New Orleans in 1814.

With the coming of peace, Franklin's naval career appeared to be over, and he was discharged on half pay. But John Barrow at the Admiralty had other plans for his officers. 'To what purpose,' he wrote in 1816, 'could a portion of our naval force be, at any one time, but more especially in time of profound peace, more honourably or more usefully employed than in completing those details of geographical and hydrological science of which the grand outlines have been sketched by Cook ... and others of your countrymen?'

In 1818 Franklin was put in command of the brig *Trent*, which accompanied Commander John Buchan aboard the barque *Dorothea* in a voyage northward through the Arctic Ocean. They were stopped by ice in the Greenland Sea to the northwest of Svalbard, but despite their limited success the voyage turned the

When he arises from sleep, half his body seems dead, till quickened into feeling by the irritation of his sores.

MIDSHIPMAN ROBERT HOOD, FRANKLIN'S DRAUGHTSMAN AND ARTIST ON HIS 1819–22 EXPEDITION, DESCRIBES THE RIGOURS OF TRAVELLING IN WINTER – AND IN A STATE OF SEMI-STARVATION – THROUGH THE CANADIAN ARCTIC.

It seems to me that the mission was projected and entered into without mature consideration and the necessary previous arrangements totally neglected.

GOVERNOR GEORGE SIMPSON OF THE HUDSON'S BAY COMPANY
COMMENTS ON FRANKLIN'S EXPEDITION OF 1819–22.

explorers into celebrities. The public flocked to see these new heroes depicted in a panorama in Leicester Square, somewhat to Franklin's embarrassment. 'I shall not venture to approach very near,' he told his sister, 'for fear passers-by should say "There goes the fellow in the panorama."'

THE MAN WHO ATE HIS BOOTS

Franklin's second expedition to the Arctic was on a far more epic scale – although more by accident than design. His brief was to follow the Coppermine River to the sea, and then either make his way west to the Mackenzie River, or east in an effort to rendezvous with William Parry, who was to attempt the Northwest Passage from Baffin Bay via Lancaster Sound. Franklin embarked on 23 May 1819 for York Factory on the west coast of Hudson's Bay, whence, with the aid of the Hudson's Bay Company and its bitter rival the North West Company, he and his party were to proceed to Fort Chipewyan on Lake Athabasca, then on to Fort Providence on the Great Slave Lake, some 1700 miles from York Factory. From here they were to head north to Fort Enterprise and the Coppermine.

Things didn't go well. Franklin himself was not best suited to his task: he was physically unfit, suffered from the cold, and had no experience of wilderness travel and the skills required. When he arrived in Canada, the trading companies failed to come up with the men and supplies they had promised, and Franklin, a stickler for procedure and orders, proved too inflexible and aloof to manage his Indian and trapper guides and boatmen with any degree of success. A first, hard winter was spent reaching Fort Chipewyan, and a second was endured at Fort Enterprise. On 14 June 1821 the party proceeded down the Coppermine in three canoes, and, reaching the sea, slowly made their way, inadequately provisioned, eastward. On 18 August, with winter approaching, they turned back at the appositely named Turnagain Point on the Kent Peninsula. With the sea becoming impossibly rough, they had no choice but to trek back across the aptly named Barren Lands to Fort Enterprise.

It was a nightmare journey, with the men succumbing one by one to starvation or the cold. They were obliged to survive on lichen – which they dubbed *tripes de roche*, and which gave them appalling diarrhoea. This Spartan diet was punctuated by scraps of putrescent carrion and the occasional piece of boiled shoe leather – hence Franklin's later reputation as 'the man who ate his boots'. Michel, one of the trapper boatmen, was suspected of killing some of his fellows and eating them. Whatever the truth, Michel became increasingly deranged, and one day shot Midshipman Robert Hood through the back of the head while the latter was comforting himself with improving readings from Edward Bickersteth's *A Scripture Help*. A few days later, Dr John Richardson, the surgeon-naturalist who was Franklin's second-in-command, took it upon himself to dispatch Michel with a shot to the head. 'His principles,' Richardson later concluded, 'unsupported by a belief in the divine truths of Christianity, were unable to withstand the pressure of severe distress.' When the survivors eventually reached Fort Enterprise, they found it had not been resupplied. Eventually some Indians helped them back to Fort Providence – but 11 men out of the party of 20 had died.

Franklin returned to England a hero. No one mentioned cannibalism, or incompetence, or poor leadership, or an inability to live off the land like a native. It had been an arduous adventure undertaken by a group of fine gentlemen, filled with the best sort of British spirit. Franklin was promoted to captain, and elected a fellow of the Royal Society. A second expedition to the Canadian northwest, in 1825–7, was more successful than the first in terms of mortality, and succeeded in surveying the coast between the Mackenzie and Coppermine rivers. After his return Franklin married Jane Griffin, his first wife having died in 1825, and a year later received a knighthood. A not altogether happy spell as lieutenant-governor of Van Diemen's Land (Tasmania) followed, from 1836 to 1843, when Franklin was recalled to England.

FOR THE HONOUR OF THE BRITISH NAME

Meanwhile, the search for the Northwest Passage had continued, and now the blank on the map was reduced to the stretch between Barrow Strait, to the west of Lancaster Sound, and Point Turnagain on the mainland, some 500 miles to the southwest as the crow flies – but no one knew how long by the winding, icebound passages that wove their way perplexingly through these bleak and uncharted wastes. The Admiralty, the Royal Geographical Society and Sir Robert Peel's government all determined that the gap should be closed.

After a number of highly experienced Arctic captains, including Parry and James Ross, declined, the choice of leading a new expedition fell on Sir John Franklin – largely thanks to lobbying by the formidable and forthright Lady Franklin. It was perhaps Franklin's amiability rather than his qualities as an explorer and a leader of men that led to his selection. There were those who thought that his age (he was now 58) and apparent unfitness should have ruled him out, and as a compromise two younger men, Captain James Fitzjames and Captain Francis Crozier, were given command respectively of *Erebus* and *Terror*, the expedition's ships, which were already specially adapted for the Arctic.

> We desire that every effort be used to penetrate to the southward and westward in a course as direct towards Bering Strait, as the position and extent of the ice or the existence of land at present unknown, may permit.

THE ADMIRALTY'S ORDER TO FRANKLIN, ON APPOINTING HIM TO COMMAND THE EXPEDITION TO FIND THE NORTHWEST PASSAGE, 7 FEBRUARY 1845

On 19 May 1845, having been seen off by 'deafening cheering', *Erebus* and *Terror* sailed down the Thames, equipped not only with state-of-the-art steam technology (both for power and heating) and propellers that could be retracted to avoid damage from the ice, but also with fine silver, porcelain and crystal for the officers' tables, and supplies intended to last three years, including a relative novelty – canned food. *Erebus* also carried a library of 1700 books: the experience of previous expeditions was that ships venturing into these far northern waters might expect to endure at least

The name of Franklin alone is, indeed, a national guarantee.

SIR RODERICK MURCHISON, PRESIDENT OF THE ROYAL GEOGRAPHICAL SOCIETY, SEEING OFF FRANKLIN IN 1845

one winter frozen into the ice, and it was important to keep up morale with entertainments of an improving nature through the long months of darkness. Franklin himself conducted regular religious services, and even set up evening classes to teach illiterate sailors to read and write. Despite these preparations, the general expectation was that they would achieve the passage in a single season, and, having passed through the Bering Strait, would revictual in Hawaii, then known as the Sandwich Islands. The hubris of all concerned (apart from a few old Arctic hands, who shook their heads gravely) was encapsulated by the president of the Royal Geographical Society, Sir Roderick Murchison: 'I have the fullest confidence that everything will be done for the promotion of science, and for the honour of the British name and Navy, that human efforts can accomplish. The name of Franklin alone is, indeed, a national guarantee.'

Reaching the north end of Baffin Bay at the end of July, the *Erebus* and *Terror* were spotted by Captain Dannett's whaler, waiting for the ice to clear from the entrance to Lancaster Sound. This was the last news heard of Franklin's expedition for quite some time.

THE FATE OF FRANKLIN NO TONGUE CAN TELL

By 1847, two years after Franklin had sailed down the Thames, some of his friends and family back at home were beginning to worry. The Admiralty pooh-poohed their concerns, and the confidence that they continued to have in their man in the Northwest Passage is attested by the fact that Franklin was made a rear-admiral in 1852. It proved to be a posthumous promotion.

Lady Franklin was at the forefront of those pressing the case for a search, and proved so irritating to the gentlemen of Whitehall that by the end of 1847 they had given the go-ahead for a rescue mission. Over the next dozen years, the fate of Franklin, the great lost hero, became a cause célèbre among the British – and indeed the American – public. Around thirty expeditions headed into the Arctic, gradually piecing together the tragic story – though at the cost of appalling suffering, frostbite, madness and several deaths. The public were not backward in coming forward with helpful suggestions: one man proposed that fleets of hot-air balloons be unleashed across the icy north, while another recommended that Arctic foxes be released with

The Relic in the White House

Among the ships sent to find Franklin in 1852 was HMS *Resolute*. She later found herself icebound to the east of Melville Island, and on 15 May 1854 she was abandoned by her crew. The following summer *Resolute* must have broken free from the ice and gradually made her way eastward through the Barrow Strait and Lancaster Sound into Baffin Bay, and then south to the Davis Strait. Here, on 17 September 1855, after a voyage of around a thousand miles, she was spotted off Cape Mercy by an American whaler, the *George Henry*. The captain, claiming salvage rights, took possession of the *Resolute*, sailed her back home and sold her to the US Navy – who graciously returned her to Queen Victoria. When the *Resolute* was eventually broken up in 1880, Queen Victoria had a desk made out of her timbers, and presented it to US President Rutherford B. Hayes. The desk still has pride of place in the Oval Office.

notes detailing the whereabouts of food caches attached to their collars. Throughout all these rescue attempts, Lady Franklin continued to play a key role, cajoling, bullying and fundraising – and even trying to join one of the expeditions herself.

In 1850, on Beechey Island at the west end of Lancaster Sound, searchers found the remains of Franklin's winter camp of 1845–6. There were three graves at the site, facing west in the Arctic tradition, and the names of the dead were inscribed on the headstones, along with the dates. One thing was curious: contrary to standard Arctic practice, there was no cairn containing a message for would-be rescuers. Although no one remarked upon it at the time, it was also curious for an expedition to lose so many men after just one winter, before the effects of scurvy began to take hold. The general consensus then was that from Beechey Island Franklin had headed north, up the Wellington Channel, although his primary orders were that he should proceed south. Thus for a while search efforts were concentrated in completely the wrong direction. Some have suspected that the Admiralty was actually more interested in looking for a navigable route to the North Pole than in locating its lost sailors.

DRIVEN TO THE LAST RESOURCE

The next clues as to the fate of Franklin's expedition emerged in 1854. In his overland travels across the Canadian north, John Rae, a tough Orcadian in the employ of the Hudson's Bay Company, had met a group of Inuit who reported that four winters previously, in 1849–50, they had come across 40 white men dragging a boat southward across King William Land (now known to be an island), some 400 miles southwest of Beechey Island. Later, the Inuit had found the bodies of 35 men on the mainland south of King William Island, a day's march from the Great Fish River (now called the Back River). Rae was able to purchase a number of items that the Inuit had collected from the grisly scene. These items clearly identified the men as belonging to Franklin's party, including as they did a silver spoon with Crozier's initials on it, and a silver plate inscribed with Franklin's name. The Inuit told Rae they had heard gunshots in the vicinity some time after discovering the bodies, which would account for the absence of five of the men among the scattered corpses. Gruesomely, the Inuit reported that the remains betrayed signs that Franklin's men had fed on one another. 'From the mutilated state of many of the corpses and the contents of the kettles,' Rae wrote to the Admiralty on 1 September 1854, 'it is evident that our wretched countrymen had been driven to the last resource – cannibalism – as a means of prolonging existence.' The public recoiled in disbelief that Englishmen should resort to such foul deeds, and Rae – who had not visited the scene himself – found himself shunned by polite society.

Five years later, in 1859, an expedition led by Francis Leopold McClintock found two written messages under a cairn on King William Island. The first, dated 28 May 1847, told how the expedition *had* succeeded in sailing north through Wellington Channel from Beechey Island; it then returned down the west coast of Cornwallis Island. It concluded 'All well.' This journey must have been made the previous summer, that of 1846. The second message, written like the first on a standard printed form stating 'Whoever finds this paper is requested to forward it to the Secretary of the Admiralty, London', was dated 25 April 1848. It told a more sombre story:

> *H.M. Ships 'Erebus' and 'Terror' were deserted on the 22nd April, 5 leagues N.N.W. of this, having been beset [i.e. frozen fast in the ice] since 12th September 1846. The officers and crews, consisting of 105 souls, under the command of F.R.M. Crozier, landed here, in lat. 69° 37′ 42″ N., long. 98° 41′ W. Sir John Franklin died on the 11th June 1847; and the total loss by deaths in this expedition has been, to this date, 9 officers and 15 men. And start on to-morrow, 26th, for Back's Fish River.*

The message was signed by Captains Crozier and Fitzjames. It was clear that after the voyage up the Wellington Channel, the expedition had, the same season, sailed down the west coast of the Boothia

Peninsula to King William Island, where the sea ice – here some of the thickest in the world, pressed against the coast by the hard northwest wind – had closed in and held the ships in its iron grip for a year and a half.

As McClintock sledged south he found two skeletons – one of them identified as Lieutenant Graham Gore of the *Erebus* – and a boat adapted as a sledge. Many items of equipment were scattered about, some of them essential, such as chocolate, cartridges and knives – but there were also relative luxuries such as handkerchiefs, towels, combs and two dozen pieces of Franklin's personal silver. One thing was particularly curious: from the direction the boat-sledge was pointing, it was clear the men had been heading back north, to where the *Erebus* and *Terror* had been abandoned in the ice. Further south, McClintock's party found even greater quantities of discarded equipment – but no stores of food. Twenty years later, the southernmost remnants of Franklin's expedition were found where the Inuit had told Rae they would be: on the Adelaide Peninsula, short of their planned destination, the Back River. The place was later named Starvation Cove.

The last resting place of Franklin himself has never been found. The memorial to him in Westminster Abbey carries lines by Alfred, Lord Tennyson:

> ## Lady Franklin's Lament
>
> There is a moving ballad, first recorded *c.*1855, that encapsulates the sadness of those widowed and orphaned in the wake of Franklin's last expedition. It is usually sung to a traditional Irish tune, 'The Croppy Boy':
>
> *We were homeward bound one night on the deep,*
> *Swinging in my hammock, I fell asleep.*
> *I dreamed a dream and I thought it true*
> *Concerning Franklin and his gallant crew.*
>
> *With a hundred seamen he sailed away*
> *To the frozen ocean in the month of May,*
> *To seek a passage around the pole,*
> *Where we poor sailors do sometimes roll.*
>
> *Through cruel misfortune they vainly strove,*
> *Their ships on mountains of ice was drove,*
> *Where the Eskimo with his skin canoe*
> *Was the only one who ever came through.*
>
> *In Baffin's Bay where the whale fish blow*
> *The fate of Franklin no man may know,*
> *The fate of Franklin no tongue can tell,*
> *Lord Franklin among his seamen do dwell.*
>
> *And now my burden gives me such pain,*
> *For my long lost Franklin I would cross the main,*
> *Ten thousand pounds I would freely give*
> *To know that on earth my Franklin do live.*

Not here! the white North has thy
*   bones; and thou,*
Heroic sailor-soul,
Art passing on thine happier voyage
*   now*
Toward no earthly pole.

The memorial, erected by Lady Franklin, notes that Franklin had died 'off Point Victory in the Frozen Ocean'. It also hails him as 'the beloved chief of the gallant crews who perished with him in completing the discovery of the North-West Passage'. Of course, Franklin's expedition had accomplished no such thing – but it would not have done to say so.

THE MARKS ON THE BONES

In the 1980s a series of expeditions by forensic anthropologists from the University of Alberta re-examined the remains on Beechey Island and King William Island. The disinterred corpses on Beechey Island were remarkably well preserved, having been mummified in the cold, dry conditions. In both locations the bodies showed unusually high levels of lead, and, on examining the empty cans abandoned by Franklin's expedition, it was thought likely that the lead used in the solder had leached into the food. If the whole expedition had gradually been poisoned by lead, that would account both for the surprisingly high mortality recorded in the second note found on King William Island, and for some of the apparently irrational decisions taken by the men, such as heading back north to the abandoned ships. The cans also betrayed evidence of shoddy procedures in the canning process, so botulism may have taken its toll. Scurvy, cold, pneumonia, tuberculosis and, of course, starvation, also played their part. Most disturbingly, on some of the bones knife cuts were apparent, showing that the bodies had been butchered. John Rae's report that the men had resorted to cannibalism was finally confirmed.

The map of the North American Arctic is now dotted with the names of the explorers who opened it up, from Martin Frobisher (Frobisher Bay) and Henry Hudson (Hudson Strait and Bay), to John Barrow (Barrow Sound), William Parry (Cape Parry) and James Ross (James Ross Strait). John Franklin also features topographically, being memorialized in Franklin Bay, between the mouths of the Mackenzie and Coppermine rivers. He is also commemorated, to the west of the Boothia Peninsula, by the Franklin Strait, down whose icy waters he and his men were lured to their doom.

It was not until 1906 that the great Norwegian polar explorer Roald Amundsen completed the first successful navigation of the Northwest Passage, in the shallow-draft *Gjøa* – a much smaller and more suitable vessel than *Erebus* or *Terror*. A century after Amundsen's epic journey, global warming was beginning to have a permanent impact on the Arctic ice, and in the summer of 2007, for the first time in recorded history, the Northwest Passage was open water from end to end.

> When I was 15 years old, the works of Sir John Franklin, the great British explorer, fell into my hands. I read them with a fervid fascination which has shaped the whole course of my life. Of all the brave Britishers who for four hundred years had given freely of their treasure, courage, and enterprise to dauntless but unsuccessful attempts to negotiate the Northwest Passage, none was braver than Sir John Franklin.

ROALD AMUNDSEN, *MY LIFE AS AN EXPLORER* (TRANSLATED 1927). IN 1906 AMUNDSEN BECAME THE FIRST MAN TO NAVIGATE THE NORTHWEST PASSAGE, AND IN 1911 HIS TEAM BECAME THE FIRST TO REACH THE SOUTH POLE.

Into the Heart of the Red Continent

Ludwig Leichhardt

(1848)

There is something other about Australia's vast, dry interior, beyond the forests and lush pastures of the coasts. To the Europeans who first ventured inland, the endless miles of red dust, broken only by clumps of sun-bleached grass and wind-scoured rocks, must have seemed as alien as the surface of Mars. Even the trees were not right: surely the grey-leaved eucalypts with their ghost-pale bark could not belong to the same creation as oak or ash or rowan? And as for the animals – what business had God creating the kangaroo, a creature that walked, like Man, on two legs? And then there was the hairy platypus with the bill of a duck, which, in defiance of received taxonomy, hatched its young from eggs. Everywhere, inescapably, was the harsh, shimmering Antipodean light, endowing every aspect of the land with a glaring, dreamlike unreality.

Into this visionary wilderness few Europeans had ever penetrated, prior to the arrival of a passionate, almost messianic figure called Ludwig Leichhardt. Leichhardt was a German naturalist of great intellect and with an enormous faith in his own capabilities. He had come to Australia in 1842, exulting in the huge natural laboratory provided by the newly settled continent, and the opportunities not only for recording its extraordinary plants and animals, but for exploring its vast unmapped tracts. In 1844–5 he made the first crossing of northeastern Australia from Moreton Bay, near Brisbane, to Port Essington, near Darwin, a journey of some 3000 miles. Buoyed up by this success, he then conceived of a plan to cross Australia from east to west, following, broadly, the same line of latitude. The last that was heard from him was a letter dated 4 April 1848, written only about 250 miles west of Moreton Bay. However, fragments of evidence that have since come to light indicate that his journey took him very much further, right into the burning heart of the continent.

THE PEAT INSPECTOR'S SON

Born in Trebatsch, Prussia, in 1813, Leichhardt was the fourth son of a farmer who doubled as the royal inspector of peat. A promising lad, Leichhardt studied philosophy and languages at the universities of Berlin and Göttingen, where he befriended a student called John Nicholson, who inspired him with an interest in medicine and the natural sciences. Leichhardt also became friends with John's younger brother, William, and in 1837 accompanied the latter when he returned to England. The two studied together at the Royal College of Surgeons and the British Museum in London, and at the Jardin des Plantes in Paris, and also carried out field studies in Switzerland and Italy. In 1841 William paid his friend's fare for the voyage to Australia, in addition supplying him with clothing and other items necessary for the journey, together with the sum of £200.

Leichhardt disembarked at Sydney on 14 February 1842, intent on exploration and discovery. He was somewhat surprised when the governor of New South Wales failed to found a national museum with him as curator, and disappointed that he was not even invited to take up the directorship of the Botanical Gardens. Instead he contented himself with private studies of the geology, botany and zoology of the Hunter River Valley, and with solo overland expeditions

The bright constellations of heaven pass unheeded over the heads of the dreaming wanderers of the wilderness ...

LUDWIG LEICHHARDT, *JOURNAL OF AN OVERLAND EXPEDITION IN AUSTRALIA* (1847)

between Newcastle (to the north of Sydney) and Moreton Bay. His hopes rose when he heard that the Legislative Council proposed an expedition from Moreton Bay to Port Essington, but the governor prevaricated, stating that such a hazardous and expensive project would need the consent of the Colonial Office back in London. Impatient with bureaucracy and delay, Leichhardt set about raising a public subscription to fund his own private expedition.

A POET IN THE WILDERNESS

It was a remarkable journey. In Sydney Leichhardt found five volunteers, and was joined by four more at Moreton Bay. On 1 October 1844 they began their journey in earnest from Jimbour, a remote sheep station on the western fringes of the Darling Downs. Leaving this last outpost of European civilization they launched themselves, in Leichhardt's words, 'buoyant with hope into the wilderness'. As they penetrated deeper and deeper into *terra incognita*, Leichhardt never allowed his scientific curiosity to slacken, however harsh the privations. His journal – published in 1847 as *Journal of an Overland Expedition in Australia, from Moreton Bay to Port Essington, a Distance of Upwards of 3000 Miles, During the Years 1844–1845* – is replete with precise descriptions of the topography, geology, fauna and flora of the changing landscapes he passed through. There are also moments of poetry:

> *The neighing of the tethered horse, the distant tinkling of the bell, or the occasional cry of night birds, alone interrupt the silence of our camp. The fire, which was bright as long as the corroborri songster kept it stirred, gradually gets dull, and smoulders slowly under the large pot in which our meat is simmering; and the bright constellations of heaven pass unheeded over the heads of the dreaming wanderers of the wilderness, until the summons of the laughing jackass recalls them to the business of the coming day.*

It was by no means all the Arcadian idyll that this passage suggests. Although they had brought with them a herd of bullocks as a living larder, they eventually ran low on provisions, with 'fat cake' – made from flour and a pinch of suet – becoming an occasional luxury, their supply of sugar having long run out. They were able in many places to shoot game to eke out their supplies. But it was water – or its absence – that occasioned more hope and despair than anything else:

> *Evening approaches; the sun has sunk below the horizon for some time, but still [the traveller] strains his eye through the gloom for the dark verdure of a creek, or strives to follow the arrow-like flight of a pigeon, the flapping of whose wings has filled him with a sudden hope, from which he relapses again into a still greater sadness; with a sickened heart he drops his head to a broken and interrupted rest, whilst his horse is standing hobbled at his side, unwilling from excessive thirst to feed on the dry grass. How often have I found myself in these different states of the brightest hope and the deepest misery, riding along, thirsty, almost lifeless and ready to drop from my saddle with fatigue; the poor horse tired like his rider, footsore, stumbling over every stone, running heedlessly against the trees, and wounding my knees! But suddenly, the note of* Grallina australis, *the call of cockatoos, or the croaking of frogs, is heard, and hopes are bright again; water is certainly at hand; the spur is applied to the flank of the tired beast, which already partakes in his rider's anticipations, and quickens his pace – and a lagoon, a creek, or a river, is before him …*

Not all Leichhardt's companions could endure the harsh life of the bushman, however, and two of them turned back for the fleshpots of New South Wales. Leichhardt was probably not too distressed at seeing the backs of the faint-hearts – elsewhere in his journal he had written: 'I had naturally a great antipathy against comfort-hunting and gourmandizing, particularly on an expedition like ours; on which we started with the full expectation of suffering much privation.'

TRAILED BY CROWS AND KITES

As the eight men remaining continued further and further into this strange but compelling new world, they were trailed by flocks of crows and kites. These seemed to Leichhardt akin to the Harpies of the *Aeneid*, ready to snatch their meals from their plates, and no doubt hoping for a heartier feast should the white men succumb. The party also found itself subject to the wary curiosity of bands of Aborigines, though the latter were more apparent than present. Around the Gulf of Carpentaria, Leichhardt writes, 'We saw smoke rising in every direction, which showed how thickly the country was inhabited', but on the whole they saw nothing but deserted fires and piles of mussel shells and fish bones.

How often have I found myself in these different states of the brightest hope and the deepest misery ...

LUDWIG LEICHHARDT, *JOURNAL OF AN OVERLAND EXPEDITION IN AUSTRALIA* (1847)

On the evening of 28 June 1845, disaster struck. They had just dined on a quartet of teal and half a dozen whistling ducks, and were settling down to sleep, when a shower of spears rained down on their tents. The Aborigines dispersed as soon as they returned fire, but two of the party, Roper and Calvert, had been skewered:

> *Several of these spears were barbed, and could not be extracted without difficulty. I had to force one through the arm of Roper, to break off the barb; and to cut another out of the groin of Mr Calvert.*

Leichhardt found a third man, Gilbert, on the ground, and, on examining him:

> *I soon found, to my sorrow, that every sign of life had disappeared. The body was, however, still warm, and I opened the veins of both arms, as well as the temporal artery, but in vain; the stream of life had stopped, and he was numbered with the dead.*

Roper and Calvert survived, and the party, now reduced to seven, continued on its way to the northwest. Six months later, on 17 December 1845, they came across a cart road, and then a garden, and then some white houses and a row of 'snug thatched cottages'. They had arrived. 'I was deeply affected in finding myself again in civilized society,' Leichhardt wrote, 'and could scarcely speak, the words growing big with tears and emotion; and, even now, when considering with what small means the Almighty had enabled me to perform such a long journey, my heart thrills in grateful acknowledgement of his infinite kindness.'

'PRINCE OF EXPLORERS'

After a month's rest in Port Essington they sailed for Sydney on board the appropriately named *Heroine*. Everybody had been convinced they had perished somewhere in the back of beyond, and the return of the heroes was greeted with outpourings of rejoicing: 'All classes pressed forward to testify their joy at our reappearance,' Leichhardt recalled with undisguised pleasure. He himself was hailed as the 'Prince of Explorers', and was honoured both by the Geographical Society in Paris and by the Royal Geographical Society in London. For its part the government of Prussia made plain its admiration for the son of the royal inspector of peat, not by awarding him a medal, but by offering him a pardon for failing to report home for military service.

Leichhardt relished the adulation: 'I was dead,' he exulted, 'and was alive again. I was lost, and was found.' It must have given him further pleasure when a public subscription raised some £1500 as a reward for the expedition members, while the Colonial Office, at the behest of the legislative council and the governor, belatedly put its hand in its pocket and bestowed a further £1000, with the caveat that 'The 50 pounds for the two Blacks [Charles Fisher and Harry Brown, who had done most of the hunting during the trip, and without whom the others might well have perished] will be lodged in the Savings' Bank, and will not be drawn out without the approval of the Vice President of that Institution.'

TOWARDS THE SWAN RIVER

Even as the colonial secretary's letter quoted above was being inserted as an appendix to Leichhardt's journal, the publisher was informing his readers in a note that Leichhardt was at that very moment embarked on another, more daring expedition, whose object was 'to explore the Interior of Australia, to discover the extent of Sturt's Desert and the character of the Western and North-Western Coast, and to observe the gradual change in vegetation and animal life from one side of the Continent to the other'.

Leichhardt had set out in early December 1846, but what the publisher of his journal did not know at the time of going to press was that after covering only 500 miles the expedition had ground to a halt, bogged down by heavy rains and weakened by fever. By August 1847 Leichhardt, undaunted, was back in Sydney, raising funds for a second attempt. His intention was to travel as directly westward from the Darling Downs as possible, although he was aware that the existence of a great desert in the interior might force him on a more northerly course, towards the Gulf of Carpentaria, in search of water.

At the beginning of April 1848 Leichhardt and six companions had arrived at the remote outpost of Cogoon, on the Darling Downs. From here they set off westward, their ultimate goal the Swan River on the far side of the continent. They never reached their destination.

A SCATTERED TRAIL OF TREES

Leichhardt had estimated that it would take him two and half years for the journey, but it was not until four years later that the government of New South Wales dispatched an expedition to see if any trace of him could be found. All they turned up was a solitary campsite, with an 'L' carved on a tree, above the letters 'XVA'. Half a dozen years passed before another expedition went in search of the missing Prussian, finding only another couple of trees inscribed with the letter L. Some felt that not enough was being done to find Leichhardt's party, and in 1865 the following anonymous lines appeared in the *Australasian*:

> *If famine, thirst*
> *Have done their worst,*
> *And low in dust the honoured head should lie;*
> *   Shame on them then,*
> *   As Christian men,*
> *The rites of Christian burial to deny.*

In 1869, rumours of a place far to the west where the bones of men and horses killed by Aborigines might be found prompted the government of Western Australia to investigate, but again nothing was found.

Some thirty years later, in 1896, the gold prospector David Carnegie, youngest son of the 9th Earl of Southesk, was working his way through the Gibson Desert and the Great Sandy Desert of Western Australia. 'What heartbreaking country,' Carnegie reported, 'monotonous, lifeless, without interest, without excitement save when the stern necessity of finding water forced us to seek out the natives in their primitive camps.' This refers to his practice, whenever his party ran out of water, of capturing an Aborigine or two and forcing them to show them the location of a nearby spring or pool. During one of these encounters, Carnegie saw that the Aborigines had in their possession the lid of a tin matchbox, an iron tent peg and a piece of metalwork from a saddle. He speculated that they might have come from Leichhardt's expedition.

More tantalizing evidence emerged some time around 1900, when an Aborigine stockman working near Sturt Creek, near the border between Western Australia and the Northern Territory, found a partially burnt shotgun hanging from a baobab tree. The gun bore a tiny brass plate engraved with Leichhardt's name, and the tree itself bore the telltale letter L. The plate came into the possession of a district clerk called Reginald Bristow-Smith, and remained in his family until in 2006 Bristow-Smith's descendants sold the item to the National Museum of Australia, whose senior curator, Matthew Higgins, supported by scientists and historians, is convinced that it is of huge significance. 'Had there not been an L on the tree,' he told the Melbourne newspaper *The Age*, 'it could have been argued the firearm was found elsewhere and traded among Aboriginal people [who] had put it in the tree.' What it did show was that Leichhardt's expedition had covered at least two-thirds of the distance to the west coast, a quite remarkable achievement in such a desolate, uncharted environment. Whether they got any further it is impossible to say, but it seems likely that they perished there, either from thirst or at the hands of hostile Aborigines. If Leichhardt had hoped that Sturt Creek would lead him to the coast, he would have been bitterly disappointed – because, like Leichhardt himself, it simply disappears into the desert.

The Man Who Was Voss

Ludwig Leichhardt was the inspiration for the eponymous hero of *Voss*, an epic novel published in 1957 by the Australian writer Patrick White, who went on to win the Nobel Prize for Literature. The other central character in the novel is Laura Trevelyan, a young woman who first meets Johann Voss in the house of her uncle, the patron of Voss's expedition, and with whom, while they are separated, Voss is bound by a form of mystic communion. White depicts Voss as a kind of Nietzschean monomaniac, convinced that by force of will he can conquer this hostile continent, an effort that White sees as doomed from the start, the nature of the land being intrinsically opposed to attempts to impose Western civilization. While Voss appears to others (and perhaps to himself) as God or Christ or Devil, the land remains indifferent to human pretensions and aspirations, and eventually all but one of his expedition perish.

But there were always those who dreamt of a better fate for 'our Leichhardt', this Germanic Australian hero. Such wishful thinking is found, for example, in an 1880 poem by Henry Kendall, entitled 'Leichhardt':

> *On the tracts of thirst and furnace – on the dumb blind burning plain*
> *Where the red earth gapes for moisture and the wan leaves hiss for rain,*
> *In a land of dry fierce thunder, did he ever pause to dream*
> *Of the cool green German valley and the singing German stream.*
> *When the sun was as a menace glaring from a sky of brass,*
> *Did he ever rest, in visions, on a lap of German grass?*
> *Past the waste of thorny terrors, did he reach a sphere of rills,*
> *In a region yet untravelled, ringed by fair untrodden hills?*
> *...*
> *Let us dream so – let us hope so! Haply in a cool green glade,*
> *Far beyond the zone of furnace, Leichhardt's sacred shell was laid!*
> *Haply in some leafy valley, underneath blue gracious skies,*
> *In the sound of mountain water, the heroic traveller lies!*

is likely to kill a man before it gets him drunk, a fact that was soon brought to Flood's attention. Flood next hypothesized that Morehouse and Briggs had been in cahoots to claim the salvage rights in the *Mary Celeste*, with Briggs first having killed his own crew. The drawback in this conjecture became apparent when it was pointed out that Briggs already had a share in the *Mary Celeste*, worth more than he would get for salvage. Unabashed, Flood concluded that Morehouse and his crew must have worked alone, massacring the entire company of the *Mary Celeste*. In the end the court discounted Flood's febrile imaginings, and awarded Morehouse one-fifth of the ship and its cargo.

MUDDIED WATERS

It was not only Frederick Solly Flood who muddied the waters. In 1884 the *Cornhill Magazine* published a piece entitled 'F. Habakuk Jephson's Statement', which purported to be an account of the *Mary Celeste's* fateful voyage by a stowaway who had survived. This was in fact a piece of fiction concocted by Arthur Conan Doyle, although it included enough true details to sow considerable confusion in the minds of many.

Further mischief was perpetrated in 1913, when the *Strand Magazine* published what it said were the papers of a recently deceased man called Abel Fosdyk, which had been found by a school-master, Howard Linford. Fosdyk, like Jephson, claimed to have been a stowaway aboard the *Mary Celeste*, and told an absurd tale of how the captain and two of the crew, to settle an argument as to how fast a clothed man could swim, dived into the water, where they were promptly devoured by sharks. The rest of the crew had clambered onto a specially built deck to watch the race, but this deck had collapsed,

The Final Fate of the *Mary Celeste*

After the mysterious events of 1872 the *Mary Celeste* went back to work, in the hands of a succession of owners. She finally came to grief on 3 January 1885 when she struck the Rochelois Reef off Haiti. It turned out that the captain had loaded her up with a pretty much worthless cargo of old boots and cat food, taken out a generous insurance policy, and deliberately run her onto the reef. Unfortunately for him, the ship would not sink, and insurance investigators soon put two and two together.

pitching them all into the sea to meet a similar fate. Only Fosdyk, clinging onto some timbers, had survived. Alert readers noted that the *Strand* specialized in the publication of short works of fiction.

TOWARDS THE TRUTH?

Giant squids, sea serpents and pirates loomed large in the explanations proffered in the popular press over the years. But the court of inquiry, on Deveau's evidence, had concluded that there was every indication that the lifeboat had been launched and that the crew had abandoned ship voluntarily. They had done so in something of a hurry, as various items scattered about bore witness, but the crew had taken enough time to collect up the ship's papers and navigational instruments.

It is likely that the *Mary Celeste's* cargo of industrial alcohol holds the key – in particular the nine barrels that were found to be empty when the ship eventually docked. If the crew had noticed the spillage and the resultant fumes, they would have been terrified that the smallest spark could blast them to oblivion. This would explain the open hatches found by Deveau, and the launching of the lifeboat. No doubt Briggs and his men planned to attach the boat to the ship by a hawser, and retreat to a safe distance until it was judged that all the alcohol had evaporated and the wind dispersed the fumes.

We know that conditions had been stormy, so it is quite possible the hawser snapped as the *Mary Celeste* ran before the wind. The lifeboat may well have been overwhelmed by a wave, taking all in it to a watery grave. Alternatively, the boat may have drifted for weeks far from sight of land, its passengers dying a slow, despairing death of thirst.

Black Bart

THE OUTLAW CHARLES E. BOLES

(1888)

One of the more curious figures of the Wild West was the mild-mannered, moustachioed stagecoach robber Charles E. Boles, the bandit who never fired a shot. Known as Black Bart, he made quite a reputation for himself in northern California and southern Oregon during the 1870s and 1880s, not least because of the poetical messages he left at the scenes of some of his escapades. His crimes eventually caught up with him, however, and he ended up in San Quentin prison for robbery. In January 1888, shortly after his release, his room in a boarding house in San Francisco was found empty, and no more was ever heard of him.

Only a few fragments are known of Charles Boles's early life. He was born in 1829, possibly in England, and at the age of 20 joined the California Gold Rush. Returning back east after a few years, he married Mary Elizabeth Johnson in 1854, later settling in Decatur, Illinois. Boles joined the Union Army in the Civil War, and rose through the ranks of the Illinois Volunteer Regiment, making sergeant within a year and ending the war in 1865 as an acting lieutenant. After the excitement of battle, Boles found it difficult to settle back into farming, and soon he was back in the West, in Idaho and Montana, prospecting for gold. He wrote occasional letters back to his wife, in one of which, dated 1871, he recounts a contretemps with some employees of Wells Fargo, and vows to get his own back. His wife then heard no more of him for many years, and presumed he was dead.

A LIFE OF GENTLEMANLY CRIME

Boles reappears in the historical record in July 1875, when he was identified as the polite, deep-voiced man who held up a stagecoach in Calaveras County, California, with the request, 'Please throw down the box.' The robber, wearing a flour sack over his head, then said, 'If he dares shoot give him a volley, boys!' This latter remark was addressed to a pile of nearby boulders, from which six rifles appeared to protrude. On later inspection, once the robbery was over, the driver of the stagecoach discovered that the 'rifles' were in fact sticks.

Having adopted the moniker Black Bart from a character in a story, Boles pursued his career as a solo stagecoach robber over the next eight years, holding up over twenty coaches and netting thousands of

Life Imitating Art

The character Black Bart, who gave Boles his *nom de guerre*, was the creation of William Henry Rhodes. Writing under the pseudonym Caxton, Rhodes introduced the outlaw Bartholomew Graham, a.k.a. Black Bart, in 'The Case of Summerfield', a story serialized in the *Sacramento Union* newspaper in 1871. A 'Wanted' poster in the story offers a reward of $10,000, and gives the following description of Black Bart:

He is five feet ten inches and a half in height, thick set, has a mustache sprinkled with gray, grizzled hair, clear blue eyes, walks stooping, and served in the late civil war, under Price and Quantrell, in the Confederate army.

The fictional Black Bart is a desperado, wanted for murder. Presumably the mild-mannered Charles Boles hoped to strike some fear into his victims by adopting his dangerous-sounding name.

Rhodes's creation itself has a real-life antecedent: Black Bart was the posthumously awarded nickname of the Welsh pirate Bartholomew Roberts who preyed on shipping off the Americas and West Africa between 1719 and 1722. In the latter year, during a *contretemps* with the Royal Navy, he was dispatched by a blast of grapeshot.

dollars – although on one occasion, a driver having asked him how much he made, he had replied, 'Not very much for the chances I take.' During another robbery he told a driver in Butte County, 'Sure hope you have a lot of gold in that strongbox, I'm nearly out of money.' This lack of funds can be explained by the fact that, when not robbing stagecoaches, Boles lived the life of a dandy about town, dining in the finest restaurants and staying in the best hotels. He was similarly gallant in his professional life: while robbing the stage from La Porte to Oroville, Boles returned a lady's purse, which she had thrown down in her panic, saying, 'Madam, I do not wish your money. In that respect I honour only the good office of Wells Fargo.'

An eyewitness described Boles as having greying brown hair, two front teeth missing, heavy eyebrows, and deep-set eyes of a piercing blue. Most striking of all was his splendid walrus moustache. He never raised his voice, he never swore, and all agreed his manner was that of a gentleman.

It was on 3 August 1877, at the scene of his robbery of a stagecoach in Sonoma County, that Boles left his first poetical visiting card. The verse in question, although lacking his usual *politesse*, neatly expresses his antipathy towards Wells Fargo, dating back to the ugly encounter of 1871:

> *I've labored long and hard for bread,*
> *For honor, and for riches,*
> *But on my corns too long you've tred,*
> *You fine-haired sons of bitches.*

This earthy effort was signed 'Black Bart, the PO8' (the significance of the last part of this signature remains a mystery). The only other authentic piece of Bartiana dates from 25 July 1878:

> *Here I lay me down to sleep*
> *To wait the coming morrow,*
> *Perhaps success, perhaps defeat,*
> *And everlasting sorrow.*
>
> *Let come what will, I'll try it on,*
> *My condition can't be worse;*
> *And if there's money in that box*
> *'Tis munny in my purse.*

A VANISHING ACT

Boles's last attempted robbery, on 3 November 1883 – at Funk Hill, the same location as his first – did not go well. Boles was in the process of dragging from the stagecoach the strongbox that Wells Fargo had inconsiderately bolted to the floor when he was shot. The wound must have been slight, as he made good his escape, but he left behind not only the valuables from the strongbox but also a number of personal items, including a handkerchief with a laundry mark. Wells Fargo's detectives traced the latter to Ferguson and Bigg's California Laundry in Bush Street, San Francisco, and thence the owner of the handkerchief to a nearby boarding house. Here Boles had lived between robberies, passing himself off as Charles E. Bolton, or as T.Z. Spalding, a mining engineer who had to make frequent business trips out of town.

Boles was sentenced to six years, but served only four on account of his exemplary behaviour and sterling work in the prison hospital. Sticking with the name Charles E. Bolton, he denied he was either Boles or Black Bart, but nevertheless carried on a correspondence with his wife, Mrs Mary Boles. On his release he was mobbed by reporters. Asked if he intended robbing any more stagecoaches, Boles insisted he was 'through with crime'. Another newsman inquired

> A person of great endurance. Exhibited genuine wit under most trying circumstances, and was extremely proper and polite in behavior. Eschews profanity.
>
> POLICE REPORT ON CHARLES BOLES AFTER HIS ARREST IN 1883

if any more poems were in the pipeline. 'Young man,' he replied, 'didn't you hear me say that I would commit no more crimes?'

A month later, Boles had vanished from his room at Nevada House, 132 Sixth Street, San Francisco. Some said that Wells Fargo had bribed Boles to get out of their hair, and it was rumoured that he had taken up residence in New York City, living a life of genteel anonymity until dying in 1917 (when a New York newspaper printed an obituary for a Civil War veteran called Charles E. Boles). He certainly never returned to his wife, who was now living in Hannibal, Missouri. Some preferred to think that he had ridden off into the sunset and the high country of Montana in search of fame and fortune, but if so, he apparently achieved neither.

On 23 January 1888, two days after Boles's release from San Quentin, the following advertisement appeared in the personal columns of a local newspaper: 'Black Bart will hear something to his advantage,' it read, 'by sending his address to M.R. Box 29, this office.' No one knows whether Boles ever saw this notice, or who had placed it in the paper.

On 14 November 1888, a few months after Boles was last seen, a man in a mask held up a Wells Fargo stagecoach, leaving the following verse:

> *So here I've stood while wind and rain*
> *Have set the trees a-sobbin',*
> *And risked my life for that damned box,*
> *That wasn't worth the robbin'.*

Disappointingly, handwriting analysis revealed that these lines were the work of an inferior imitator, a pretender to Black Bart's crown as king of the robber-poets.

Three Men Dead

The Keepers of the Flannan Isles

(1900)

Out in the Atlantic, a score of miles beyond the Western Isles and about as remote as one can be from the mainland of Scotland, lie the rugged rocks of the Flannan Isles. It was in the 7th century that St Flannan built his chapel on Eilean Mór, the largest of the seven islets. Here, in the wind-filled emptiness of the open ocean, with only fulmars and razorbills and puffins for company, he sought refuge from the temptations of this world, and a closer communion with God.

Many centuries later, in 1899, St Flannan's chapel on Eilean Mór was joined by another structure, a lighthouse. The Flannan light was designed by David Alan Stevenson, a cousin of the writer Robert Louis Stevenson, and a member of the family responsible for so many lighthouses around Scotland's coasts. The year following its construction the lighthouse on Eilean Mór became the scene of a notable unsolved mystery. On Boxing Day 1900 the *Hesperus*, the relief vessel of the Commissioners of Northern Lights, arrived at Eilean Mór. But of the three keepers – James Ducat, Thomas Marshall and Donald McArthur – there was no sign.

PROPITIATING THE *GENIUS LOCI*

Apart from St Flannan and a succession of lighthouse keepers who lived here until the light was automated in 1971, there is no record of permanent habitation on the Flannan Isles, also known as the Seven Hunters. People from the Isle of Lewis, 21 miles across the open sea to the east, used to make an annual pilgrimage to worship in the chapel, and small numbers of Lewismen visited the islands every summer until the 1920s to net seabirds and tend the sheep they pastured there. Visiting in the early 16th century, Dean Munro said the Seven Haley ('holy') Isles, as he called them, were inhabited only by 'infinit wyld sheipe', which, for some reason, 'cannot be eaten by honest men'.

The islands seem to have possessed a certain aura in the minds of the Gaels. Martin Martin, in his *Description of the Western Isles of Scotland* (1695), notes that anyone landing on the Flannan Isles, if not versed in the customs of the place, 'must be instructed perfectly in all the punctilioes observed here before landing'. Foremost among the necessary observances was that all members of the party, once they had clambered up the ladder from the landing place, should 'uncover their heads, and make a turn sun-ways round, thanking God for their safety'. Martin continues:

The first injunction given after landing, is not to ease nature in that place where the boat lies, for that they reckon a crime of the highest nature, and of dangerous consequence to all their crew; for they have a great regard to that very piece of rock upon which they first set their feet, after escaping the danger of the ocean.

There were also very strict requirements as to the rituals to be observed close to the altar in the chapel, including the diktat that all visitors should 'strip themselves of their upper garments at once'. Further taboos included a prohibition on killing a seabird with a stone, or before ascending the ladder, or after evening prayers. There was also a ban on using the standard word for various things. Thus:

Visk, which in the language of the natives signifies Water, they call Burn; a Rock, which in their language is Creg, must here be called Cruey, i.e., hard; Shore in their language, expressed by Claddach, must here be called Vah, i.e., a Cave; Sour in their language as expressed Gort, but must be here called Gaire, i.e., Sharp; Slippery, which is expressed Bog, must be called Soft; and several other things to this purpose.

It is unclear what terrors motivated these propitiations, apart from a general sense that to do otherwise would result in disaster. Martin was intrigued:

I had this superstitious account not only from several of the natives of the Lewis, but likewise from two who had been in the Flannan Islands the preceding year. I asked one of them if he prayed at home as often, and as fervently as he did when in the Flannan Islands, and he plainly confessed to me that he did not: adding further, that these remote islands were places of inherent sanctity; and that there was none ever yet landed in them but found himself more disposed to devotion there, than anywhere else.

THE MEN WHO WERE NOT THERE

On the night of 15 December 1900 the steamship *Archtor*, passing the Flannan Isles en route from Philadelphia to Leith, noted the absence of a light. Before this news had arrived in Oban, the relief ship *Hesperus*, captained by James Harvie, had already set sail, but her plan to visit Eilean Mór on 20 December, to replace one of the keepers as part of the regular rotation, was delayed by atrocious storms. It was not until midday on 26 December that the *Hesperus* arrived off the landing place on Eilean Mór. The ship's whistle went unanswered, and no flag flew on the island's flagpole.

A dreadful accident has happened at the Flannans. The three keepers, Ducat, Marshall and the Occasional [McArthur] have disappeared from the Island. The clocks were stopped and other signs indicated that the accident must have happened about a week ago. Poor fellows must have been blown over the cliffs or drowned trying to rescue a crane or something like that.

CAPTAIN JAMES HARVIE OF THE *HESPERUS*, SIGNAL TO THE NORTHERN LIGHTHOUSE BOARD, 26 DECEMBER 1900

On entering the lighthouse, the relief keeper, Joseph Moore, found a table laid with an untouched meal of cold meat, potatoes and pickles. The lamp had been prepared for lighting, and the log was complete up to 13 December, with notes up to 9 a.m. on the 15th. The gate and door of the lighthouse had been firmly closed, and nothing seemed amiss – apart from one chair that had been knocked over, and the absence of two sets of oilskins. Also absent were the three keepers, despite a thorough search being conducted of the entire island by Moore, together with the second mate of the *Hesperus* and a seaman. At the west landing there were, however, signs of the recent fierce storms, with damage caused by huge waves apparent at the top of the cliff over 200 feet above the sea.

GIANT WAVES AND SEA SERPENTS

The official report by Robert Muirhead, superintendent of the Commissioners of Northern Lights, dated 8 January 1901, concludes:

> *I am of the opinion that the most likely explanation of the disappearance of the men is that they had all gone down on the afternoon of Saturday, 15 December to the proximity of the West landing, to secure the box with the mooring ropes, etc and that an unexpectedly large roller had come up on the Island, and a large body of water going up higher than where they were and coming down upon them had swept them away with resistless force.*

The question arises, however, as to why one man had gone out in such appalling conditions without his oilskins. If the other two had been in trouble, their shouts would not have been heard by the third man – and if he had rushed out without his oilskins in an emergency, why had the door and gate been so carefully closed?

We landed ...
Each wishing he was safe afloat,
On any sea, however far,
So it be far from Flannan Isle.
    WILFRED WILSON GIBSON, 'FLANNAN ISLE' (1912)

All kinds of wild speculation ensued in the press. It was suggested by some that one keeper, driven mad by his solitary existence, had murdered the other two, then thrown himself in the sea. Others blamed sea monsters, or the Secret Service, while the locals suspected the disappearance had something to do with the otherwordly nature of the place. The most likely explanation is similar to the official one: two of the keepers were at the west landing when the third, from the lighthouse, spotted one or more large waves approaching them, and rushed down to warn them – but was overwhelmed himself.

The mystery inspired the 1979 opera *The Lighthouse* by the Orkney-based composer Peter Maxwell Davis, and, most famously, the spine-tingling ballad 'Flannan Isle', written in 1912 by Wilfred Wilson Gibson. The ballad is told from the point of view of Joseph Moore, the relief keeper, and concludes:

> *We seemed to stand for an endless while,*
> *Though still no word was said,*
> *Three men alive on Flannan Isle,*
> *Who thought on three men dead.*

The Man Who Knew Too Much?

RUDOLPH DIESEL

(1913)

On 1 October 1913 the *New York Times* carried the following news, received via Marconi Transatlantic Wireless Telegraph: 'London, Sept. 30.—Dr Rudolf Diesel, the famous inventor of the Diesel oil engine, has disappeared in most mysterious circumstances. He left Antwerp yesterday to attend in London the annual meeting of the Consolidated Diesel Engine Manufacturers.' The report continued: 'Dr Diesel had a cabin to himself. On the arrival of the vessel at Harwich at 6 o'clock this morning he was missing. His bed had not been slept in, though his night attire was laid out on it.' This is the bare outline of a tale whose strangeness lies in the absence of much more in the way of actual facts.

Although few are aware of the mysterious circumstances of his death, Diesel is familiar across the world through the engine that bears his name. His parents were Bavarian, from Augsburg, although he himself was born and raised in Paris. With the outbreak of the Franco-Prussian War in 1870 his family left for England, sending the 12-year-old Rudolph to study in Augsburg, from where he proceeded to the prestigious Munich Polytechnic.

DIESEL AND HIS ENGINES

Always fascinated by engines – as a boy in Paris he had been captivated by an 18th-century steam-powered gun carriage at the Museum of Arts and Crafts – Diesel came to the conclusion that it would be possible to build a much more efficient engine than those powered by steam. The result was his compression-ignition internal combustion engine. His experiments were not without risk – on one occasion he almost lost his head, literally, when a cylinder head blew off a prototype. But he persisted, and went on to perfect his invention, founding his own manufacturing company in Augsburg in 1899. Although he had no talent for business, the company did well.

I will see you in the morning.

RUDOLPH DIESEL'S LAST RECORDED
WORDS, c.10 P.M., 29 SEPTEMBER 1913 ·

Diesel was a great promoter of his engine. It could run on a variety of fuels: initially he tried coal dust, but then settled on refined petroleum oil. In 1911 he anticipated the biodiesel fuels of the future: 'The diesel engine can be fed with vegetable oils and would help considerably in the development of agriculture of the countries which use it.' The following year he declared: 'The use of vegetable oils for engine fuels may seem insignificant today. But such oils may become in course of time as important as petroleum and the coal tar products of the present time.'

THE EMPTY CABIN

On 29 September 1913 Diesel boarded the SS *Dresden* at Antwerp in Belgium, accompanied by a fellow director, George Carels, and Herr Luckmann, his chief engineer. Carels later told the press that all three of them had dined together, then strolled on deck, talking and smoking. Dr Diesel was 'in the very best of spirits', and the conversation was 'cheery and buoyant'. Around 10 o'clock that night, with the lights of Flushing still visible on the Dutch coast, they descended to their cabins. Diesel entered his, then re-emerged, walked along the corridor to Carels' cabin, shook his hand and wished him goodnight. 'I will see you in the morning,' were the last words anyone heard him speak.

When they docked in Harwich the next morning, there was no sign of Diesel. Carels first looked in Diesel's cabin: 'An inspection of the bed showed it had not been slept in. The coverlet was turned down and a nightshirt lay ready for Dr Diesel on the bed. His keys were in the lock of his little handbag, and he had hung his watch on the side of the bed in such a position that he would be able to see it from where he lay.' Carels continued: 'Everything appeared orderly in the cabin. I could not say whether any money was missing, because I do not know how much he had in his possession, but there was nothing to indicate any interference with his belongings.' Diesel's landing ticket was still there, so he could not have disembarked before his colleagues, and there was no sign of him anywhere on board the ship. 'We could not think otherwise,' Carels concluded, 'than that he disappeared overboard in the course of the night.'

> *The theory of suicide in a sudden fit of aberration is entirely unsupported.*
>
> BARON SCHMIDT, DIESEL'S SON-IN-LAW, OCTOBER 1913

ACCIDENT, SUICIDE OR MURDER?

The British Board of Trade conducted an inquiry, but came up with nothing. Similarly fruitless was a search of Diesel's private papers back in Bavaria. Although some have suggested that he was in financial difficulties at the time of his death, it seems, on the contrary, that Diesel had made considerable sums of money from his invention. Carels attested to his good humour the night before, so suicide appears highly unlikely. 'If one has to put aside the thought of accident,' Carels commented, 'I can only think that something must suddenly have given way in his brain. He was most abstemious, did not smoke, and, so far as I know, did not suffer from giddiness.'

The following day, Baron Schmidt, Diesel's son-in-law, declared that 'the theory of suicide in a sudden fit of aberration is entirely unsupported.' However, Schmidt reported that when Diesel had recently visited his daughter in Frankfurt, after a shooting holiday in the Bavarian Alps, he had complained that he had 'overstrained' himself, and that this had exacerbated the weakness of the heart from which he had suffered for some years. But even if Diesel – now aged 55 – had suffered a heart attack, it is unlikely that he could have hauled himself over the ship's rail at the same time.

There is one particularly suspicious circumstance surrounding Diesel's disappearance. His trip to London was not just for the sake of the meeting of the Consolidated Diesel Engine Manufacturers; he also had an appointment with the British Admiralty. This was at a time when Britain and Germany were locked in a naval arms race, an aggressive rivalry that was to contribute to the outbreak of the First World War the following year. During that conflict, one of Germany's main strategic weapons, used to starve Britain of food and raw materials, was its fleet of submarines – powered by diesel engines. It certainly would have been in Germany's interest if Diesel had never kept his appointment. However, no evidence of an assassination has ever emerged.

The Devil's Lexicographer

Ambrose Bierce

(1913)

The misanthropic American writer Ambrose Bierce earned a reputation as a man who made more enemies than friends. Nevertheless, there runs through his life and work a vein of dark sardonic humour that can still raise a wry smile; and his *Devil's Dictionary*, an eminently quotable collection of cynical apothegms, has rarely been out of print.

Something of the character of the man and his obsession with the grotesque and the morbid can be gleaned by the titles of his works – *The Fiend's Delight, The Dance of Death, Cobwebs from an Empty Skull, Black Beetles in Amber, The Monk and the Hangman's Daughter.* Becoming increasingly disillusioned with contemporary American civilization, at the end of 1913 he set off for Mexico, then ravaged by civil war, claiming to be in search of 'the good, kind darkness'. No more was ever heard of him.

BLOODIED AT SHILOH

Ambrose Bierce's father, Marcus Aurelius Bierce, was a book-loving no-hoper who managed to scratch a hard living from the soil of Indiana. He also managed to father a large brood of children, all of whose names began with A. So alongside Ambrose there were also Abigail, Amelia, Ann, Addison, Aurelius, Augustus, Almeda, Andrew, Albert, Arthur, Adelia and Aurelia. Although his elder siblings found life in Kosciusko County just fine (his younger brother and twin sisters all died in infancy), Ambrose was a withdrawn youngster, and rejected the rustic idyll, later writing with loathing of

> *The scum-covered duck pond, the pigsty close by it,*
> *The ditch where the sour-smelling house drainage fell ...*

The opportunity to escape came with the outbreak of the Civil War in 1861. Young Bierce was only 18 when he joined the Union Army as an enlisted man in the 9th Regiment Indiana Infantry; he was later promoted lieutenant. In April 1862 he saw action at Shiloh, a battle of unprecedented ferocity that ushered in the era of total war; Shiloh accounted for more American dead than the Revolutionary War, the War of 1812 and the Mexican War put together. Bierce was later to describe the battle in a memoir, 'What I Saw of Shiloh'. At one point he comes across a Union sergeant with half his head shot away, but still breathing. Bierce wonders how a man 'could get on, even in this unsatisfactory fashion, with so little brain'. One of his men offers to put the sergeant out of his misery, but Bierce turns down the request. 'Too many were looking,' he says.

The following day he finds himself in a ravine where hundreds of Federal troops have been shot to pieces by Confederate marksmen on either lip:

> *The woods had caught fire and the bodies had been cremated. They lay, half buried in ashes; some in the unlovely looseness of attitude denoting sudden death by the bullet, but by far the greater number in postures of agony that told of the tormenting flames. Their clothing was half burnt away – their hair and beard entirely; the rain had come too late to save their nails. Some were swollen to double girth; others shrivelled to manikins. According to degree of exposure, their faces were bloated and black or yellow and shrunken. The contraction of muscles which had given claws for hands had cursed each countenance with a hideous grin.*

No one up to this time had written with such brutal honesty about the horrors of war. But Bierce breaks off his description with a dismissive gesture: 'Faugh! I cannot catalogue the charms of these gallant gentlemen who had got what they enlisted for.' A dozen or more battles followed – including Kennesaw Mountain, where, in June 1864, Bierce himself suffered a serious wound to the head.

THE LONG PEACE

It has been said no American writer prior to the First World War acquired more direct experience of conflict than Ambrose Bierce. The Civil War informed a number of his later short stories, including 'An Occurrence at Owl Creek', a twisting tale of the hanging of a Confederate sympathizer. Although Bierce had marched off to war a confirmed abolitionist and convinced of the rightness of the Union cause, coming face to face with the realities of total war made him cynical of the motives and morals of politicians – and, indeed, of men in general. He had entered, he said, 'a world of fools and rogues, blind with superstition, tormented with envy, consumed with vanity, selfish, false, cruel, cursed with illusions – frothing mad!'

> ## From *The Devil's Dictionary*
>
> BATTLE, *n.* A method of untying with the teeth a political knot that would not yield to the tongue. ...
>
> HISTORY, *n.* An account, mostly false, of events, mostly unimportant, which are brought about by rulers, mostly knaves, and soldiers, mostly fools. ...
>
> PEACE, *n.* In international affairs, a period of cheating between two periods of fighting.

On Christmas Day 1871 Bierce married Mollie Day, but there was little joy in it; Bierce later wrote that marriage consists of 'a master, a mistress and two slaves, making in all two'. In 1888 he left Mollie after coming across letters to her from another man, although this may well have just been a convenient excuse. The following year their older boy, Day, became infatuated with a factory girl called Eva, but she turned him down and married his best friend, Neil Hubbs. In a fit of jealousy, Day – who habitually packed a pistol – opened fire on the happy couple. Eva only suffered a pierced ear, but Hubbs – who had returned Day's fire but missed – took a fatal shot to the stomach. Still conscious, he managed to hit Day over the head. This seems to have had a calming effect on the young firebrand: 'My God, Neil,' Day cried. 'What have I done?' He then fled to his room and blew his brains out. He was only 17. The other son, Leigh, declined into alcoholism, and in 1901, when he was meant to be delivering Christmas presents to the children of the New York slums on behalf of the local newspaper, he got hopelessly drunk, gave away all the presents before they could get to their intended recipients, contracted pneumonia, and died. He was just 26. Bierce divorced his wife three years later, in 1904, and within another year she too was dead.

> *Man is long ago dead in every zone,*
> *The angels are all gone in graves unknown;*
> *The devils, too, are cold enough at last,*
> *And God lies dead before a great white throne!*
> AMBROSE BIERCE, 'VISIONS OF THE NIGHT'

In the meantime, Bierce's own career had thrived. For a quarter of a century he had pursued it in California, where he was known as 'the wickedest man in San Francisco'; in 1897 he moved to Washington DC. Bierce was well known as a satirist and journalist (he worked for William Randolph Hearst from 1887 until 1906), and also published many fine short stories, together with volumes of poetry and essays. Younger writers feared his merciless judgements (one critic dubbed him 'the literary dictator of the Pacific coast'), but those he did admire he encouraged and inspired. He could also make politicians and businessmen quake: one of his most notable campaigns was against the bill introduced into Congress to excuse the Union Pacific and Central Pacific railroad companies the $130 million debt they owed the government following the construction of the First Transcontinental Railroad. When Collis P. Huntingdon of Central Pacific approached Bierce on the steps of the Capitol and asked him to name his price, Bierce replied: 'My price is one hundred thirty million dollars. If, when you are ready to pay, I happen to be out of town, you may hand it over to my friend, the Treasurer of the United States.' Bierce's response was reported in newspapers across the country, and the bill was defeated.

A PRETTY DEFINITE PURPOSE

In 1912, during his last visit to California, Bierce confided in one of his few remaining friends that he was 'sleepy for death'. He was now in his seventies, and seemingly enveloped in gloom, sick of the ways of men and the world. Yet there was perhaps something wilful, even playful, in his despair. 'My work is finished,' Bierce wrote in January 1913, 'and so am I.' That same month he transferred to his daughter Helen ownership of the cemetery plot where Mollie, Day and Leigh were buried, telling her:

> I do not wish to lie there. That matter is all arranged, and you will not be bothered about the mortal part of
>> Your Daddy

On a last, affectionate visit to his daughter in Illinois that spring, he had seemed in good health, but restless. He made it clear that he found old age objectionable: 'Old people are cranky and fussy and infernal bores,' he said. 'I'll never be like that.' He also dropped hints about heading south to take a look at the revolution then in progress in Mexico, where General Carranza and Pancho Villa and Emiliano Zapata were taking on the forces of the federal government. 'This fighting in Mexico interests me,' he told Helen. 'I want to go down and see if these Mexicans shoot straight.' He dropped

What this country needs – what every country needs occasionally – is a good hard bloody war …

AMBROSE BIERCE,
LETTER, 15 FEBRUARY 1911

similar hints to others, adding spice with the suggestion that he would be putting himself in mortal danger, lured as he was by the siren song of the guns beyond the Rio Grande. In one of his last letters, to his niece Lora Bierce on 1 October 1913, he wrote:

> Goodbye – if you hear of my being stood up against a Mexican stone wall and shot to rags please know that I think that a pretty good way to depart this life. It beats old age, disease, or falling down the cellar stairs. To be a Gringo in Mexico – ah, that is euthanasia!

This may have been self-dramatization: in fact the warring parties in Mexico were carefully avoiding any outrage against American citizens or their property, for fear of a military intervention from the north.

Bierce had dropped other hints – of going on to South America, of having 'a pretty definite purpose … not at present disclosable'. This purpose – if there ever was one – never was disclosed, unless it was the fulfilment of his apparent death wish. But before he left for Mexico, he embarked, on 2 October 1913, on a tour of the battlefields he'd known half a century before. At Shiloh, the ravine where he'd wandered among the incinerated corpses was now covered over in grass, with no hint of the horror that lay beneath. Proceeding on to New Orleans, he told a local reporter that he had 'never amounted to much' since his fighting days. He also said he wouldn't be entering Mexico 'if I find it unsafe for Americans to be there', and expressed his intention of returning to

There are so many things that might happen between now and when I come back ...

AMBROSE BIERCE, TO A
REPORTER OF THE NEW ORLEANS
STAR, OCTOBER 1913

the States after his trip, which he declared was a well-deserved 'rest' now that he had retired from writing. 'There are so many things that might happen between now and when I come back,' he concluded. 'My trip might take several years, and I'm an old man now.' When he sent a cutting of this article to his niece Lora on 5 November, he told her, 'You need not believe all that these newspapers say of me and my purposes. I had to tell them something.' This only serves to thicken the mystery – and one cannot but feel that the thickening was deliberate. It seems that Bierce himself was to be the central character in his last, most perplexing story.

DOWN MEXICO WAY

Very little was heard of Bierce after this. From New Orleans he travelled through Texas, and by the end of November he appears to have crossed over the Mexican border at El Paso. Journalists who talked to him there reported that he had told them he was going to offer his services to Pancho Villa's revolutionary army, and that if he was not accepted for active service, he was going to 'crawl into some out-of-the-way hole in the mountains and die'.

In his last known letter, written on 26 December, Bierce says he is on his way to Chihuahua City to post it. He tells his secretary, Carrie Christiansen, that he is accompanying Villa's army – by whom he has been 'cordially received' – and that on the morrow they are to depart for Ojinaga. We know that Villa seized the town of Ojinaga on 11 January 1914 after a ten-day siege, and it has been generally assumed that Bierce was killed during the fighting, his body perhaps burnt to avoid the further spread of a typhus epidemic. However, none of the other American journalists at the battle or with Villa's forces mentioned Bierce – and the presence of such a lion of American letters would not have escaped their notice. Villa himself later said he had never met Bierce (it had been alleged, without any evidence, that he had had Bierce killed), and many of Villa's followers also denied any knowledge of the man. Over the following years, various inquiries instigated by the American authorities failed to come up with any information as to Bierce's fate.

Doubt has been expressed as to whether Bierce ever entered Mexico at all, or, if he did, as to whether he ever joined up with Villa. The American consulate at Chihuahua City had no record of his presence, although it kept close tabs on all Americans who were in the area for any length of time. Bierce's letter from Chihuahua does not survive – only the transcription made by his secretary, Miss Christiansen. The story that Bierce was anxious to fight for Villa also seems entirely out of character – Bierce had throughout his career condemned radicals, socialists and revolutionaries, and had denounced Villa as nothing but a bandit. One persistent theory, though without any hard evidence to back it up, holds that Bierce had gone not to Mexico but to the Grand Canyon, and there shot himself with his German revolver. Wherever he ended up, that he died alone – probably sometime in early 1914 – seems likely, as no one ever came forward with any information about his last days. His end was almost certainly – given all his dark hints – as he had planned.

There is a Latin epitaph that an earlier and equally fierce satirist intended for himself, but which could as well be fitted to the man they called Bitter Bierce: '*Ubi saeva indignatio ulterius cor lacerare nequit.*' Wherever his corpse lies mouldering, Bierce, like Dean Swift, now lies where savage indignation can no longer tear his breast.

No Known Grave

THE DEAD OF THE MENIN GATE

(1914–18)

If you find yourself in Flanders in the cathedral city of Ieper, pause a while and make a diversion to the east. There, standing gaunt and alone on the road to the small town known in Flemish as Menen, stands the Menin Gate, a brick and limestone memorial dedicated in 1927. Up and down the great panels that line the interior are inscribed the names of 54,896 soldiers from Britain and the British Empire who died in the First World War, but whose last resting place is unknown.

Ieper is better known by its French name, Ypres, altered to 'Wipers' by the hundreds of thousands of Tommies who spent long years defending the Ypres Salient against repeated onslaughts by the Germans. There were four main battles here: in the autumn of 1914, in the spring of 1915, through much of the second half of 1917 – this is the battle whose horror lives on in the British folk memory as Passchendaele – and finally in the spring of 1918, during the Kaiser's last desperate throw of the dice.

THE MEMORIAL AND ITS CEREMONIES

The original Menin Gate was just a gap in the star-shaped fortifications erected around Ieper by Louis XIV's military engineer, Vauban. This side of the town was chosen for the memorial as it was the gate nearest to the fighting – although constant danger of shelling meant that Allied troops actually left for the front via another route.

It was in 1921 that Sir Reginald Blomfield first came up with his design for the memorial, in the form of a triumphal arch in a heavy neoclassical style. At the dedication ceremony on 24 July 1927, heard by millions on the wireless throughout Britain, Field Marshal Lord Plumer declared:

> *It was resolved that here at Ypres, where so many of the 'Missing' are known to have fallen, there should be erected a memorial worthy of them which should give expression to the nation's gratitude for their sacrifice and its sympathy with those who mourned them.*
>
> *A memorial has been erected which, in its simple grandeur, fulfils this object, and now it can be said of each one in whose honour we are assembled here today: 'He is not missing. He is here.'*

Every day since 1928, at eight o'clock in the evening, the road that runs through the memorial is closed, and buglers from the local volunteer fire brigade play the Last Post, followed by a minute's silence.

MECHANIZED MASS SLAUGHTER

Visiting the memorial, you are almost overwhelmed by the number of names. But then you must remember that these are only a portion of the missing. When the monument was completed it was found that there was not room to include all of them, and the 34,984 British soldiers who went missing in action after 15 August 1917 are inscribed elsewhere, in the Tyne Cot Memorial six miles northeast of Ypres, while no names from either New Zealand or Newfoundland are included. The 89,880 names listed on these two memorials – which would take some 75 hours to read out loud – comprise only a fraction of the estimated 9.7 million soldiers killed in the First World War. Their names would take nearly a year to recite; their graves are found in rank after rank, row after row, in vast military cemeteries across Flanders, Picardy, Champagne, Alsace, Lorraine, and on all the other fronts where men died like cattle in the mechanized mass slaughter of the First World War.

Their Name Liveth for Evermore

INSCRIPTION ON THE MENIN GATE MEMORIAL

What passing-bells for these who die as cattle?
Only the monstrous anger of the guns.

WILFRED OWEN, 'ANTHEM FOR DOOMED YOUTH' (WRITTEN 1917). OWEN,
WHO SERVED AS AN INFANTRY OFFICER ON THE WESTERN FRONT, WAS KILLED
ON 4 NOVEMBER 1918 – JUST A WEEK BEFORE THE ARMISTICE WAS SIGNED.

What did it mean in the context of the First World War to be missing in action? It was a war in which the technology of military defence – the artillery piece and the machine gun, combined with barbed wire, trenches and concrete-lined dugouts deep beneath the surface – far outstripped the offensive tactics available to the attackers. Men sent over the top to attack the enemy, often only a few hundred yards away, had to stumble through ground churned into a swamp by their own artillery. This same shellfire had an uncanny knack of being unable to destroy the ubiquitous barbed-wire entanglements. For the defenders the advancing infantry made easy targets. A burst of machine-gun fire could saw a man in two, shrapnel would shred a body into pieces. A direct hit from an artillery shell meant instant oblivion, with no identifiable body parts left on the ground even if stretcher bearers managed to reach the spot. Private Harry Patch, one of the few soldiers of the Great War to survive into the 21st century, recalled an attack in 1917:

> *All over the battlefield the wounded were lying down, English and German all asking for help. We weren't the Good Samaritan in the Bible, we were the robbers who passed by and left them. You couldn't help them. I came across a Cornishman, ripped from shoulder to waist with shrapnel, his stomach on the ground beside him in a pool of blood. As I got to him he said, 'Shoot me.' He was beyond all human aid. Before we could even draw a revolver he had died. He just said 'Mother.' I will never forget it.*

THE MUD OF PASSCHENDAELE

In many battles mud became the greatest enemy – no more so than at Passchendaele in the late summer and autumn of 1917. Lieutenant Edwin Campion Vaughan recalled:

> *I stood up and looked over the front of my hole. There was just a dreary waste of mud and water, no relic of civilization, only shell holes ... And everywhere were bodies, English and German, in all stages of decomposition.*

For Corporal Jack Dillon it was the smells that remained most vivid in the memory:

> *At Passchendaele the smells were very marked and very sweet. Very sweet indeed. The first smell one got going up the track was a very sweet smell which you only later found out was the smell of decaying bodies ... When you were walking up the track a shell dropping into the mud and stirring it all up would release a great burst of these smells.*

Inside the shell-hole was the dead body of a Boche who had been there a very long time and who floated or sank on alternate days according to the atmosphere.

LIEUTENANT DOUGLAS WIMBERLEY OF
THE MACHINE GUN CORPS, REMEMBERING
THE BATTLE OF MENIN ROAD RIDGE, 1917

Private Richard W. Mercer remembered the terror of drowning in the mud – a fate met by thousands:

Passchendaele was just a terrible, terrible, terrible, terrible, terrible, terrible place. We used to walk along these wooden duckboards – something like ladders laid on the ground. The Germans would concentrate on these things. If a man was hit and wounded and fell off he could easily drown in the mud and never be seen again. You just did not want [to] go off the duckboards.

Bombardier J.W. Palmer, like all those who served here, found himself in a nightmare from which he could not awake:

It was mud, mud, everywhere: mud in the trenches, mud in front of the trenches, mud behind the trenches. Every shell-hole was a sea of filthy oozing mud. I suppose there's a limit to everything, but the mud of Passchendaele – to see men sinking into the slime, dying in the slime – I think it absolutely finished me off.

On one occasion a party moving up to the front came across a man who was stuck fast in mud, up above his knees. They tried to heave him out with rifles beneath his armpits, but to no avail. Eventually they were obliged to leave him, and move up to the front line as they were ordered. Two days later they returned the same way. The mud had reached up to the man's neck, and he had gone stark staring mad.

Topped by its monstrous stone lion, symbol of British imperial pomp, and with its rhetoric of glorious sacrifice, the Menin Gate Memorial has seemed to some a memorial to nothing but blind brutality and folly. In 1927 Siegfried Sassoon, one of the greatest of the poets to emerge out of the blood and mess of the trenches, visited the site and bore witness to 'these intolerably nameless names'. For him the 'pile of peace-complacent stone' only served to deride the memory of 'the Dead who struggled in the slime'.

Who will remember, passing through this Gate,
The unheroic Dead who fed the guns?
Who shall absolve the foulness of their fate, –
Those doomed, conscripted, unvictorious ones?'

'ON PASSING THE NEW MENIN GATE' (1928)

Lost Between
Earth and Heaven

George Leigh Mallory
and Andrew Irvine

(1924)

On 8 June 1924 the British mountaineers George Leigh Mallory and Andrew Irvine set off from their small tent at 26,800 feet on the north flank of Mount Everest intent on becoming the first men to stand on the highest point on earth, just over 2200 feet above them. 'Perfect weather for the job!' Mallory had scrawled in a note he sent down with the porters who had helped them make camp. The next day dawned clear, but before long wreaths of mist began to unwind across the north face.

At 12.50 p.m., as the clouds briefly parted, Mallory and Irvine were seen by Noel Odell, a fellow team member some 2000 feet below them. They were, Odell said, making progress along the northeast ridge, heading for the summit pyramid. But then they were shrouded again in mist, which Odell said had a kind of luminous quality.

Over the next few days, those below waited anxiously for news. Howard Somervell, who prior to Mallory and Irvine's attempt had himself reached 28,000 feet before turning back drained to exhaustion in the thin air, wrote in his diary:

> June 11th.—*No news. It is ominous. A few people here have filtered back to Base, very pessimistic. It is very disappointing to think that Mallory and Irvine may have failed – but they may never come back. They may be dead. My friend and fellow-climber, Mallory, one in spirit with me – dead? – I can hardly believe it.*
>
> June 12th.—*They are all arriving at the Base now. No signs of Mallory and Irvine. Odell went up on the 9th to 27,000 feet, and found the tent there empty. There are only two possibilities – accident or benightenment. It is terrible. But there are few better deaths than to die in high endeavour, and Everest is the finest cenotaph in the world to a couple of the best of men.*

'A COUPLE OF THE BEST OF MEN'

Even allowing for the very British principle of *De mortuis nil nisi bonum* ('about the dead say nothing unless it be good'), Mallory and Irvine, were, it was generally agreed, very 'decent sorts'. In a letter from Base Camp at the beginning of the 1924 expedition, Somervell had written frankly about the other team members to his brother. He had this to say about the 22-year-old Andrew ('Sandy') Irvine:

> *Irvine, our blue-eyed boy from Oxford, is much younger than any of us, and is really a very good sort; neither bumptious by virtue of his 'blue' [he had rowed for Oxford in its 1923 victory against Cambridge], nor squashed by the age of the rest of us. Mild but strong, full of common sense, good at gadgets ... He's thoroughly a man (or boy) of the world, yet with high ideals, and very decent with the porters.*

Many years later Somervell – who became a medical missionary in India – described Mallory in his book *After Everest* (1936) as:

> *A man whose outlook on life was lofty and choice, human and loving, and in a measure divine ...*

For his part, Mallory described Irvine, whom he first met on the 1924 expedition, as 'sensible and not highly strung, he'll be one to depend on, for everything except conversation'.

Irvine – in Somervell's words, 'a stout and hefty lad' – was too young, perhaps, to have gained much in the way of encomiums by the time he was lost on Everest. Mallory, however, had been about a bit. A boy of strikingly good looks, considerable athleticism and no mean intellect, he had been introduced to Alpine climbing by Graham Irving, the senior master of his house at the elite private school, Winchester College. In his obituary of Mallory for the *Alpine Journal*, Irving described Mallory thus:

> *He had a strikingly beautiful face. Its shape, its delicately cut features, especially the rather large, heavily lashed, thoughtful eyes, were extraordinarily suggestive of a Botticelli Madonna, even when he had ceased to be a boy – though any suspicion of effeminacy was completely banished by obvious proofs of physical energy and strength.*

THE GOLDEN BOY

The aura that surrounded Mallory intensified when he went up to Cambridge in 1905. It was here that he found himself on the fringes of the Bloomsbury Group, caught up in the hothouse homoerotic atmosphere that appears to have prevailed at Cambridge in the years prior to the First World War. He was pursued by the extravagantly homosexual writer and critic, Lytton Strachey, but preferred Lytton's brother James (who later translated Freud into English, and with whom Mallory had his only homosexual encounter, which turned out to be unsatisfactory to both parties). James Strachey, meanwhile, pined for the poet Rupert Brooke, who directed Mallory in a minor role in a production of Milton's *Comus*. Lytton Strachey, writing to fellow Bloomsbury-ites Clive and Vanessa Bell in 1909, could barely contain himself:

> *Mon Dieu! George Mallory! When that's been written, what more need be said? My hand trembles, my heart palpitates, my whole being swoons away at the words – oh heavens, heavens! I found of course that he'd been absurdly maligned – he's six foot high, with the body of an athlete by Praxiteles, and a face – oh incredible – the mystery of Botticelli, the refinement and delicacy of a Chinese print, the youth and piquancy of an imaginable English boy. I rave, but when you see him, as you must, you will admit all – all!*

Mallory's physical beauty also drew the attention of the Bloomsbury painter Duncan Grant, who made two nude portraits of him, and who was certain that Mallory liked to be admired. In a letter to Grant, Mallory stated that 'I am profoundly interested in the nude me.' This pride and pleasure in his own body continued into his thirties: a photograph survives of one of the approach marches to Everest in which Mallory strikes a heroic pose after a river crossing, dressed only in a hat and a rucksack.

SCHOLAR, TEACHER, SOLDIER

But Mallory was more than just a gilded youth. Shortly after leaving Cambridge, where he studied history, he published a study of James Boswell, the biographer of Dr Johnson. Later, when stormbound in a tent high on Everest, he would read to his companions poems by Shelley, Coleridge and Emily Brontë, from Robert Bridges's anthology, *The Spirit of Man*. After Cambridge he became a teacher at Charterhouse, a prestigious private school in the south of England. Among his pupils there was the future poet and novelist Robert Graves, and it was here that Mallory began to evolve ideas about a less hidebound, discipline-led form of education for boys, one that

> *That young man will not be alive for long.*
>
> KARL BLÖDIG ON GEORGE MALLORY IN 1911, AFTER A DAY'S CLIMBING WITH HIM ON THE CRAGS OF SNOWDONIA, NORTH WALES. BLÖDIG WAS AN AUSTRIAN DENTIST WHO BECAME THE FIRST MAN TO CLIMB ALL 57 OF THE PEAKS IN THE ALPS OVER 4000 METRES.

would bring out their humanity and their individual spirit. Graves said he was one of the very few 'really decent masters' at the school.

Although Mallory continued to have close relations with a number of men, these were all platonic, intellectual friendships, mostly centred around climbing. Mallory pioneered a number of difficult new routes up the mountain cliffs in North Wales and the Lake District, and also acquitted himself well on many of the *grandes courses* of the Alps. It was while mountaineering there that he first met a vivacious young woman called Cottie Saunders, with whom he struck up an enduring friendship, even though she ended up marrying someone else. On holiday in Italy at Easter 1914, Mallory met his soul-mate, the astonishingly beautiful Ruth Turner, whom he referred to as his 'one true vision … brave and true and sweet', and whom he introduced to the joys of mountain climbing. They married at the end of July that year, just a few days before Britain declared war on Germany, and went on to have two daughters and a son.

Mallory was keen to volunteer to fight, but it was not until December 1915 that his headmaster would allow him to join the army, which he did as an artillery officer. The following year he witnessed the terrible fighting at the Somme: '"Oh the pity of it!" I very often exclaim when I see the dead lying out, and anger when I see corpses quite inexcusably not buried.' After the war he returned to teaching at Charterhouse. 'If I haven't escaped so many chances of death as plenty of others,' he wrote to his father, a clergyman, 'still it is surprising to find myself a survivor, and it's not a lot I've always wanted. There has not been much to be said for being alive in the company of the dead. Anyway, it's good to be alive now.'

Teaching did not turn out to be so fulfilling for Mallory. His humanist, child-centred ideas about education held no sway at Charterhouse. He began to ponder what else he could do with his life, when, on 23 January 1921 he received a letter from the secretary of the Alpine Club: 'It looks as though Everest would really be tried this summer. Party would leave early April and get back in October. Any aspirations?'

The invitation put an end to Mallory's uncertainties. The only doubt in his mind was his responsibility to his wife and young family. Ruth told him to go. Mallory took the plunge, resigned his teaching post, and seized what he called 'the opportunity of a lifetime'.

THE OPPORTUNITY OF A LIFETIME

Mallory went on three expeditions to Everest. The first was small in scale, and involved reconnoitring an approach through Tibet to the northern side of the mountain. Mallory pioneered a way up to the North Col, which turned out to be the key to a possible way to the summit. The second expedition, in 1922, was thwarted by bad weather and marred by the deaths of seven porters in an avalanche, although Mallory reached 26,985 feet without bottled oxygen. It was a daunting,

The highest of mountains is capable of severity, a severity so awful and so fatal that the wiser sort of men do well to think and tremble even on the threshold of their high endeavour.

GEORGE LEIGH MALLORY, WRITING AFTER THE 1921
RECONNAISSANCE EXPEDITION TO EVEREST

A Poignant Coincidence

On 8 June 1924 – the day that Mallory and Irvine were making their fateful summit bid on Everest – Mallory's old friend and climbing mentor, the poet and writer Geoffrey Winthrop Young, was on the summit of a far lower, but equally significant, mountain in the Lake District. The peak in question, Great Gable, was where in 1886 the sport of rock climbing had begun in Britain. Now, in 1924, Young was there for a more sombre purpose, the unveiling of a bronze plaque in memory of all the members of the Fell and Rock Climbing Club who had fallen in the First World War. Young himself had lost a leg during the fighting, but this did not stop him climbing, with the aid of an artificial limb. When he heard what had happened on Everest, and that Mallory might have succeeded in surmounting the Second Step, he wrote: 'After nearly twenty years' knowledge of Mallory as a mountaineer, I can say that difficult as it would have been for any mountaineer to turn back, with the only difficulty past, to Mallory it would have been an impossibility.'

draining, dangerous game, made perilous by thin air, treacherous snow slopes, bitter cold and storms of unparalleled violence. 'We were not playing with this mountain,' Mallory later wrote; 'it might be playing with us.'

It was another two years before a third attempt could be mounted. When he had been asked by an American reporter in 1923 why he wanted to climb Everest, Mallory famously responded, 'Because it is there.' Whether he was being flippant, or whether his famous words encapsulated an existential necessity, is uncertain, but it appears that he felt that the 1924 expedition would be his last chance at the summit. Prior to setting off, he seems to have been troubled by premonitions. He was apparently discomfited by a meeting with the widow of Captain Scott, who had died on his way back from the South Pole in 1912, and after the meeting confided in a friend that he did not want to return to Everest. He told another friend, Geoffrey Keynes (brother of the great economist), that it would be 'more like a war than adventure, and that he did not believe he would return alive'.

But once confronted again with the reality of the mountain, Mallory buckled down to the business of climbing it. He was part of a strong team, led, like the 1922 expedition, by General Charles Bruce. They faced even worse storms than the previous attempt, however, and it wasn't until after the middle of May that the weather cleared sufficiently to make a summit bid thinkable. There would only be time for two attempts before the monsoon snows arrived, making progress up or down the mountain impractical.

The first attempt, by Mallory and Geoffrey Bruce, fizzled out at 25,200 feet when their porters refused to continue, making it impossible for them to establish a camp high enough to make a summit bid. The second team, of Howard Somervell and Edward Norton, had better luck, and set up Camp 6 at 26,800 feet. They started off for the summit the next morning, without bottled oxygen, making painfully slow progress, unable to take more than a dozen steps without stopping to rest. Eventually first Somervell and then Norton ground to a complete halt. 'We realized that it would be madness to continue,' wrote Somervell.

THE THIRD ATTEMPT

In the meantime, Mallory had decided to make a third attempt, this time with oxygen, and chose as his partner Andrew Irvine. Irvine may not have been a very experienced climber, but he was as strong as an ox – and a mechanical genius, able to fiddle and adjust the primitive and temperamental breathing apparatus whenever required. While Somervell and Norton, when they turned back, 'were somehow quite content to leave it at that', Mallory seems to have had a very different attitude: 'I can't see myself coming down defeated,' he had written to Ruth.

Early on the morning of 8 June Mallory and Irvine set off for the summit. The terrain above Camp 6, though not technically difficult, is treacherous, with the rock shelves sloping downward, like tiles on a roof, and the coverings of gravel and ice and powder snow making each step a throw of the dice, a Herculean effort seized by the failing body from the thin air.

At 12.50 their team mate, Noel Odell, looked up from far below:

... there was a sudden clearing of the atmosphere, and the entire summit ridge and final peak of Everest were unveiled. My eyes became fixed on one tiny black spot silhouetted on a small snow-crest beneath a rock-step in the ridge; the black spot moved. Another black spot became apparent and moved up the snow to join the other on the crest. The first then approached the great rock-step and shortly emerged at the top; the second did likewise. Then the whole fascinating vision vanished, enveloped in cloud once more.

After that – nothing. The next day, Odell climbed up to Camp 5 to see if there was any trace of the two men, and the day after continued on up to Camp 6. From there he struggled on for a couple of hours, but could find no sign of them. Returning to the tent, he dragged out a couple of sleeping bags and laid them out in the snow in the shape of a 'T'. The prearranged signal to those watching far below meant 'No trace can be found – given up hope.' Ruth received the news by telegram while on holiday with her children at the seaside.

THE UNANSWERED QUESTION

What happened to Mallory and Irvine? In 1933 another British expedition found Irvine's ice axe well below the First Step, and a used oxygen cylinder nearby. Five decades later, a story began to filter through to the West that in 1975 a Chinese climber had found 'an old English dead' high on the mountain. Prompted by this story, in 1999 an American research expedition found Mallory's body, face down and with a broken leg, at 26,760 feet on the north face of the mountain, more or less below the place where Irvine's ice axe had been found on the ridge above. The body was well-preserved in the cold, dry air, and showed signs that Mallory had fallen. He was buried where he lay. Irvine's body has still not been found.

It is not difficult for me to believe that George's spirit was ready for another life and his way of going to it was very beautiful ...

RUTH MALLORY, LETTER TO GEOFFREY WINTHROP YOUNG, 1924

Could they have reached the summit? Odell had thought that he had seen them above the Second Step, a rock barrier on the northeast ridge. If that was the case, they were making good progress and might well have reached the summit. But it seems from other evidence that they were, at the highest, just above the First Step. Later climbers have reported that the Second Step is as hard as anything Mallory had climbed at sea level, and quite beyond anything that Irvine had attempted – but there are still those who believe that Mallory was capable of it. It has also been pointed out that between them they did not have sufficient oxygen to reach the summit. It is of course possible that Mallory went on alone, taking Irvine's spare cylinder.

Mallory's daughter Clare always believed that it was her father's intention to place a photograph

Britons Lost on Everest

Everest was always a very British obsession. After the ill-fated 1924 expedition, it was another nine years before a fourth attempt was made, and almost three decades before the 1953 British expedition succeeded in putting Edmund Hillary (a New Zealander) and Tenzing Norgay (a Nepali Sherpa) on the summit.

It was not until 1975, however, that the first Britons – Dougal Haston and Doug Scott – reached the top, having climbed the mountain by the very difficult southwest face. Following in their footsteps on the same expedition, the climbing cameraman Mick Burke was last seen heading alone for the summit in stormy conditions. He never returned, but it is possible that he made it.

In 1982 another strong British expedition set out to make the first ascent of Everest's formidable north-northeast ridge. The two leading climbers, Pete Boardman and Joe Tasker, disappeared high on the mountain. In 1992 Boardman's body was found by climbers from Kazakhstan near the Second Pinnacle. He was in a sitting position, and 'looked as if he were asleep'.

of Ruth on the summit. But there was no photograph among his possessions when his body was found – confirming Clare in her belief that her father had reached the summit.

In a letter to a friend, Tom Longstaff, who had been on Everest with Mallory in 1922, wrote:

It is obvious to any climber that they got up. You cannot expect of that pair to weigh up the chances of return. I should be weighing them still. It sounds a fair day. Probably they were above those clouds that hid them from Odell. How they must have appreciated that view of half the world. It was worthwhile to them. Now, they will never grow old and I am very sure they would not change places with any of us

Mallory's son John, who was only three when his father died, echoed the views of many mountaineers when he said: 'To me the only way you achieve a summit is to come back alive. The job is half done if you don't get down again.' He would far rather have had a father, he said, than a legend.

All his life he sought after whatsoever things are pure and high and eternal. At last in the flower of his perfect manhood he was lost to human sight between earth and heaven on the topmost peak of Mt Everest.

INSCRIPTION IN MEMORY OF GEORGE LEIGH MALLORY IN ST WILFRID'S CHURCH IN THE SMALL CHESHIRE VILLAGE OF MOBBERLEY, WHERE MALLORY'S FATHER HAD BEEN RECTOR WHEN MALLORY WAS A BOY. IT WAS ON THE WALLS AND ROOF OF THIS MEDIEVAL GOTHIC CHURCH THAT IN THE EARLY 1890S THE YOUNG GEORGE HAD BEGUN TO TEST HIS SKILLS AS A ROCK CLIMBER.

The Quest for Z

Colonel Percy Fawcett

(1925)

In many respects, the life of Colonel Percy Harrison Fawcett – soldier, surveyor, mystic and fantasist – spilt over into fiction. A friend of both H. Rider Haggard and Arthur Conan Doyle, Fawcett spent many years exploring the remoter reaches of Amazonia, his descriptions of the rock-girt, forest-covered plateaux of the Serra Ricardo Franco giving Conan Doyle the inspiration for his novel *The Lost World*. In 1925 Fawcett mounted an expedition into the dense jungles of the Mato Grosso, determined to find a lost city he referred to simply as 'Z'. He never returned, but his maverick personality, and his Boy's Own-style adventures – he claimed to have shot a 62-foot anaconda and to have discovered a wild dog with two noses – are said to have inspired the character of Indiana Jones in Steven Spielberg's *Raiders of the Lost Ark* and its various sequels.

On the surface of it, Fawcett's upbringing and early career were conventional enough. Like many boys brought up in the Victorian era, his childhood was, in his own words, 'devoid of parental affection'. After attending Westminster School he became an army cadet, and was commissioned as an officer in the Royal Artillery in 1886. His first posting was in Ceylon (now Sri Lanka), where he met Nina Paterson, They married in 1901, and went on to raise two sons. Shortly after the wedding, Fawcett's life began to take on a bit more colour, when the Foreign Office asked him to undertake undercover intelligence work in Morocco.

EARLY ADVENTURES IN SOUTH AMERICA

Fawcett also trained as a surveyor, and in 1906 he was seconded by the army to the Royal Geographical Society, which had been commissioned as a disinterested third party by the governments of Brazil and Bolivia to establish the border between the two countries, an area rich in rubber, gold and diamonds. Although the two countries had agreed that the border should follow various rivers, the precise courses of these rivers was as yet unknown.

The task was a daunting one, but one that Fawcett relished. Not only was the area thickly forested and infested with dangerous animals, it was also inhabited by largely unknown Indian tribes, who, angered by the attempts of the local European rubber barons to force them to work as virtual slaves, were known to attack any intruder into their territory. Fawcett seems to have got

> It is quite true that [Fawcett] has a reputation of being difficult to get on with, and has a queer manner in many ways, being a mystic and a spiritualist, but all the same he has an extraordinary power of getting through difficulties that would deter anybody else.
>
> SIR JOHN KELTIE, SECRETARY OF THE ROYAL GEOGRAPHICAL SOCIETY, LETTER TO SIR MAURICE DE BUNSEN OF THE FOREIGN OFFICE, 10 MARCH 1920

round the hostility of the local peoples with a combination of gifts and diplomacy, and the success of his first border survey led to further commissions. Having resigned from the army, in 1911 he undertook the exploration of the unknown upper reaches of the Rio Heath, nominated as the border between Bolivia and Peru. It seems that around this time he became intrigued by stories of remains of ancient civilizations in the depths of the forest.

'THE QUEST'

Thus began what Fawcett described as 'The Quest'. To the modern cynic, legends of giant crystals, monuments inscribed with mysterious writing and towers that emit a strange light sound like so much hokum, but Fawcett belonged to a different age, one in which the vast, impenetrable wastes of the Amazonian jungle held unimaginable possibilities. No one had yet flown over the dense forests of Amazonia: the only way to get through them was on foot or by canoe, a slow and dangerous process. Might there not be something behind Indian stories of hidden cities and tribes with pale skins? To the European mind immersed in imperialist ideology and notions of racial superiority, the concept of fair-skinned civilizations existing in as yet unexplored parts of the world did not seem unduly ridiculous – such a notion underlay Rider Haggard's novel *She*, the story of a white-skinned queen in darkest Africa.

Fawcett's search was curtailed by the outbreak of the First World War. He rejoined the army, served as an artillery officer on the Western Front and was promoted to lieutenant-colonel; a curious aspect of his wartime service was his insistence on using an ouija board to locate German gun batteries. After the war he rejoined his family in Devon, but by 1920 he was back on 'The Quest' in South America, where, in the national library in Rio de Janeiro, he came across an account of the discovery in 1753 of a vast, deserted city somewhere deep in the jungle. During the course of the following year he made a number of journeys into the interior, claiming that he had found various things that made a return trip a necessity – although he would not elaborate on the nature of his discoveries.

TOWARDS THE HIDDEN CITY

It was some years before Fawcett was able to return. Back in England he set about raising funds for an expedition consisting of himself, his eldest son Jack, and Jack's old schoolfriend, Raleigh Rimell. In seeking sponsorship, Fawcett had to balance his desire for secrecy with the need to present a plausible outline of where he intended looking for 'Z', as he named the lost city. In London he approached the Royal Geographical Society, which had come to regard him with some suspicion, and also a group of London financiers known somewhat mysteriously as 'The Glove'. From England he sailed to New York, where he gained the support of the National Geographic Society and sold exclusive newspaper rights to the North American Newspaper Alliance (NANA).

The expedition arrived in Rio in February 1925, and proceeded to the town of Cuiabá, situated near the headwaters of the Paraguay River system and at the foot of the Mato Grosso plateau, the watershed between the Paraguay and the Amazon. From Cuiabá the party, having purchased horses and mules, headed north. After covering some 400 miles of difficult terrain, towards the end of May they had crossed the Upper Xingu, a tributary of the Amazon, and reached Dead Horse Camp, so-called because in 1921 Fawcett's horse had died there. At this point Fawcett ordered his Brazilian assistants back to Cuiabá, sending with them a message to his wife, dated 29 May, telling her 'you need have no fear of failure'. Nothing more was ever heard of him, his son Jack, or Raleigh Rimell.

SEEKING COLONEL FAWCETT

Over the years various reports emerged from the jungles of the Mato Grosso of encounters with an old, ill white man. The first came from a Frenchman, Roger Courteville, who said he had come across such a person, who claimed he was Fawcett. Nina Fawcett tried to persuade her remaining son Brian to go out to Brazil to locate this man, but nothing came of this. A later report of an elderly European with long white hair was discounted, as Fawcett had been bald for many years. In 1928 NANA sponsored a search party, but nothing was found bar some equipment Fawcett had abandoned in 1920. Two year later, another search expedition penetrated the Mato Grosso, but never re-emerged – having failed to heed Fawcett's injunction that no one should try to find them should they fail to return.

Two decades later, in 1951, a Brazilian working with the Indian tribes of the Mato Grosso said a Kalapalo chief had admitted on his deathbed that he had killed Fawcett and the two younger men after a quarrel, but the bones disinterred from the place where the chief indicated Fawcett had been buried turned out not to belong to the colonel. It is quite possible that the three men died of natural causes, although the Kalapalo have continued to prove hostile to outsiders: the members of a 1996 expedition were held captive until they handed over all their equipment. In all, over a dozen separate expeditions have tried to find out what happened to Colonel Fawcett, and a hundred people have died in the attempt. But no clear evidence as to the fate of the colonel and his companions has ever emerged.

The Sith Hypothesis

In the early 21st century an intriguing new theory emerged, suggesting that Fawcett's 'disappearance' was entirely deliberate. The writer and director Misha Williams, having been given access to the Fawcett family archives, came to the conclusion that the colonel, influenced by the then fashionable tenets of theosophy, was planning to set up a mystical community in the jungle, centred around the worship of his son Jack. Apparently dozens of fellow-believers were waiting to follow them out from England into the green wilderness of the Mato Grosso. 'The English go native very easily,' Fawcett once said. 'There is no disgrace in it. On the contrary, in my opinion it shows a creditable regard for the real things in life.' Fawcett had already emphasized to would-be sponsors of his last expedition the suitability of his son and his friend, not because of their physical toughness, but because they were resistant to the charms of alcohol, tobacco and sex. Mixed in with Fawcett's vision of a utopian community there seems to have been a 'sith', an ageless female 'spirit guide' known only to the Fawcett family, who, like an erotic siren, lured them into the jungle. Whatever the truth of it, such a theory is entirely in keeping with this strange, obsessional man and his dreams of the Lost City of Z.

Mrs Christie's Ten-Day Absence

Agatha Christie

(1926)

For ten days in 1926 Agatha Christie, the Queen of Crime, was involved in a real-life mystery. Late on the night of Friday 3 December she left her home at Styles, in Sunningdale, Berkshire. The following morning her car was found abandoned off the road in the Surrey Downs. The public was agog, the police baffled, and the press had a field day. But it was little more than a seven-day wonder. On 14 December, Mrs Christie was positively identified in a hotel in Harrogate, Yorkshire. She never explained what had happened, or why she had absented herself from her family and friends.

It has been suggested that she was suffering a mental breakdown, accompanied by amnesia, following the sudden death of her mother, and the announcement by her husband, Colonel Archie Christie, that he wanted a divorce. Others felt that the disappearance was a way of getting back at her husband. Many at the time believed it was simply a publicity stunt to boost sales of her detective novels.

THE LADY VANISHES

Nothing in the way that Agatha Christie behaved in the week before her disappearance suggests anything untoward. She spent some time in London, had a meeting with her publishers, and bought a new negligee. Back at Styles, on the morning of her disappearance, according to a maid, she had a tumultuous row with her husband – although he later denied this. In the afternoon, with her seven-year-old daughter Rosalind, she visited her mother-in-law, who commented that Agatha was not wearing her wedding ring, at which the younger woman 'sat perfectly still for some time, gazing into space, and giving an hysterical laugh, turned away and patted Rosalind's head'. Agatha was apparently aware that her husband was spending the weekend with his mistress, Nancy Neele, in Godalming.

That evening she dined alone, and around 10 or 11 o'clock told a servant she was going out for a drive. At 8 o'clock the following morning a Morris car was found abandoned at Newlands Corner, a beauty spot on the North Downs near Guildford, a few miles to the northeast of Godalming. The police report stated that the car 'was found in such a position as to indicate that some unusual proceeding had taken place, the car being found half-way down a grassy slope well off the main road with its bonnet buried in some bushes'. One witness reported having earlier seen 'a woman in a frenzied condition standing by a motor car near the top of Newlands Corner Hill'. According to this witness, 'she was wearing only a thin frock'. The police contacted Colonel Christie, and took him to view the car. He confirmed it was his wife's.

THE SEARCH

The case attracted maximum publicity. Vast numbers of volunteers – including the detective writer Dorothy L. Sayers – helped the police. Many assumed Agatha Christie had taken her own life – or had been done away with. '10,000 Motorists to Scour Surrey Downs', shouted one newspaper headline, continuing: 'The Downs have been exhaustively explored, ponds have been dragged, and woods combed and recombed in the hope of finding the

I am inclined to think that my daughter-in-law planned her end and deliberately drove the car to where it was found.

MRS HELMSLEY, AGATHA CHRISTIE'S MOTHER-IN-LAW, IN AN INTERVIEW WITH THE *DAILY MAIL*, DECEMBER 1926

> *It is quite true that my wife had discussed the possibility of disappearing at will*
>
> COLONEL ARCHIE CHRISTIE, IN AN
> INTERVIEW WITH THE *DAILY MAIL*,
> 10 DECEMBER 1926

missing woman.' The pond in question was the nearby Silent Pool, which had featured in one of Agatha Christie's stories. But no sign of the missing woman turned up anywhere in the neighbourhood. A clairvoyant suggested her body would be found in a log cabin in the woods. It wasn't.

Suspicion fell on the husband – it was even said that the police tapped his phone. In a press interview, he said he doubted his wife *had* killed herself, and suspected that she had deliberately staged the disappearance. To another journalist he complained that he had been 'badgered and pestered like a criminal'. His mother believed Agatha Christie had killed herself: 'It is my opinion,' she told a reporter, 'that in a fit of depression and not knowing where she was going or what she was doing, my daughter-in-law abandoned her car at Newlands Corner and wandered away over the Downs.'

THE LADY FOUND

Agatha Christie had in fact made her way by train halfway up the country, and on 4 December had checked into the Hydropathic Hotel in Harrogate, Yorkshire, under the name 'Mrs Teresa Neele' – using the same surname as her husband's mistress. After the newspapers had splashed her photograph repeatedly across their pages, staff at the hotel began to have an inkling that their guest, who 'seemed normal and happy', was not who she said she was. They contacted the police, who contacted Colonel Christie, who travelled to Harrogate, where he confirmed that Mrs Neele was indeed Mrs Christie. The unhappy couple left by the back door, in an attempt to escape the pack of waiting pressmen.

Two doctors who examined Agatha Christie declared that she had been suffering from amnesia, Colonel Christie informed the papers. After this, neither friends nor family would speak to journalists, and the writer herself omits the whole affair from her posthumously published autobiography. At the time, the press pursued the deliberate hoax theory, and

> *I felt like a fox, hunted.*
>
> AGATHA CHRISTIE, ON THE PRESS CAMPAIGN
> TO PERSUADE HER TO CONFESS THAT SHE HAD
> PERFORMED AN ELABORATE HOAX

criticized Agatha Christie for wasting police time, public money and the efforts of many voluntary searchers. Janet Morgan, who published the authorized biography in 1984, believes that Agatha Christie may have suffered concussion when her car went off the road, and subsequently entered a 'hysterical fugue', a condition in which the subject, following some great emotional trauma, enters a wandering state, barely aware of past or present; afterwards, the subject has no memory of the episode.

In February 1928 Agatha Christie took herself off to the Canary Islands to get away from it all. The divorce went through in April that year, and gradually she took back control of her life. In 1930 she married Sir Max Mallowan, an archaeologist 14 years her junior, to whom she remained married – reasonably happily, despite his affairs in the later years – for the rest of her life.

Gas is Running Low

AMELIA EARHART

(1937)

'0742 KHAQQ calling *Itasca*. We must be on you but cannot see you but gas is running low. Been unable to reach you by radio. We are flying at 1000 feet.' This was one of the last radio messages received from Amelia Earhart by the *Itasca*, a US Coastguard cutter positioned on watch off Howland Island, a tiny speck of land in the middle of the Pacific Ocean. After a gruelling flight of over 2500 miles, from Lae in New Guinea, Earhart and her navigator, Fred Noonan, were attempting to locate Howland and its rudimentary airstrip. They never found it.

Despite a huge search-and-rescue operation mounted by the US Navy over the course of the following 17 days, no traces of Earhart or Noonan or their Lockheed Electra aircraft were ever found. It wasn't long before rumour-mongers, hoaxers and conspiracy theorists set to work, creating a web of speculation and misinformation. Some claimed to have picked up SOS signals from remote atolls in the Pacific, others that Earhart had faked her own disappearance in order to leave her husband. Most persistently, there were those who believed she had been on an espionage mission for the US government, and had been shot down by the Japanese. The weaving of half-truths, might-have-beens and downright fictions around a famous person has become familiar to us in our age of celebrity culture, but then the process represented something new. The stories that were told about Amelia Earhart all had one thing in common – the desire to find a fitting end to the heroic myth that she herself had created.

THE TOM-BOY FROM SMALL-TOWN KANSAS

Full-mouthed, bright-eyed, crop-haired – Amelia Earhart may have looked like an innocent gamine, but she had a will of steel. Born in 1897 in the small Kansas town of Atchison, Amelia was the daughter of Edwin Earhart, a none-too-successful lawyer, and Amy Otis, the daughter of a retired federal judge. Amy brought her two daughters up to be independent-minded and tough – an attitude that Amelia found increasingly necessary as her father declined into alcoholism. Amelia tried in vain to save Edwin Earhart from himself, on one occasion pouring his whiskey down the sink. He was furious, and tried to hit her. When he was found drunk at his desk he was fired from his job with a railroad company. Edwin and Amy separated, although they were later reconciled. For her part Amelia adopted an outgoing manner, involving herself in numerous projects. She gave little indication of an inner life, avoiding any intimacy. Her closed exterior was no doubt a reaction to what she thought of as her father's betrayal.

AE, as she became known, was determined to show that women could do anything that men could do. She had set her sights on either Bryn Mawr or Vassar, the two top women's universities in America, but the family's financial circumstances made this impractical. During the First World War

> *AE was something of a prima donna. She had a façade of being shy and humble, but she really had an ego, and she could be as tough as nails when the occasion required it.*
>
> CAPTAIN HARRY MANNING OF THE US NAVY, WHO SOMETIMES FLEW WITH EARHART AS CO-PILOT OR NAVIGATOR

she espoused pacifism, working as a nurse's aide in Toronto, and in 1919 enrolled as a medical student at Columbia University, although she left a year later to join her parents in California. She subsequently tried her hand at social work and teaching English, but she had already, in Toronto, been thrilled at an air display when a stunt plane dived straight at her. 'I believe that little red airplane said something to me as it swished by,' she recalled. Her first ride in an aeroplane, in 1920, clinched her ambition, and she determined to learn to fly.

'FIRST LADY OF THE AIR'

By January 1921 AE had saved enough from her earnings in a variety of odd jobs to begin flying lessons. Six months later she bought her first plane, in which she flew to an altitude of over 14,000 feet, setting a new record for a woman pilot. A string of other records followed. In 1928 she became the first woman to fly across the Atlantic, although she was not at the controls – something she rectified four years later when she repeated Charles Lindbergh's feat and flew across the Atlantic solo, battling with iced wings and an engine fire. The flight earned her the nickname 'Lady Lindy' – a title she loathed. Other newspapers called her 'Queen of the Air' or 'America's First Lady of the Air'. In 1931 she flew to over 18,000 feet in an autogyro, and in 1935 she flew solo from Honolulu to California, from Los Angeles to Mexico City, and from Mexico to Newark, New Jersey – all firsts.

In the 1920s and 1930s aviation was the great new field of adventure, attracting huge coverage in the press. AE exploited this to the full, cultivating her androgynous image by making sure she was photographed in her trademark garb of trousers, man's shirt, scarf and scuffed leather jacket. She was taken up by the wealthy publisher George P. Putnam (known as GP), a brilliant publicist who had been looking for an aviatrix to participate in one of the schemes he was promoting, the 1928 flight across the Atlantic. Putnam, ten years AE's senior, subsequently proposed to her on a number of occasions, and the two eventually married in 1931. On the day of the wedding, AE handed GP a note: 'Let me go in one year if we find no happiness together.' By this time GP had already turned his wife into a celebrity, and the Amelia Earhart brand had become a hot commercial property: she delivered lectures, wrote articles, endorsed products ranging from children's toys to luggage, and modelled her own range of elegant and very feminine couture. At the same time she energetically promoted a feminist message, showing women that there was more to life than the kitchen, the nursery and the bedroom.

ONE LAST FLIGHT

AE was only too well aware of the strains and hazards of pioneering long-distance flights along new routes – over oceans, mountains, jungles and deserts, without the sophisticated navigational instruments available to today's pilots, and often out of radio contact with the rest of the world. The fatigue involved could be tremendous, with AE having to pilot her plane for 14, 17 or even 19 hours non-stop. Her husband repeatedly urged her to give up these dangerous attempts, but the two agreed on one final, glorious adventure, on a scale much greater than anything she had previously attempted. 'I have a feeling that there is just about one more

I know that if I fail or if I am lost you will be blamed for allowing me to leave on this trip ... But it's my responsibility and mine alone.

AMELIA EARHART TO HER HUSBAND
GEORGE PUTNAM, 31 MAY 1937

good flight left in my system,' she told a journalist in May 1937, 'and I hope this trip is it.' The 'trip' in question was to be the first flight all the way around the world, sticking as close as possible to the equator.

Her plane, a silver Lockheed Electra 10E, was a twin-engined, twin-tailed, state-of-the-art machine, purchased for her by Purdue University, where she counselled women on careers and acted as a technical adviser to the Department of Aeronautics. In the posthumously published *Last Flight*, compiled from her journal entries, she describes the cockpit:

> *The dimensions of my cubbyhole are four feet eight inches high, four feet six inches fore and aft … nearly every inch of floor, wall and ceiling is covered with equipment. There are considerably more than a hundred gadgets in a modern cockpit that the pilot must periodically look at or twiddle.*

Her navigator's working space was some way behind her, and the two communicated by passing notes via a fishing line or on the end of a cleft bamboo pole.

In planning the flight, George Putnam, who knew everyone and who could persuade anyone to do anything, prevailed upon the US Navy to provide support ships at strategic points across the Pacific. The USA had only just recently laid claim to Howland Island, which is approximately half way between Hawaii and New Guinea, and in anticipation of AE's flight a rudimentary airstrip was built there, so that she could take on fuel. GP also paid considerable attention to the commercial spin-offs, arranging the post-flight lecture tour, and printing 10,000 special envelopes for AE to carry and post from various exotic locations en route. The envelopes could be purchased for $2.50 – or $5.00 with 'Miss Earhart's autograph'.

With all the arrangements in place, including permissions to fly across many other countries' territories, AE took off from Oakland in California on 17 March 1937, with Fred Noonan as navigator and two other crew. Just under 16 hours and 2400 miles later she landed in Honolulu, having taken an hour off the record held by the Boeing Clipper flying boats run by Pan Am. The loneliness and isolation of these pioneering trans-oceanic flights can be gauged from AE's account of spotting one of the Clippers 'silhouetted against a towering bank of cumulus, sun-flecked clouds … this was the first time I had ever seen another plane at sea, and later I was to learn that in all their Pacific crossings up to then Pan American pilots had never sighted each other'.

This first round-the-world attempt was to be short-lived, however. After a 24-hour rest to recover from her fatiguing flight, AE piloted the Electra down the runway at Luke Field, near Pearl Harbor. Around a thousand feet into her run, the Electra, weighed down with fuel, swung out of control. The undercarriage collapsed, and the plane skidded along the runway on its belly, eventually coming to rest. Luckily, no fire broke out, and AE and her crew managed to scramble free, but the machine was badly damaged. When asked by a radio reporter if she'd try again, she replied 'Of course.'

THE SECOND ATTEMPT

The cost of repairing and rebuilding the Electra was down to AE and her husband. 'I more or less mortgaged my future,' she said. 'Without regret, however, for what are futures for?' AE blamed her crash at Luke Field on a technical failure, but many experienced pilots suspected human error – despite her many achievements, AE was not the most proficient of fliers. Some of her colleagues also felt there had been inadequate technical preparation for her second attempt, which began on 21 May. This time she was flying round the world the other way, her first leg taking her from Los Angeles to Miami. She took with her just one crew member: navigator Fred Noonan. Before leaving Miami, AE told her husband: 'I know that if I fail or if I am lost you will be blamed for allowing me to leave on this trip; the backers of the flight will be blamed and everyone connected with it. But it's my responsibility and mine alone.' Later, GP recalled their parting in a dingy hangar:

There in the dim chill we perched briefly on cold concrete steps, her hands in mine. There is very little one says at such times. When Bo called that all was ready, Amelia's eyes were clear with the good light of the adventure that lay before her. But as she walked out ... she seemed to me very small and slim and feminine ...

AE's departure was surrounded by celebrity gossip. She had apparently confided in a friend that she might be pregnant, and in fact on several occasions during the flight experienced nausea in the morning, blaming it on fuel fumes. There were also persistent rumours that AE intended to divorce GP after the flight, although the identity of the man she was supposedly going to marry varied.

The planned flight took AE and Noonan in a series of hops: across the Caribbean, down the coast of the Guianas and Brazil, across the Atlantic to Senegal, then over the southern fringes of the Sahara. From Khartoum they crossed the Red Sea, following the coast of Arabia to the mouth of the Persian Gulf and then across to the Indian subcontinent and on down through Burma, Thailand and Malaya to Singapore. A few more hops from island to island in the Dutch East Indies took them to Darwin in Australia, and on 29 June they landed in Lae, in eastern New Guinea. The trip was not without its adventures: crossing the Atlantic AE preferred to follow her own intuition rather than Noonan's calculations and ended up in St Louis, Senegal, 163 miles north of their intended destination, Dakar. On 17 June they had a close escape taking off from a rain-sodden airfield in Calcutta: 'That take-off was precarious, perhaps as risky as any we had. The plane clung for what seemed like ages to the heavy sticky soil before the wheels finally lifted, and we cleared with nothing at all to spare the fringe of trees at the airdrome's edge.'

INTO THE WIDE BLUE YONDER

By the time AE and Noonan reached Lae they had flown some 22,000 miles. The Electra's parachutes had been abandoned in Darwin, on the grounds that they would be no use during the 7000-mile crossing of the Pacific Ocean that still lay ahead. AE's plan – with a sharp eye on the significance of the date – was to arrive back in California on 4 July, but poor weather in Lae and various technical problems meant that this timetable had to be abandoned. Both AE and Noonan were suffering from fatigue, partly due to lack of sleep. Noonan, known to be a heavy drinker, apparently went on a bender after a row with AE – but only after they had decided not to fly the next day. Noonan in particular faced a very tricky task on the next leg: it was up to him to locate an island of no more than one square mile in area, and nowhere higher than 18 feet, in the vast expanse of the Pacific Ocean. But he was absolutely confident that he could find it. On the morning of 2 July the weather cleared, and AE made the decision to take off for Howland Island.

The flight almost ended in disaster before it had begun. The Electra had never taken on such a massive load of fuel, required for the 2556-mile flight to Howland. The 1000-yard runway at Lae ended in a 25-foot drop into the sea, and it was only 50 yards before the end that the Electra made it into the air. In a moment it had dropped down within a few feet of the surface of the sea, the propellers churning up spray. One eyewitness reported that the plane 'had not climbed to more than 100 feet before it disappeared from sight'. Nevertheless, the local pilots were full of admiration at the way AE had handled such an overloaded craft. The time was 00.00 GMT.

Although there had been virtually no wind during takeoff – which was why it was such a hair's-breadth affair – during the flight AE encountered stronger than expected headwinds, reducing her average groundspeed to only 118 mph, compared to an airspeed of 150 mph. By 08.00 GMT the Electra was 800 miles into its flight, near the Nukumanu Islands. This was AE's last radio contact with Lae. What happened thereafter is shrouded in confusion, and there were no subsequent reports of anybody on the ground seeing the Electra overhead. The USS *Ontario*, on watch for the flight some 400 miles east of the Nukumanu Islands, received no response from AE to its Morse signal. Another

> *We are circling but cannot hear you ...*
>
> AMELIA EARHART, RADIO
> SIGNAL TO THE USS COASTGUARD
> CUTTER *ITASCA*, 2 JULY 1937

500 miles beyond the *Ontario*, at 14.15 GMT, when the Electra was somewhere over the Gilbert Islands, the *Itasca*, standing off Howland, picked up a faint transmission from AE, but nothing could be made out bar the words 'cloudy and overcast'. Over the next few hours the *Itasca* continued to transmit signals to AE at the allocated times and on the allocated frequencies – but AE only made some of her half-hourly time slots in response, and some of her transmissions were too faint to be understood. At 18.15 GMT she reported that she was 'About 100 miles out.' At 19.12 GMT – 07.42 ship's time on the *Itasca* – her voice was clear: 'We must be on you but cannot see you but gas is running low. Been unable to reach you by radio. We are flying at altitude 1000 feet.' The high-frequency direction finder on Howland Island could not locate the Electra, and the *Itasca* resorted to the low-tech tactic of making heavy black smoke, which should have been visible to a radius of 20 miles. The *Itasca* continued to transmit, but received no response.

By now AE and Noonan had been in the air for over 19 hours. They were running short of fuel, and could see no sign of either the *Itasca* or Howland Island. Neither could they hear the *Itasca's* radio signals – if they had, AE could have deployed her own direction-finding apparatus. At 19.28 GMT she again called the *Itasca*: 'We are circling but cannot hear you ...' At 20.14 GMT the radio operators on board the *Itasca* heard Amelia's voice for the last time: 'We are on the line of position one five seven dash three three seven. Will repeat this message on 6210 kilocycles. We are running north and south.' The *Itasca* continued to transmit on all frequencies until 21.30 GMT. At that point the ship's captain, Commander Warner K. Thompson, assuming that AE had ditched in the sea having run out of fuel, ordered a search to begin.

THE FOUR MILLION DOLLAR SEARCH

The fact that AE had said at 19.12 GMT that she was flying at 1000 feet indicated to Commander Thompson that she was keeping below a cloud ceiling, as otherwise she would have flown much higher in order to get a better view of Howland. Thompson noted that the only cloud cover was to the north and northwest of Howland, and so concentrated search efforts in that sector. Gradually the area of search was broadened to take in the Phoenix Islands to the south of Howland. On the assumption that the Electra could float on its empty fuel tanks if it ditched, and aware that AE was an all-American heroine close to the heart of his electorate, President F.D. Roosevelt authorized the deployment of nine ships of the US Navy, including the battleship USS *Colorado*, the aircraft carrier *Lexington* and 66 aeroplanes, at an estimated cost of $4 million.

But no sign of AE or Noonan or the Electra was found, and the search was eventually called off on 19 July 1937. George Putnam told reporters, 'If Amelia is dead it is the way she would have chosen.' Nevertheless, he offered a reward of $2000 for any information, and pressed for further searches of the Phoenix Islands, the Gilbert Islands and the Marshall Islands, the latter a Japanese mandated territory since the end of the First World War. Although – poignantly – Putnam continued to receive letters that Amelia had sent him from her various stop-off points around the world, no further hint of her fate emerged..

A SECRET MISSION?

Subsequent to AE's disappearance, various politicians began to question the sums the government had spent on the search effort. The US government responded by pointing out that the overflights made by Navy planes of hitherto little known islands had made a valuable contribution to the knowledge of the geography and operating conditions 'in a part of the Pacific which is becoming of increasing strategic importance'.

The USA by this stage was becoming concerned about Japan's ambitions in the region, and was no doubt anxious to learn the extent of any military build-up in the Japanese-controlled Marshall Islands that might threaten America's own interests and territories in the Pacific. It is not inconceivable that the support that AE received from the US government and the US Navy was in return for her carrying out photo-reconnaissance over the Marshall Islands, under the guise of losing her way during her round-the-world flight, and that she was shot down by the Japanese.

The Bones on Gardner Island

A week after AE's last radio message, an aeroplane from the USS *Colorado* flew over Gardner Island (now Nikumaroro) in the Phoenix group (now part of Kiribati). Gardner had not been inhabited for some forty years, but the report on the flight stated:

> Here signs of recent habitation were clearly visible but repeated circling and zooming failed to elicit any answering wave from possible inhabitants and it was finally taken for granted that none were there ... Given a chance, it is believed that Miss Earhart could have landed her aircraft in [the] lagoon and swum or waded ashore.

In 1940 a British colonial officer reported that he had found a skeleton and a sextant box on Gardner Island. The bones were taken to Fiji, where, in 1941, detailed measurements were made. At the time it was concluded that the skeleton belonged to a stocky male, although analysis of the recorded data by forensic anthropologists in 1998 (the actual bones had been lost) suggested that the remains belonged to a 'tall white female of northern European ancestry'. Subsequent expeditions to Nikumaroro found further artefacts, some of which could have related to AE, Noonan and the Electra, but the evidence remains inconclusive.

However, there is no direct evidence that this was the case, despite the efforts of a variety of conspiracy theorists to knit together a convincing narrative – no doubt encouraged by the 1943 movie *Flight for Freedom*, a wartime morale-booster that depicted a character akin to AE carrying out an espionage mission against the Japanese. Supposed eyewitness accounts of AE's captivity and execution on Saipan, in the Japanese-occupied Marianas Islands, were recorded decades after the event, and cannot be relied upon. However, rumours that AE was held by the Japanese were persistent enough for the US government, after the Second World War, to ask George Putnam to listen to the voices of the various European women known as 'Tokyo Rose', who broadcast Japanese propaganda in English during the war, to see if one of them might have been AE. However, GP failed to identify any of the voices as that of his wife.

The truth is likely to be more prosaic, and less satisfactory – as the truth often is. The generally accepted conclusion as to AE's fate, supported by a range of aviation experts, is that through a small navigational error AE and Noonan missed Howland Island and, out of gas, ditched in the sea. Unless the waters are exceptionally calm, any crash landing in the sea is likely to result in the violent disintegration of the aeroplane. Even if they had managed to land without breaking up, experts now believe that the plane would have rapidly nose-dived to the bottom of the ocean. And it is there, almost certainly, that the remains of Amelia Earhart lie.

For AE it may not have been the worst of fates. 'Please know I am quite aware of the hazards,' she had said before her last flight. 'I want to do it because I want to do it. Women must try to do things as men have tried. When they fail their failure must be but a challenge to others.'

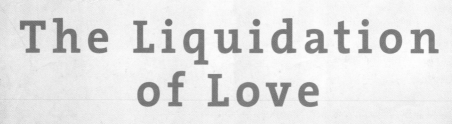

The Liquidation
of Love

Rose Cohen

(1937)

For seventy years the old mansion at 8/1 Nikolskaya Street in Moscow held a terrible secret. In the 19th century it had belonged to a merchant called Chizhyov, a friend of the author of *Dead Souls*, Nikolai Gogol. After the October Revolution the place became a Red Army dormitory, and then an outpost of the nearby Lubyanka, the headquarters of the NKVD – Stalin's infamous secret police. The Military Collegium of the Supreme Court of the USSR, the body responsible for handing down the death penalty, was also conveniently close at hand.

Under Russia's new free-market economy, 8/1 Nikolskaya Street is being converted into an entertainment centre and cinema. On Wednesday 3 October 2007, during the renovation process, builders enlarging the basement came across the skeletons of 34 people, along with a rusty 1903 Browning revolver. When the police began to investigate they found bullet marks on skull fragments, showing that the people had been shot at close range. 'Forensic examinations will be needed,' a police spokesman told journalists, 'but according to the specialists' initial conclusions these people were killed in the 1930s. Most likely they were the victims of political repression ...'

THE KNOCK ON THE DOOR

Stalin's Great Purge began on 1 December 1934 with the assassination of Sergei Kirov, the party leader in Leningrad. Although Stalin himself may have ordered the killing, distrusting Kirov's growing popularity, he used the death of his old friend and ally as an opportunity to 'liquidate' anybody who he thought might threaten his power, accusing them of being in league with his exiled rival, Leon Trotsky – or with the British or the Japanese or the Germans. After Kirov's assassination he introduced the infamous 'Law of First December', which laid down that prosecutors could question suspects in court without the presence of witnesses or defence lawyers, and order their immediate execution following conviction. There was no right of appeal. A further law in 1935 declared that all family members of an 'enemy of the Motherland' were by definition also guilty, and all children over the age of 12 were liable to prosecution.

The first to go were old Bolsheviks such as Kamenev, Zinoviev and Bukharin, the heroes of the revolutionary struggle. Absurd confessions were extracted under torture and aired at public 'show trials', at which the accused were invariably sentenced to death. As Stalin's daughter Svetlana later recalled. 'Years of friendship and fighting side by side in a common cause might as well never have been. He could wipe it all out at a stroke ...'

Through the later 1930s Stalin widened the net, hauling in Communist Party officials, army officers, 'dangerous ethnic elements', kulaks – the wealthy peasants – and even members of the NKVD itself. Stalin's paranoia knew no bounds: on 2 July 1937 a decree was issued that ordered all local NKVD troikas to fulfil quotas of those to be charged with crimes against the state. During 1937 and 1938 the NKVD arrested and detained some 1.5 million people, of whom nearly 700,000 were shot, usually at prepared mass burial sites

Anyone who by his thoughts and actions – yes, his thoughts – encroaches on the unity of the socialist state, we will destroy.

JOSEPH STALIN IN 1935,
TOASTING THE ANNIVERSARY
OF THE 1917 REVOLUTION

well away from the main urban centres. Some historians put the figures at several times those cited above. Hundreds of thousands – possibly millions – more died in the Gulag, the network of punitive labour camps that extended across the more hostile parts of the Soviet Union. The most notorious were in Kolyma, in the far northeast of Siberia, where the gates of each camp bore the edifying slogan: 'Labour is a matter of honour, valour and heroism.' The prisoners themselves had a rhyme:

> *Kolyma, wonderful planet,*
> *Twelve months winter, the rest summer.*

Only a tiny proportion of victims were given a show trial and their sentence announced to the world. The majority would simply receive a knock on the door in the middle of the night. '*Za chto?*' they would ask the men arresting them – 'What for?' Their friends and neighbours would know they had been taken away, but no one could be sure of their subsequent whereabouts, or of their ultimate fate.

He sought to strike, not at the ideas of his opponent, but at his skull.

LEON TROTSKY ON STALIN, 1936

'ALL MY LIFE IS YOURS'

It was not just Soviet citizens who became Stalin's victims. For many young idealists around the world, the USSR had become a beacon of hope in a world of exploitation and injustice. Communist parties had been formed in many countries following the Russian Revolution of 1917, mostly created on the direct orders of Stalin's predecessor, Lenin, who controlled them via a Moscow-based institution, the Communist International – known as the Comintern. Many foreigners came to work for this and other Soviet bodies in Russia, among them an attractive, vivacious and highly intelligent young Englishwoman called Rose Cohen.

Rose Cohen was born in London in 1894 of Jewish parents who had been forced by persecution to flee from Poland. Rose's mother and father worked in the garment trade in London's East End, struggling to make ends meet. After primary school, Rose continued to study with the help of the Workers' Educational Association, and found employment with the Labour Research Organization, a left-wing think-tank. In 1920 she became a founder-member of the Communist Party of Great Britain. With her charm, her winning smile, her brown eyes and long dark hair, she turned not a few heads, including that of another founder member, a young man called Harry Pollitt. For all his life Pollitt was a dedicated communist, becoming general secretary of the party in 1929, and remaining the most important figure in the British Communist Party for nearly three decades.

The photograph that opens this chapter shows Rose Cohen (back, right) and Harry Pollitt (back, left) with some other British communists in Moscow in the 1920s. On the back is a caption in Pollitt's handwriting that includes the words:

> *Rose Cohen, who I am*
> *in love with, and*
> *who has rejected me 14 times.*

According to a friend of Rose's, Pollitt once promised her: 'Rose, all my life is yours, at any time you want it.'

The man Rose chose over Pollitt was an old Bolshevik some ten years her senior called Max Petrovsky, whom she first met in 1921. In 1924 Petrovsky – who used a number of aliases, including Lipetz, Goldfarb and Bennett – became the Comintern's representative in Britain, and thus the effective controller of the British Communist Party. Rose herself was already working as an agent of the Comintern, carrying funds and messages to communist parties around Europe. In 1927 she went to Moscow with Petrovsky, and settled there permanently. Pollitt, meanwhile, had given up hope of ever winning Rose's heart, and in 1925 had married Marjory Edna Brewer, a school teacher and fellow-communist.

'WHY DO YOU NEED ME TO DIE?'

In Moscow the Petrovskys were members of the Soviet elite, forging, as they believed, a new and better world. Max was in charge of the Comintern department responsible for agitation and propaganda, and was appointed to the praesidium of the Supreme Soviet Economic Council. Rose, meanwhile, became a leading journalist on the *Moscow Daily News*, an English-language paper. They acquired a luxurious flat in Moscow and a dacha in the country, where they entertained their many friends. Rose's success seems to have inspired the envy of some of the other British residents in Moscow, one or two of whom found Rose 'snobby' and 'conceited'. Her success might also, as the purges began, have made her complacent. And like many – or even most – communists of the time, she came to believe that those who were arrested as 'Trotskyite saboteurs' or 'fascist agents' were exactly that, despite their apparent loyalty to the party.

Max seems to have shared Rose's complacency. When in 1937 Nikolai Bukharin, Stalin's old revolutionary comrade, was hauled before the Central Committee, he was questioned by Stalin himself. Petrovsky, who was present, seems to have expressed some doubt regarding something Stalin said. Condemned to death in March 1938, Bukharin sent a note to Stalin, addressing him by his old revolutionary nickname: 'Koba, why do you need me to die?' He pleaded to be allowed to take poison, rather than be shot, but his wish was denied.

The NKVD had come for Petrovsky a year before, on 11 March 1937. Writing to her sister in London a month after Max's arrest, Rose,

Better that ten innocent people should suffer than that one spy get away. When you cut down the forest, wood chips fly.

NIKOLAI YEZHOV, HEAD OF THE NKVD FROM 1936 TO 1938, WHO GAVE HIS NAME TO THE PERIOD OF THE PURGES: THE YEZHOVSHCHINA. WHEN HE HIMSELF WAS ARRESTED IN APRIL 1939 HE DECLARED, 'HOW LONG I HAVE WAITED FOR THIS!' HE WAS EXECUTED ON 4 FEBRUARY 1940.

knowing that her letter would be read by the NKVD, would only say 'Max is away'. The inner core of the British Communist Party – which was never quite trusted by Stalin – were informed of Petrovsky's arrest, and those who had known him in London were instructed to provide denunciations of the 'wrecker'. Harry Pollitt sent a letter to Rose to try to cheer her up. She never received it. At three o'clock in the morning on 13 August 1937 Rose herself was taken from her flat. None of her friends or colleagues ever saw her again.

'A THOROUGHLY UNDESIRABLE PERSON'

Some historians believe that the arrests of Rose and Max were just a prelude to Stalin's real target, the Communist Party of Great Britain and its general secretary, Harry Pollitt, who had proved not as malleable as Stalin would have wished. Not least among Pollitt's crimes was the fact that, when required to denounce Petrovsky, he had instead defended him.

> *I wonder whether Miss Cohen is now solid or liquid?*
>
> R.H. HADOW, A SENIOR OFFICIAL OF THE BRITISH FOREIGN OFFICE, 1938

Pollitt was actually in Moscow at the time of Rose's arrest, so the NKVD may have hoped that, once put under pressure, she would say something to compromise him. He had already been denounced under torture by the Hungarian communist Béla Kun as one of his 'Trotskyite co-conspirators', so the secret police may have been casting around for one last nail to put in Pollitt's coffin. Blissfully unaware of the danger he was in, Pollitt made a discreet plea on behalf of both Rose and Max to Georgi Dimitrov, the general secretary of the Comintern. Pollitt later said his conversation with Dimitrov was 'one of the most helpful things that I remember', but never elaborated. Dimitrov presumably advised him not to pursue Rose's case any further. Shortly afterwards, Pollitt returned to Britain.

It was not until some months later that the Soviets announced that Rose had been sentenced to ten years hard labour, but refused to say why, or where she was being held. She and Max – like hundreds of thousands of others – were simply referred to as 'enemies of the people'. The British Communist Party, via its organ, the *Daily Worker*, publicly asserted that the Soviet Union had every right to try its own citizens 'according to the forms of Soviet justice'. The British government seems to have agreed, choosing to believe that Rose had surrendered her British passport (which was not in fact the case), and declining to press the Soviet government on her behalf. A Foreign Office official called Lascelles described her as 'a thoroughly undesirable person', while another, R.H. Hadow, in a handwritten margin note, callously wondered 'whether Miss Cohen is now solid or liquid?'

REHABILITATING THE DEAD

Harry Pollitt never raised a finger ever again to protest about the crimes committed by the Soviet Union in the name of socialism. But he never forgot Rose Cohen.

To dedicated communists around the world, the four-hour 'secret' speech made by Nikita Khrushchev on 25 February 1956 to the 20th Congress of the Communist Party of the Soviet Union came as a terrible shock. Some in the audience that day suffered heart attacks, while others committed suicide shortly afterwards. During the speech, Khrushchev, who had won the struggle to succeed Stalin after the latter's sudden death in 1953, denounced his predecessor not only for developing a cult of personality, but for 'grave perversions of party principles, of party democracy, of revolutionary legality'. In particular, he detailed the mass liquidations in 1937–8 of party activists who 'were never actually enemies, spies, wreckers, etc., but were always honest communists'.

Five months after Khrushchev's speech, Harry Pollitt took his courage in his hands and wrote to the Central Committee of the Communist Party of the Soviet Union. 'Dear Comrades,' he began, 'The relatives of Comrade Rose Cohen asked me to try to obtain some information about her ...' The reply Pollitt received dashed any last lingering hopes that he might see his beloved Rose again:

In the case of Cohen, Rose Morisovna … sentenced by the Military Collegium of the Supreme Court of the USSR on 28 November 1937 … to be shot, with confiscation of property.

Cohen was found guilty of having been a member of an anti-Soviet organization … and a resident agent of British Intelligence.

In the conclusion of the Chief Military Prosecutor it is incumbent to rescind the sentence in relation to Cohen and to quash the case against her in the absence of evidence …

Rose – whom the British believed to be a Soviet agent and the Soviets believed was a British spy – had been executed within hours of the sentence being passed, just one of the thousand or so victims that the NKVD shot every day through 1937 and 1938. Now, twenty years later, like so many of the dead, Rose had been rehabilitated.

Pollitt himself had long been inured to the horrors of Stalinism. He was privately indignant with Khrushchev for besmirching his hero's reputation, refusing to take down the portrait of Stalin in his living room. 'He's staying there as long as I'm alive,' he said. But the revelations of the secret speech, and the Soviet repression of the Hungarian Rising later that year, precipitated mass resignations from the British Communist Party, and Pollitt stood down as general secretary. He died four years later, on 27 June 1960, of a cerebral haemorrhage. In 1971 the Soviet navy named a ship after him.

> *The history of the Russian revolution shows that the 'Bloomsbury Bolshevik' or 'parlour pink' is the first to go to the wall.*
>
> AN OFFICIAL OF THE BRITISH FOREIGN OFFICE, BRIEFING THE FOREIGN SECRETARY ON ROSE COHEN'S CASE, 1938

Since the collapse of the Soviet Union, the last resting places of tens of thousands of victims of Stalin's purges have begun to come to light. Twenty thousand corpses were found at Moscow's Butovo shooting range alone. Whether Rose Cohen's body was buried there, or sealed up in the cellar at 8/1 Nikolskaya Street, or left to rot in one of many other burial sites round Moscow for victims of Stalin's purges, we will probably never know.

Amy, Wonderful Amy

Amy Johnson

(1941)

The Gilbert and Nicholls song 'Amy, Wonderful Amy' was just one of a number of tributes composed in 1930 to celebrate the homecoming of Amy Johnson following her solo flight from England to Australia. The journey, undertaken in a flimsy biplane made of nothing more than wood and fabric, had been full of adventure. It was particularly remarkable given that Amy had only taken up flying two years previously.

Further record-breaking attempts followed through the 1930s, and 'Wonderful Amy' became the darling of the British public. During the Second World War she volunteered to pilot military aircraft from factories to aerodromes around Britain, and it was on one such mission that she was forced to bale out over the Thames Estuary. Her body was never found.

ADVENTURES IN THE SKIES

Amy Johnson was born in Hull, Yorkshire, in 1903, the daughter of a wealthy businessman who became one of the strongest supporters of her flying career. Unusually for women of the day, Amy went to university, graduating with a degree in economics from Sheffield in 1925, and then began work in London as secretary to a solicitor. In 1928 she joined the London Aeroplane Club and started to learn to fly. 'It makes me happy to be taking these lessons,' she wrote to her father, 'and gives me an interest in an otherwise very monotonous life and gives me a chance to meet people.' This sounds as if she wasn't yet completely fired by the romance of flying – it was more just a break from office routine and an opportunity to socialize. But she went on to assure her father that she had 'an immense belief in the future of flying'. Joining the technical school of the aircraft designer and manufacturer Geoffrey de Havilland, she became the first woman to qualify as a ground engineer, and in the same year – 1929 – she gained her pilot's licence.

Having gained her wings, her ambition began to soar. On 5 May 1930 she took off from Croydon aerodrome, south of London, in her Gipsy Moth biplane *Jason*, aiming to beat the 15½-day record for the England–Australia flight set by Bert Hinkler in 1928. She later recalled: 'The prospect did not frighten me, because I was so appallingly ignorant that I never realized in the least what I had taken on.' Flying over Turkey she only just missed the Taurus Mountains, which suddenly and unexpectedly loomed out of the mist. On the fourth day she was forced by a sandstorm to land in the Syrian desert. For several hours she held her gun tightly, convinced that the wild dogs she could hear barking were about to attack. Later, flying across the Indian subcontinent, realizing that she did not have enough fuel to make her scheduled stop, she was obliged to land at an army barracks, scattering the soldiers on the parade ground. Her onward progress was hindered by bad weather, and by the repairs to the plane made necessary by a number of rough landings, and in the end she completed her flight four days behind Hinkler's record. Nevertheless, her achievement was hailed around the world, and Amy became a role model for independent-minded young women everywhere.

Had I been a man I might have explored the Poles or climbed Mount Everest, but as it was my spirit found outlet in the air

AMY JOHNSON, IN MARGOT ASQUITH (ED.), *MYSELF WHEN YOUNG* (1938)

More remarkable flights followed. In 1931 Amy and her co-pilot Jack Humphreys flew in a De Havilland Puss Moth non-stop from London to Moscow – a distance of 1760 miles – in 21 hours, and then continued on across Siberia to Tokyo. The following year she knocked 10 hours off the time previously achieved by her new husband, Jim Mollison, on the flight from London to Cape Town in South Africa. Mollison had proposed to her in Australia, just after her 1930 flight, having only known her for eight hours. More dramatic exploits followed, including a flight from South Wales to the USA in 1933 with her husband. Both were injured when they crash landed in Connecticut.

DARKER DAYS

Amy's marriage to Jim Mollison was not a success: both were individually ambitious, and Mollison was a playboy, a heavy drinker and a philanderer. In 1938 the couple divorced, and Amy resumed the use of her maiden name. She had never relished the limelight, and she had made her last long-distant flight in 1936, when she regained her England-to-South-Africa record.

In 1940, following the outbreak of war, Amy joined the Air Transport Auxiliary, which recruited men considered too old or disabled to fly with the RAF, and a limited number of women pilots. Women were barred from combat duty, but undertook the still dangerous task of ferrying military aircraft around the country. Amy was one of the most experienced flyers to join the ATA – but, having been a solo flyer, at first she kicked against the discipline:

I dislike intensely being with the ATA; although I know that most of us at present are having to do jobs we don't like. I'm too much of an individualist to work as a cog in a wheel …

During the period of the Phoney War it was boring and unglamorous work, the women being restricted to flying old trainers. They particularly resented the gibes of the 'Brylcreem Boys' of the RAF, who claimed ATA stood for 'Always Terrified Airwomen'. However, following the fall of France, the evacuation from Dunkirk and the beginning of the Battle of Britain, the work of the ATA took on a new urgency, and the women were allowed to fly larger, faster machines.

THE LAST FLIGHT

Amy's regular route involved shuttling planes between Prestwick in southwest Scotland and Hatfield in Hertfordshire, just north of London. At the beginning of January 1941 – at the height of the Blitz, when night after night German bombers dropped their deadly loads on British cities – she was detailed to take a new Airspeed Oxford, a large, cumbersome twin-engined plane, from Prestwick to RAF Kidlington, near Oxford. She broke the journey at Blackpool, Lancashire, where she stayed the night with her sister Molly. Conditions on her flight south from Scotland had been poor, with mist reducing visibility. In addition Amy was worried that her compass might be slightly out – a cause for concern, as she was aware she was not the best of navigators, although she assured her sister that she could 'smell her way' to Kidlington.

Amy left her sister's house on the morning of Sunday 5 January. Molly said she had never seen Amy looking so well and happy. At Squire's Gate aerodrome visibility was still very poor, and the flight controller advised against take-off, but Amy chose to ignore the warning, saying she would fly above the ceiling of low cloud. She took off at 11.49.

The one and only thing I am simply terrified of is a parachute descent.

AMY JOHNSON IN 1938

High above the clouds, relying on a compass that may not have been accurate, it would have been difficult for Amy to know when to make her descent to Kidlington. Beneath the cloud there were clusters of barrage balloons, intended to defend key sites from German air attack, but equally hazardous to friendly aircraft. Those on the ground at Kidlington waited anxiously; by 15.30 Amy was two hours overdue.

Another ATA woman flying an Airspeed Oxford that day noticed that it was icing up, even as low as 800 feet. The Oxford had no facility for de-icing its wings. There were snow flurries, and by mid-afternoon the sky was beginning to darken. Unable to find a gap in the clouds, and unsure where she was, it seems that Amy flew east, perhaps hoping the cloud cover would end at the coast, and that she would be able to recover her bearings.

INTO THE DARK, ICY WATERS

When Amy emerged from the clouds she was over the Thames Estuary and running out of fuel. But she may have thought she was over land, misled by the barrage balloons attached to fishing boats anchored in a line extending southward from Shoeburyness on the Essex shore, or the balloons attached to some of the ships of Convoy CE21, then inching its way up the estuary towards London, hoping to avoid attack from German submarines and E-boats.

Hurry, please, hurry!

AMY JOHNSON'S LAST WORDS

To parachute over land was dangerous enough; to parachute into the sea in the middle of winter meant almost certain death, from drowning or hypothermia. Amy had, in 1938, confided to *Women's Illustrated*: 'The one and only thing I am simply terrified of is a parachute descent. Even if the wing falls off an aeroplane it still feels like solid earth to me … I know inside me that I could never, never pull the cord and trust myself to the air.'

At 15.30 Lieutenant Henry O'Dea, an officer on the bridge of HMS *Haslemere*, one of the convoy vessels, saw an aeroplane break through the cloud cover, and, about 500 feet up, a parachute. The convoy was then in an area dotted with sandbanks about 11 miles north of Herne Bay on the Kent coast. There was a bitter wind blowing and driving sleet, along with a big swell and a choppy sea. Lieutenant-Commander Walter Fletcher, the captain of the *Haslemere*, ordered his ship to make full steam ahead towards where the parachute would land. When the plane hit the water, witnesses said it floated for a moment, then nosedived straight to the bottom. In its haste, the *Haslemere* ran aground on a sandbank, but both O'Dea and Seaman Raymond Dean noticed two bodies in the water, drifting past the grounded vessel. One raised an arm and called 'Hurry, please, hurry!' They realized it was a woman. The crew tried to throw her a line, but each time the current swept it from her grasp. Dean scrambled onto the ship's outer board, on the side of the hull, and stretched out his hand, but as the cold numbed and exhausted him the woman slipped away, disappearing under the stern of the boat.

Dean began to shed his clothes, apparently intent on diving in, but Fletcher ordered him back on board. Then Fletcher himself stripped off and dived into the dark, icy water, heading for the second figure. Reaching it, he supported it for two or three minutes, but in that cold the body quickly succumbs and he had to let go. Fletcher struggled in the direction of a lifeboat rowing towards him through the heavy swell, sometimes disappearing from view. 'For God's sake, lad, tell them to pull!' he shouted. When he was eventually hauled on board a motor launch by a boat hook he had been in the water for twenty minutes. He never regained consciousness, and five days later died from the effects of hypothermia. He is buried in a naval cemetery in Gillingham, and was posthumously awarded the Albert Medal, the lifesaving equivalent of the George Cross for gallantry.

THE MYSTERIOUS MR X

Shortly after Fletcher was taken from the water the convoy came under attack from a German Junkers Ju-88 fighter-bomber. HMS *Berkeley*, a destroyer with the convoy, repelled the attack with anti-aircraft fire, and then began a search of the area. Two pieces of luggage were found, one marked 'AJ', the other 'Amy Johnson'. Later, a fragment of Amy's Airspeed Oxford was found floating in the water, with part of the serial number on it. Amy's parents were informed that she was 'Missing believed killed'; they later sent a wreath to Fletcher's mother. Both Amy's recovered handbag and the piece of wreckage from the plane subsequently disappeared.

On Tuesday 7 January the Admiralty issued a statement that mentioned the two bodies in the water. This was quickly denied by the Ministry of Aircraft Production. Harry Banks, a member of the ground crew at Squire's Field, who had been on board Amy's plane just before take-off, was sure she had been alone. Speculation was rife in the press as to the identity of the mysterious 'Mr X' – there was even a suggestion (without a shred of evidence) that he was a German friend of Amy's whom she was returning home. The talk in the RAF, Amy's father heard, was that Amy was not off route at all, but had been heading to the Continent on a secret mission – and not for the first time – so in this case the assumption was that 'Mr X' was an agent, picked up somewhere in England after her departure from Squire's Field. However, we know now that such operations were carried out at night, using unmarked Lysanders, not by day in cumbersome Oxfords clearly marked as British.

Obtaining a death certificate without a body was not an easy matter in those days, and it was

Let no one grieve for me or wish me any other fate.

AMY JOHNSON IN 1937 ·

not until 1943 that Amy's case came to court. There was some confusion and discrepancies among the witnesses from the convoy, but six men were sure there had been two figures in the water. It has been suggested, however, that what they thought was a second body was in fact one of the pieces of Amy's luggage that was later picked up, which, in the difficult conditions attending the attempted rescue, could have been mistaken for the upper part of a body, bobbing about in the water. Alternatively, it could have been the door of the Oxford, jettisoned as Amy made her jump.

Some of the witnesses aboard the *Haslemere* were convinced the 'body' wore the helmet and scarf typical of a Luftwaffe pilot, so the figure could have been an earlier victim of aerial combat in the area.

In 1988 a man who had been a sailor on the *Berkeley* claimed it was his ship's anti-aircraft guns that had shot down Amy's plane in error. A similar claim emerged a decade later from a member of an anti-aircraft battery on the Kent coast. He had been told by officers to keep the incident quiet, and waited almost sixty years before unburdening himself. But in neither case does the evidence stack up, regarding either timing or location, and it is almost certain that Amy was not a victim of friendly fire, nor of conspiratorial cover-ups, but simply of the appalling conditions that bleak, midwinter Sunday. Her body was never recovered, and it is likely that when she disappeared under the stern of the *Haslemere* she was cut to pieces by the ship's propeller, a gruesome detail the witnesses on board may have preferred to keep to themselves.

'If I fail to find my Mid-Pacific island,' Amy had written in 1937, referring to the fate of her friend and fellow flyer Amelia Earhart, 'let no one grieve for me or wish me any other fate. We all must finish our lives some time, and I infinitely prefer this end to the flu or senile decay. Rather grieve if I never have the chance to try.'

Nacht und Nebel

Noor Inayat Khan

(1943)

On 7 December 1941 SS Reichsführer Heinrich Himmler issued what became known as the *Nacht-und-Nebel Erlass* – the Night-and-Fog Decree. 'After lengthy consideration,' he announced, 'it is the will of the Führer that the measures taken against those who are guilty of offences against the Reich or against the occupation forces in occupied areas should be altered. The Führer is of the opinion that in such cases penal servitude or even a hard labour sentence for life will be regarded as a sign of weakness. An effective and lasting deterrent can be achieved only by the death penalty or by taking measures that will leave the family and the population uncertain as to the fate of the offender. Deportation to Germany serves this purpose.'

The decree was signed and implemented by Field Marshall Wilhelm Keitel, chief of staff of the armed forces of the Reich. Keitel stated: 'Efficient and enduring intimidation can only be achieved either by capital punishment or by measures by which the relatives of the criminals do not know the fate of the criminal. The prisoners are, in future, to be transported to Germany secretly, and further treatment of the offenders will take place here; these measures will have a deterrent effect because – A. The prisoners will vanish without a trace. B. No information may be given as to their whereabouts or their fate.'

The policy was aimed principally at political activists and resistance fighters in the occupied territories. Just one of the many victims who were lost in the 'Night and Fog' of the death camps was an agent of the British Special Operations Executive, a young Indian princess called Noor Inayat Khan.

SETTING EUROPE ABLAZE

After the Fall of France in June 1940, Britain faced Hitler alone. The new prime minister, Winston Churchill, was defiant, and, even though British forces had been withdrawn from continental Europe, he was determined to take the war to the enemy. With this in view, on 16 July 1940 he instructed Hugh Dalton, minister of economic warfare, to set up a new organization known as the Special Operations Executive (SOE). It was to send agents into Nazi-occupied territories to support local resistance movements in acts of sabotage and other aspects of guerrilla warfare. The aim was, in Churchill's words, to 'set Europe ablaze'.

SOE recruited individuals from a wide range of backgrounds, both men and women, some already in the services, some not. Many were upper-middle-class City types, some were left-wing intellectuals, and a few were convicted criminals, recruited for their skills at forgery or safe-cracking. No one applied to join SOE. Typically one received a summons from the War Office to attend a meeting in a hotel in central London. Here, in a room with blacked out windows, furnished only with two folding chairs and a naked light bulb, the potential recruit would be interviewed by a man who rarely divulged his name, and who never let any expression appear on his face. This was Selwyn Jepson, the recruiting officer for F Section, the French section of SOE. Jepson – who sometimes conducted the interview as a captain in the Royal Navy, sometimes in civilian dress, and sometimes as a major in the Buffs – had faced 'a good deal of opposition' when he had started to recruit women, but had obtained the direct authority of Churchill himself. The prime minister had agreed it was 'very sensible', and had wished Jepson good luck.

During this initial interview Jepson would probe the character of the prospective agent – who at this stage would have no idea why he or she was being interviewed. Fluency in French, and a good knowledge of France, seemed to be required. Perhaps the War Office needed interpreters or bilingual secretaries, the candidate would wonder. After the interview, if the candidate seemed to be the right kind of person, Jepson would ask MI5 to run security checks, and, if all was well, he would invite the candidate back for another 'chat'. Here he would outline what he had in mind, and warn the candidate that the odds of returning from France alive were about fifty-fifty. He would then say both he and the candidate should think it over for a day or two, 'I have to decide whether I can risk your life,' he would say, 'and you have to decide whether you're willing to risk it.'

AN INDIAN PRINCESS

On 10 October 1942, in Room 238 of the Hotel Victoria in Northumberland Avenue, Jepson met a potential recruit he would never forget. 'There is one ... above all the others remembered more often and vividly ... not only in the dark hours of solitude with which we must all contend but at unexpected moments in daytime activity; it is as though a shutter opens in a familiar wall which I know has no shutter in it, and she is there, briefly, the light filling my eyes. She does not haunt me as do some of the others who but for me, that "me" of the war, might still be alive. She is simply with me, now and again, for a little moment. And she is Inayat Khan.'

Noor Inayat Khan –the first name means 'light of womanhood' – was the daughter of Hazrat Inayat Khan, a great-grandson of Tipu Sultan, the ruler of Mysore who died defending his capital against the British in 1799. Hazrat was a musician and a teacher of Sufism (a pacific, mystic order within Islam), who met Noor's mother, Ora Ray Baker, while travelling in the United States. Noor herself was born in Moscow, on 1 January 1914.

The family moved to London shortly after the outbreak of the First World War. After the war, in 1920, they settled in France. Noor's father died in India in 1927, and three years later the family went out to erect his tomb. Still based in France, the family travelled extensively within Europe, visiting Hazrat's disciples. Noor herself was completely Europeanized both in manner and appearance, fluent in both French and English, and also able to speak German and Spanish. She studied child psychology at the Sorbonne, and subsequently earned money writing children's stories. Before the war she used to read these on Radio Paris, and in 1941 one of her stories was broadcast on the BBC's Children's Hour.

I wish some Indians would win high military distinction in this war. It would help to build a bridge between the English and the Indians.

NOOR INAYAT KHAN

When France fell to the Nazis in June 1940 the family escaped to England. On 19 November, she joined the Women's Auxiliary Air Force (WAAF) to train as a wireless operator.

BEHIND ENEMY LINES

After nearly two years in the WAAF, and now an experienced wireless operator, Noor received a fateful summons from the War Office to go to a certain hotel in central London. Jepson recalled that she had a 'great gentleness of manner', but at the same time he thought she had 'an intuitive sense of what might be in my mind for her to do'. Prior to Noor, women SOE agents had only worked as couriers; Noor would be the first to work as a wireless operator behind enemy lines. Jepson saw that she was painstaking and patient, and would be 'almost perfect' in this role.

As usual, I stressed immediately the extreme danger, that in the event of capture she would be interrogated by the Gestapo – a thing no human being could face with anything but terror – that since she would not be in uniform she would have no protection under the international rules of warfare – in short that she might not return.

Noor appeared undeterred, and stated quite simply 'that she would like to undertake it'. There was something about Noor that persuaded Jepson that she knew her mind. He agreed to take her on.

A rigorous programme of training followed, involving unarmed combat, small arms, explosives, cipher, security and general tradecraft. Noor, now known as 'Nora Baker', attracted varying opinions from her instructors as to her capabilities. 'Active, plenty of spirit and could be relied on to come up to scratch when the occasion arose,' reported one. 'Completely self-effacing and unselfish ... not quick, studious rather than clever. Extremely conscientious,' wrote another. 'She has an unstable and temperamental personality and it is very doubtful whether she is really suited to work in the field,' thought a third – but he was overruled in response to an urgent request from Paris for a wireless operator.

Without having finished her training, Noor was given the codename 'Nurse', the field name 'Madeleine' and a cover identity as 'Jeanne-Marie Regnier', an identity that overlapped with her own – Jeanne-Marie had an American mother and had been educated at the Sorbonne. On the night of 16/17 June 1943 she was flown by Lysander to a field in northern France, from where she made her way to Paris. It was a bad time for the Resistance and F Section: the night before, members of the 'Archdeacon' network had been arrested, and just a week later the SD (Sicherheitsdienst), the security service of the SS, began to roll up the 'Prosper' network to which she was attached. After a month and a half, Noor was the only wireless operator in the network still in action.

> *She felt that she had come to a dead end as a WAAF and was longing to do something more active in the prosecution of the war, something which would make more call on her capabilities and perhaps demand more sacrifice.*
>
> ONE OF HER INSTRUCTORS, A LIEUTENANT HOLLAND, REPORTING ON NOOR DURING HER SOE TRAINING, 19 APRIL 1943

Noor was given the opportunity by her controllers in Britain to return, but she refused. Knowing that the SD would be trying to get a fix on her position, she continually moved around with her transmitter, sending out messages from other agents and facilitating the escape of Allied airmen shot down in France. She had a very close shave once on the Métro, when two German officers demanded to know what was in her case. She had no choice but to show them, explaining that it was a cinematograph projector. 'There are the little bulbs,' she said. 'Haven't you seen one before?' Her bluff came off. On another occasion she actually persuaded a German neighbour to help rig up her aerial, telling him that it was a washing line.

BETRAYAL

Noor's luck ran out in October 1943. She was betrayed – probably by a Frenchwoman who was jealous of her attachment to another SOE agent. The SD put a tail on 'Madeleine', but Noor managed to shake him off. After a few hours, however, she was arrested, and taken to the headquarters of the SD in the Avenue Foch.

It's grand working with you – the best moments I have had yet...

UNDATED MESSAGE FROM NOOR IN OCCUPIED FRANCE TO HER CONTROLLERS IN BRITAIN

One German officer attempting to interrogate her got nowhere, later recalling: 'She glared at me as if she was a caged tiger, but she wouldn't speak.' Noor does not seem to have been tortured. However, she had made one fatal error. She had misinterpreted an ambiguous instruction on her operation order before she departed: 'We should like to point out here that you must be extremely careful with the filing of your messages.' What had been meant by the word 'filing' was the sense in which a journalist would use it – submitting copy. Noor interpreted it in the more generally received sense, and kept a complete record in Paris of all the messages she had transmitted and received. This allowed the Germans to access all her security checks, and so to 'play back' her radio set to her controllers in Britain for several more months. The result of what the Germans called the *Englandspiel* ('England game') was that seven SOE agents, when they landed in France, found themselves greeted not by a reception committee from the Resistance, but by the Gestapo. All seven were killed in concentration camps.

INTO THE NIGHT AND FOG

What happened to Noor after she was taken to the Avenue Foch was only pieced together gradually after the war, partially through the testimony of Germans standing trial for war crimes, and partly through the assiduous efforts of Vera Atkins, who had been assistant to the head of SOE's F Section, Maurice Buckmaster. After the war, on her own initiative, Vera Atkins determined to discover the fate of all those agents who had disappeared in occupied France.

Noor made two attempts to escape from the Avenue Foch. The second might well have succeeded had not an air-raid siren gone off, at which point the SD followed the normal procedure and checked on all the prisoners in their cells. The result was that Noor was taken to Germany and imprisoned at Pforzheim. In 1946 the prison's governor, Wilhelm Krauss, told a war crimes investigation unit:

I remember that in November 1943 an English woman was delivered into Pforzheim prison. I was told that she was to be treated in accordance with regulations for Nacht und Nebel *prisoners and moreover that she was to be chained hand and foot. This order was carried through.*

Krauss later removed the chains from her hands out of pity, but was ordered by the Gestapo to put them back on. Noor, kept in solitary confinement, remained uncooperative, and appears to have been beaten up by one of her jailers.

In May 1946 Vera Atkins, examining the records at Karlsruhe prison, just 15 miles from Pforzheim, assumed that Noor – using the *nom de guerre* Sonia Olschanezky – was among a group of women sent in July 1944 to an unnamed concentration camp, which Atkins believed to be Natzweiler. On 29 May 1946 she testified in the trial of nine SS men from Natzweiler, who were accused of responsibility for the deaths of four women SOE agents on 6 July 1944. They had all been killed by lethal injection.

Violette Szabo

Violette Szabo, who, like Noor, was awarded a posthumous George Cross, is perhaps SOE's most famous woman agent, partly because of her portrayal by Virginia McKenna in the 1958 film *Carve her Name with Pride*. Violette was a crack shot, and in 1944 was sent on two missions to France to coordinate sabotage operations by the Resistance. On the second mission, in June, she was captured. She was tortured by the SD in Limoges, then in late August sent under the *Nacht-und-Nebel* decree to Ravensbrück concentration camp. She was forced to work under gruelling conditions out of doors all through the winter, alongside two other SOE agents, Denise Bloch and Lilian Rolfe. Some time in February 1945 orders came from Berlin that the three of them were to be executed. The SS camp overseer later told the British investigator Vera Atkins that they had been shot through the back of the neck.

Just over a year after this trial, new information came to light. It transpired that on 11 September 1944 Noor, along with three SOE agents held at Karlsruhe – Yolande Beekman, Eliane Plewman and Madeleine Damerment – were sent to Dachau concentration camp, walking the last part of the journey in the dark. According to an official report by Major N.G. Mott of the War Office, dated 26 June 1947: 'They spent the night in the cells and between 8 and 10 the following morning, 13th September, they were taken to the crematorium compound and shot through the back of the head and immediately cremated.'

Noor, who was only 30 when she died, was posthumously awarded the Croix de Guerre and the George Cross – the latter being Britain's highest award for gallantry off the field of battle. It was only when *The London Gazette* carried her George Cross citation on 15 April 1949 that the world at large heard about Noor Inayat Khan and what she had done, refusing to abandon 'what had become the most important and dangerous post in France'.

In 1958 a former Dutch prisoner of the Nazis known only as 'A.F.' wrote to Jean Overton Fuller, Noor's biographer, claiming to have witnessed Noor's last moments:

> *The SS undressed the girl and she was terribly beaten by Ruppert [Wilhelm Ruppert, a notorious sadist executed for war crimes in 1946] all over her body. She did not cry, neither said anything. When Ruppert got tired and the girl was a bloody mess he told her then he would shoot her. She had to kneel and the only word she said, before Ruppert shot her from behind through the head, was 'liberté'.*

This document, along with Noor's full file, was only released by Britain's National Archives in 2006.

Noor was just one of 118 agents of F Section who disappeared during the war, just one of thousands who were condemned to die unknown deaths in the night and fog – and just one of the millions who perished at the hands of one of the most monstrous tyrannies the world has ever known. Himmler, the man who had issued the *Nacht-und-Nebel* decree in 1941, and who had been in overall charge of the SS, the Gestapo and the extermination camps, was arrested by British troops in May 1945. He committed suicide before he could be brought to trial. Field Marshal Keitel, who signed and implemented the *Nacht-und-Nebel* decree, was tried at Nuremberg on charges of crimes against peace; of planning, initiating and waging wars of aggression; of war crimes; and of crimes against humanity. He was hanged on 16 October 1946.

The Romantic
Airman

ANTOINE DE SAINT-EXUPÉRY

(1944)

Antoine de Saint-Exupéry – writer, poet, philosopher, pioneering aviator – actually disappeared twice. In 1935, while making a bid to fly from Paris to Saigon in record-breaking time, he and his mechanic André Prévot crashed their Caudron C-630 Simoun in the Libyan Desert. They had, Saint-Exupéry recalled, nothing to sustain them but grapes, an orange and some wine, which ran out after a day. It was four days before they were found by a Bedouin, by which time they were hallucinating and so dehydrated they could not even sweat.

This was just one of many lucky escapes in the career of a man who was among the most remarkable figures in the history of aviation – a career made more remarkable by Saint-Exupéry's ability to transmute his experiences into a series of highly poetic and often philosophical works, from *Courrier-Sud* (1929) and *Vol de nuit* (1931) to *Terre des hommes* (1939, translated as *Wind, Sand and Stars*) and *Pilote de guerre* (1942; *Flight to Arras*).

Saint-Exupéry is perhaps best known for *Le Petit Prince* (1943; *The Little Prince*), a children's fable for adults about an aviator stranded in the Sahara. In the desert he comes across the young prince of the title, who is visiting Earth from a tiny asteroid called B612. The book is a meditation on what is important in life, providing a perspective often lost to adults: 'It is only with the heart that one can see rightly; what is essential is invisible to the eye.' The year after *Le Petit Prince* was published, Saint-Ex disappeared again, this time for good.

IN SEARCH OF A DREAM

Born in Lyon in 1900 of an impoverished aristocratic family, Saint-Ex – as he was known to friends and colleagues – was something of a flop at school, and in 1919 failed the entrance exams for the French navy. He drifted aimlessly and impecuniously around Paris for the next two years, conscious that while France welcomed home her victorious soldiers he himself had been too young to fight in the Great War. He was desperately searching for a purpose to his life, something against which he could measure his talents and test his courage.

A Place Among the Stars

Saint-Exupéry, poet of the sky and the stars, has been honoured by astronomers in a number of names chosen for newly discovered asteroids. One such body found in 1975 is officially known as 2578 Saint-Exupéry, while a small asteroid moon discovered in 1998 was in 2003 given the name Petit-Prince, in honour of the eponymous hero of Saint-Exupéry's fable *Le Petit Prince*. The Little Prince himself comes from a small asteroid called B612, which gave rise to the official name of another asteroid, 46610 Bésixdouze: the number 46610 is represented in hexadecimal notation as 'B612', while 'Bésixdouze' is French for 'B-six-twelve'.

As a boy in 1912 he had had a glimpse of a different, braver, more thrilling world, when he had badgered a pilot giving a flying display to take him up. The ecstasy that the young Saint-Ex experienced can be gauged from the breathless lines he scribbled down once back on earth:

Les ailes frémissait sous le soufflé du soir
Le moteur, de son chant, berçait l'âme endormie,
Le soleil nous frôlait de sa couleur palie ...

(The wings tremble under the evening breeze, / The engine, with its song, rocks the sleeping soul, / The sun's pale colour shines down on us ...)

It was his call-up for military service that saved Saint-Ex. The papers arrived in the spring of 1921: he was to report to the French Air Force. By the following year he had obtained his pilot's licence, and was writing to his mother: '*Maman*, I adore this *métier*. You cannot imagine the calm, the solitude, one finds at twelve thousand feet alone with one's engine.' He describes the comradeship back on the ground, the 'stories of marvels ... fairy-tale adventures' that they tell each other, the exhilaration of admitting one's fear. It was not long before he had his first accident: in the spring of 1923 while performing acrobatics over a fête at Versailles he ran out of fuel, tried to glide beyond the crowd and stalled. When he regained consciousness in hospital he murmured, 'Strange, I'm dead, yet I have all the sensations of a living man.'

The world teaches us more about ourselves than any number of books, because it resists us; a man discovers himself only when he faces up to its challenge ...

ANTOINE DE SAINT-EXUPÉRY,
Terre des hommes (1939),
OPENING SENTENCE

LOVE INTERPOSES, THEN WITHDRAWS

At the time of this first accident Saint-Ex was about to finish his period of military service, and was considering applying for a permanent commission. Then he fell in love, passionately, recklessly, with Louise de Vilmorin, a budding novelist and the youngest daughter of a large landowning family. When she went to Switzerland for the sake of her delicate health, Saint-Ex pursued her there, and proposed. She accepted. Her family did not think much of Louise's choice – an impoverished airman who would turn up with dirty fingernails and oil-stained clothes at all times of day and night. So to measure up to the expectations of the de Vilmorins, Saint-Ex chucked in the air force and took a drudging but stable job as a trainee accountant with a tile manufacturer. He knew the job might kill his restless spirit, but he sacrificed all for love. In some ways it must have come as something of a relief when Louise changed her mind and broke off the engagement. It was, perhaps, a lucky escape in more ways than one: Evelyn Waugh, who knew Louise well, described her as 'an egocentric maniac with the eyes of a witch'.

Saint-Ex was free again to pursue his vocation, but did not immediately return to flying. Instead, he took up as a travelling salesman of motor trucks – a job he had no aptitude for, but it was better than being stuck in an office. What he most enjoyed was working with the mechanics and engineers, getting to know how the ten-ton trucks ticked. 'What constitutes the dignity of a craft,' he wrote in *Terre des hommes*, 'is that it creates a fellowship, binds men together, and fashions for them a common language.'

AIRBORNE AGAIN

In 1926 a mutual friend arranged for Saint-Ex to see Beppo de Massimi, the head of the Latécoère Airline Company, which was pioneering the first airmail services between France and her colonies in North and West Africa. At the urging of Saint-Exupéry's family – who feared that their son would throw away his life, both figuratively and literally, if he took up again as a pilot – de Massimi offered the young man an administrative job, but Saint-Ex made it clear that he was only interested in flying. De Massimi had lost so many experienced pilots that he eventually relented.

In those days aeroplanes were very basic, lacking much in the way of instrumentation, and demanding a great deal from the pilot's skills and instincts. Most of Latécoère's planes were obsolete models, left over from the war, and the pilots were obliged to take many risks – crossing the Pyrenees in all weathers, battling with turbulence and icing; flying non-stop across the Mediterranean by night as well as day to beat the mailboats; being forced to make emergency landings in the Sahara, where they faced not only heat and thirst but sometimes also hostile and bloodthirsty tribesmen. Saint-Ex thrived on the dangers, and in his first novel, *Courrier-Sud*, he pays homage to 'those elemental divinities – night, day, mountain, sea and storm'.

Saint-Ex continued his adventures in South America, where in 1929 he was appointed director of the Argentine airmail service, and in this role pioneered routes across the Andes in the teeth of the storms that slam into the mountains of Patagonia with the impact of a screaming freight train. In 1931,

In the night reason disappears, only the lines of things remaining.

ANTOINE DE SAINT-EXUPÉRY, *VOL DE NUIT* (1931)

back in France, he published *Vol de nuit*, and in the same year married Consuelo Gómez Carillo, a Salvadorean widow. The marriage was a stormy one, and Saint-Ex conducted a number of affairs with other women throughout the 1930s. During this period he developed his skills as a writer, while working variously as a test pilot, publicity officer for Air France and journalist, reporting on, among other things, the Spanish Civil War.

Adventure in the air was never far away, and fed both his writing and his need for heroic action. He came perhaps nearest to death after the 1935 crash landing in the Libyan Desert en route to Saigon. From the crash site he and Prévot walked considerable distances in a number of directions, becoming weaker and weaker from lack of food and water, but found no sign of other humans. Eventually, heading northeast and unable to make more than two hundred yards at a time, they came across a Bedouin caravan. Before their rescue, as they faced death, Saint-Ex found an inner calm, as if this was what gave his life meaning. He describes the experience in *Terre des hommes*:

> I had thought myself lost, had touched the very bottom of despair; and then, when the spirit of renunciation had filled me, I had known peace; I know now what I was not conscious of at the time – that in such an hour a man feels that he has finally found himself and has become his own friend.

PHONEY WAR TO BLITZKRIEG

Saint-Ex was visiting Germany in the early spring of 1939 when the Nazis marched into Czechoslovakia. The Germans were keen to impress this hero of the air, but Saint-Ex turned down an invitation to meet Goering, himself a former pilot. Saint-Ex had no time for his hosts:

> The Nazi respects only what resembles him … He denies the creative contradictions, ruins any hope of man's ascent and, for a thousand years, in place of man, creates an ant-hill robot. Order for order's sake deprives man of his essential power which is to transform the world and himself.

In August, as tensions continued to build in Europe, Saint-Ex was in New York, publicizing the US edition of *Wind, Sand and Stars*. He returned to France a week before war was declared. His mood was one of growing pessimism.

Saint-Ex loathed the war, but saw its necessity. 'War is not an adventure,' he wrote in *Flight to Arras*. 'It is a disease. It is like typhus.' He was frustrated when he volunteered for the air force in September 1939 to be confined to duties as an instructor in Toulouse, and lobbied hard to be given a combat role. Initially the authorities resisted on the grounds of his age and injuries (his left arm was partly paralysed), then offered him a place in the Ministry of Information under the distinguished dramatist and diplomat, Jean Giraudoux, where he could exploit his prestige and exercise his literary talents. This would not do either. Eventually, in November, he was attached to an air reconnaissance group in eastern France, and over the next few months flew many missions across the German border and over the Rhineland. One of his colleagues at this time recalled: 'In the air he was always light-hearted and even hilarious, but sometimes in the mess he would fall into a moody silence, and then the only thing to do was to leave him alone.'

The Phoney War ended with the German Blitzkrieg in May 1940. Almost every day Saint-Ex's unit was forced to establish a new base, retreating deeper and deeper into central France. The attrition was appalling: nearly three-quarters of the air crews in his unit were lost. On 23 May Saint-Ex made the flight to Arras that inspired the book of that name. During the flight his plane was hit by machine-gun fire, but survived:

> *Forward of my plane I suddenly saw three lance-strokes aimed at my machine. Three long, brilliant, vertical twigs. The paths of tracer bullets fired from a small calibre gun. They were golden. Suddenly, in the blue of the evening, I had seen the spurting glow of a three-branched candelabra.*

In June his unit retreated from Paris to Bordeaux, and on the 17th was ordered to move on to Algiers. In August, in the confused political situation, Saint-Ex was demobilized and returned to France, which had by now fallen to the Nazis. From there he managed to leave for the United States, travelling via Lisbon in neutral Portugal.

EXILE

The French exiles in New York were as divided as those back in France, between Pétainist collaborationists and Free-French Gaullists. Saint-Ex favoured neither group. He was furious when he heard that Marshal Pétain, who had set up the pro-German Vichy regime in France, had made him an honorary councillor of state, and was obliged to refute the appointment in the press. As for the Gaullists, he disliked many of them personally; he mistrusted their insistence that they had a monopoly on patriotism, dubbing them the 'Fifth Avenue Resistance'. For their part, they circulated rumours that Saint-Ex was a Nazi agent. The squabbles and petty jealousies that affect any group of political exiles got him down, and he became increasingly prone to mood swings. None of the other exiles had seen action; he had, and he determined to tell the world about it. The result was *Flight to Arras*.

Flight to Arras is not just a gripping account of a mission; it is a meditation on what Saint-Exupéry seems to think of as the crisis of civilization, and humanity's need for a greater sense of mutual responsibility. The pilot starts his flight in a mood of pessimism, an isolated individual haunted by a sense of futility, but as he rises above the world and faces danger, he comes to appreciate the 'brotherhood among men', and that civilization is 'founded upon the reverence for Man present in all men'. It is a lesson he seems to think France could only learn in the humiliation of defeat.

RETURN

Saint-Ex became increasingly homesick in New York, and frustrated that he could not do more for the war effort. In the summer of 1942 he tried to persuade the US Office of Strategic Services (the forerunner of the CIA) to use his local knowledge of Morocco, and his contacts there, to support an Allied invasion of northwest Africa. He was dismissed as a dreamer – he might be a poet and a

Saint-Exupéry had that quality so little associated with the idea of a Frenchman yet relatively frequent among the best of them – the quality of moral fearlessness which rises above both shyness and display, and which lends to the countenance a beauty there is no missing.

LEWIS GALANTIÈRE, SAINT-EXUPÉRY'S FRIEND AND TRANSLATOR, IN A LETTER TO THE *TIMES LITERARY SUPPLEMENT*, c.1952

heroic pilot, but he was no military strategist. Ironically, on 8 November, Allied forces *did* land in northwest Africa, and subsequently Saint-Ex broadcast a call to all Frenchmen to unite against the common enemy. Some time later Saint-Ex heard that his old unit was being re-formed in Algeria, under US command. As he had done in 1939, he used all his persistence and powers of persuasion to secure a passage back across the Atlantic to resume active service. Eventually the authorities gave in, and he embarked at the end of March 1943.

Saint-Ex's carelessness about practical things, his scruffy clothes, his bearing, 'which was both heavy and ill at ease on this planet', according to a fellow-pilot, all seemed to indicate a detachment from the day-to-day business of the world. This carelessness even seemed to extend to his flying, and he suffered a number of accidents. At 43 he conceded that his reactions were not what they were, nor was his physical strength – 'my physical condition makes everything as difficult as climbing the Himalayas,' he wrote to a friend. And now he was faced with piloting one of the fastest aircraft in the world, the twin-boomed Lockheed P-38 Lightning, a plane intended to be flown by fit young men in their 20s or early 30s, capable of dealing with high G forces, sudden changes in atmospheric pressure and a service ceiling of 44,000 feet. His unit's role was photo reconnaissance, which meant that the Lightnings would be unarmed, for the sake of speed and altitude.

At the unit's desert base, the rows of high-tech machines, the massed arrays of hangars, barracks, workshops, the men marshalled into models of military efficiency – all seemed to signify the coming of a soulless, mechanized world in which the individual spirit would be lost. In an unsent letter found amongst his papers after his death, Saint-Ex voiced his increasing despair: 'I am sad for my generation, empty as it is of all human content … a generation that thinks of bars, Bugattis and calculating machines as forms of the spiritual life …'

TOWARDS THE BLUE HORIZON

At the end of July 1943 Saint-Ex made his first operational flight in a Lightning, to photograph the Rhône Valley. He was thrilled to see France again, after an absence of three years, albeit from an altitude of 30,000 feet. Four days later he embarked on his second mission, but made a technical error with the braking mechanism on his return, and crashed into a vineyard – with little damage to the aircraft and none to himself. But the US command insisted on grounding him. Saint-Ex spent the next eight months morosely, neurotically in Algiers – a hotbed of political intrigue and rivalry between the various French factions – begging to be sent again on active service, anywhere. He worked on his next book, *The Wisdom of the Sands*, which, with a certain premonition, he described as his 'posthumous work'. He never finished it, and an honest critic would characterize it as an incoherent ragbag. It does however give a flavour of his thinking and mood at this time. In common with other men past their prime, Saint-Ex was now drifting into cultural pessimism and mistrust of the masses, decrying freedom and equality and advocating the values of discipline, constraint and hierarchy.

In the early spring of 1944 Saint-Ex's badgering paid off, and he was attached to a squadron of B-26 Marauders based in Sardinia. He flew a number of missions – but as radio operator or bomb aimer, as he was still barred from piloting. Further badgering saw Saint-Ex back with his unit of Lightnings, with permission to fly five more missions. Something of his youthful vigour and childlike playfulness returned, with this new lease of life. 'Once again I am experiencing the joys of high-altitude flights,' he wrote in *Life* magazine. 'They are like a diver's plunges into the depths of the sea: one enters forbidden territory, decked out in barbarous equipment, encased in a framework of dials and instruments and gauges; and high above one's country one breathes oxygen manufactured in the United States … At the controls of this light, fleet monster, this Lightning P.38, there is no feeling of movement, but, rather, of being fixed and immobile at one and the same moment, over a whole continent.'

His missions were not without incident. On one occasion at 27,000 feet his oxygen ran out, and he had to dive rapidly to avoid passing out. In another incident, the port engine failed, and he ended up limping home over northern Italy, pursued by enemy fighters and taking invaluable low-altitude photographs of German positions. On 7 July the unit moved to a new base, near Bastia in Corsica, and on 31 July, at 8.45 in the morning, Saint-Ex took off one more time, despite having exceeded his five permitted missions.

It was a perfect summer's day, hot and clear, as his plane cleared the Corsican mountains, aiming for the blue horizon and the coast of occupied France. From here he intended to continue north, to Annecy and Grenoble, tracking German troop movements. Just under half an hour after take-off, he was detected by radar as he crossed the French coast. At midday the radar should have picked him up again as he returned. But no blip came, and the screen remained empty. His comrades in the operations room waited anxiously, but as the hours dragged slowly on, hope began to fade. By 14:30 Saint-Ex's fuel would have run out. At 15:30 the interrogation officer, Vernon Robison, filled out his report card for the mission: 'PILOT DID NOT RETURN AND IS PRESUMED LOST … NO PICTURES.'

A saint in short, true to his name, flying up here at the right hand of God. The good Saint-Ex! And he was not the only one. He was merely the one who put it into words most beautifully and anointed himself before the altar of the right stuff.

TOM WOLFE, *THE RIGHT STUFF* (1979)

He disappeared without trace, like a god of antique legend in a mysterious ascension.

JEAN LELEU, OPERATIONS OFFICER OF 1ST SQUADRON, GROUP 2-33 – SAINT-EX'S UNIT

Clutching at straws, some suggested he might have made it to neutral Switzerland, others that he might have bailed out and be sheltering with the Resistance. His political enemies whispered that he had gone over to Vichy, while some of his friends suggested his plane might have been sabotaged. Many decades later, in 1998, a tiny bit of evidence emerged when a fisherman retrieved a silver chain bracelet from the sea south of Marseille. It bore the name of Saint-Ex's wife, Consuelo, and was attached to a piece of fabric. Two years later, in the same area, divers came across the wreck of a Lightning P-38 on the seabed. In 2004 this was positively identified as the Lightning – No. 223 – that Antoine de Saint-Exupéry had taken off in sixty years before. There was no sign that the plane had been hit by enemy fire, reinforcing the evidence of the German combat records for 31 July 1944, which report 'strong enemy reconnaissance activity in the entire southern France area', but make no mention of an Allied plane being shot down. Despite this, in 2008 a former Luftwaffe pilot, Horst Rippert, came forward with a claim that he had shot down a Lightning that day, and that Saint-Ex might have been the pilot – but he could not be completely sure. 'In our youth, at school, we had all read him,' Rippert said. 'We loved his books. If I had known, I would not have opened fire. Not on him!'

If Rippert was mistaken, and it wasn't Saint-Ex whom he shot down, then it is likely that the crashed Lightning recovered in 2000 had suffered some technical failure, in both engines or the oxygen supply. But there may have been an element of pilot error. Saint-Ex had become increasingly careless in his routines: when, for example, he had crash-landed into a vineyard in August 1943 it had been because he had forgotten to pump up his brake pressure before landing. This was a symptom of his increasing alienation from what he saw as a soullessly mechanized world, itself an aspect of his growing pessimism and frequent moods of despair. Where once he had revelled in machines and the company of mechanics, now he felt more the slave than the master of the shiny new American monsters, with their dials and instruments and gauges. Even if he did not deliberately crash his Lightning into the Mediterranean that day, perhaps something in him yearned to be free from a post-heroic age, an age in which the striving human spirit had no place. In a letter he wrote to General Chambe some time before his death, but never sent, he articulates this anguish:

There is but one problem, one sole problem for the world – how to give men back a spiritual significance … Man today no longer has significance.

Perhaps in the end it was this despair that brought about his destruction that clear summer's day.

Major Miller
is Missing

Glen Miller

(1944)

At 13.45 on Friday 15 December 1944 Major Glenn Miller, accompanied by Lieutenant-Colonel Norman F. Baessell and piloted by Flight Officer John R.S. Morgan, took off from an RAF aerodrome at Twinwood Farm, near the village of Clapham in Bedfordshire. They were on board a single-engined Noorduyn Norseman UC-64, a small Canadian bush plane designed to take off and land on rough ground.

Their destination was Paris, where Miller was to entertain the Allied troops who had liberated the city from the Nazis that August. The rest of Miller's band was to follow the next day in three C-47 transport aircraft. Miller's plane never made it, but what happened to the plane, its pilot and its passengers remains unknown.

THE MAESTRO OF SWING

Glenn Miller led one of the most successful big bands of the swing era. Numbers such as 'In the Mood', 'Moonlight Serenade' and 'Chattanooga Choo Choo' conjure up images of GIs dancing with their sweethearts, the warmth and sentiment of the music bringing an escape from the deprivations and horrors of the Second World War. Miller himself, a tall, bespectacled man with a somewhat ascetic mien, had, according to his friend and colleague Paul Dudley, 'a heart of warm mush hiding behind a quick-freeze kisser'.

Miller started his career as a jazz trombonist in the early 1920s, but it was not until 1937 that he formed his first band and began to develop his distinctive sound, based on a combination of clarinet and saxophones. The band did not at first make much of a mark, but from 1939 they hit the spot.

MILLER JOINS UP

When the USA entered the Second World War in December 1941 Miller was 37 – too old to be called up, but anxious to serve. In August 1942, having been turned down by the navy, he offered his services to Brigadier-General Charles Young, asking to be allowed to lead 'a modernized army band', with the aim of putting 'a little more spring into the feet of our marching men and a little more joy into their hearts'. The first ensemble Miller formed in the army was a large marching band, but his attempt to jazz up traditional military marches caused consternation among conservative senior officers. *Time* magazine said the army was now 'swinging its hips instead of its feet'.

But the ordinary soldiers loved Miller's music. The army soon recognized this, and decided that the band could make its best contribution to the war effort in the ETO – the European Theatre of Operations. So on 28 June 1944 Miller and his players – now officially known as the Army Air Forces Band (Special), and more informally as the American Band of the AEF (Allied Expeditionary Force) – disembarked from the liner *Queen Elizabeth* at Gourock on the Clyde, from where they travelled overnight to London. For the next six months the band toured Britain, giving hundreds of morale-boosting performances to hundreds of thousands of GIs and other Allied servicemen and women, and making numerous radio broadcasts on the BBC. On 29 July, after an out-of-doors concert at Wycombe Abbey, Lieutenant-General James H. Doolittle, commanding general of the Eighth Air Force, took the microphone, shook Miller by the hand and said, 'Next to a letter from home, Captain Miller,

Miller had America's music pulse, he knew what would please the listeners.

HERMAN 'TRIGGER' ALPERT, BASS PLAYER IN GLEN MILLER'S BIG BAND, SPEAKING IN 2004

your organization is the greatest morale-booster in the ETO.' For his part, Miller told a journalist, 'My job is to carry out orders, as any man in uniform must do. My job is to play to the men and women of the Allied Forces, and that is what I'm doing.' On 8 August he was promoted to major.

FLIGHT TO FRANCE

By the autumn of 1944, as the Allied armies pressed against the German frontier, Paris became the centre of rest and recreation for combat troops, and it was decided that the men should be provided with some star-quality entertainment. On 15 November Miller was flown to SHAEF (Supreme Allied Headquarters Allied Expeditionary Force) at Versailles, just outside Paris, and it was agreed that he and his band should play in France for six weeks, from mid-December.

Shortly before Miller was due to cross the English Channel, Maurice Gorham, director of his BBC shows, said to the major as he left his office for the last time, 'Now, Glenn, there's only one more thing. For heaven's sake make sure the boat they put you on is seaworthy. We don't want to lose you all.' It had, however, been decided to fly rather than go by sea. On 4 December Miller wrote to his brother Herb: 'By the time you receive this letter we shall be in Paris, barring of course a nose-dive into the Channel.'

Owing to bad weather, regular service flights to Paris were cancelled, but on 14 December Colonel Norman F. Baessell, a boisterous Southerner who had befriended Miller in England, offered him a lift the following day on a small plane that was taking him to Paris, then on to Bordeaux. That night, Miller played poker at the Officers' Club at Milton Ernest Hall, and later talked into the small hours with his friend and associate, Lieutenant Don Haynes, chatting about their plans once the war was over. In the morning the weather was still poor, but by lunchtime had improved sufficiently for the flight to obtain clearance. The rain had eased, but there was a steady drizzle, the temperature was near freezing, and the cloud ceiling was low.

What the hell, Miller, do you want to live forever?

LIEUTENANT-COLONEL NORMAN F. BAESSELL,
MILLER'S FELLOW PASSENGER ON THE ILL-FATED
NORSEMAN UC-64, 15 DECEMBER 1944. MILLER HAD
ENQUIRED WHERE THE PARACHUTES WERE.

As they boarded the Norseman, Baessell sat next to Morgan, the pilot, while Miller took one of the eight passenger seats behind them. 'Where are the parachutes?' Miller apparently inquired. 'What the hell, Miller,' Baessell replied, 'do you want to live forever?' The plane took off at 13.45, and was due to land in Paris around three hours later.

THE REST IS SILENCE

The bad weather delayed the flight of Haynes and the other band members until Monday 18 December. When they arrived at Orly airfield, near Paris, at 13.45 that day they were surprised that Major Miller was not there to meet them, and neither were the buses that were supposed to take them to their hotel. Haynes phoned SHAEF to see if they had heard from Miller or Baessell. They hadn't – but in the confusion of recent events that was perhaps not surprising. Just two days earlier the Germans – taking advantage of the appalling weather that had grounded Allied planes – launched an unexpected counter-attack in the Ardennes, catching the American 1st Army on the hop. This was the start of the Battle of the Bulge, a major offensive that threatened the Allied advance into Germany.

> *I'm afraid Major Miller has had it.*
>
> MAJOR-GENERAL R.W. BARKER OF SHAEF,
> TO MILLER'S FRIEND AND COLLEAGUE,
> LIEUTENANT DON HAYNES, 18 DECEMBER 1944 ·

In the middle of the bomb-damaged airfield, Haynes told the band members what he knew, which wasn't much. Miller hadn't been heard from, he said, and everybody was looking for him. Sergeant Harry Katzman, one of players and a graduate of the prestigious Julliard School of Music, later recalled his reaction: 'If a man is missing for three or four days, now then he's really lost.' The band eventually made their way to Paris. They were cold and hungry, and the news was that the Germans were only 150 miles away. It was even said that German soldiers disguised as GIs were already on the loose in the city, picking off those Americans foolish enough to go out on their own.

Haynes and Sergeant Paul Dudley – producer and scriptwriter on Miller's radio shows – took a car out to report to General Barker at SHAEF in Versailles. Barker had been making inquiries. There was a record of a single-engined plane flying over the south coast of England on 15 December, heading for France. But there was no report of the plane reaching the French coast. 'It looks very bad, lieutenant,' Barker told Haynes. 'I'm afraid Major Miller has had it.'

As the days passed, there was still no news – no reports of any crashes, or discovery of wreckage. Barker believed the plane could have been shot down having strayed over enemy territory (there were still isolated German positions around Dunkirk, for example), in which case those on board would either be dead or in captivity. Alternatively, the plane had crashed somewhere remote and had not yet been found (some have subsequently suggested the Chiltern Hills, west of London, but this has generally been discounted). The third possibility – now assumed to be the most likely – was that the plane had ditched in the Channel. The Norseman had no de-icing equipment, so it is possible that it had iced up in the freezing conditions and plunged into the sea. Even if Morgan had managed to make a safe water landing on the surface of the sea, in midwinter nobody can survive more than a few minutes in the cold grey waters of the English Channel.

In 1984 a former RAF navigator, Fred Shaw, recalled how on 15 December 1944 he was returning from an aborted bombing raid on Germany when his Lancaster jettisoned its bombs over the Channel. Too late, they noticed a small plane beneath them, which lost control when it was hit by the blast. However, subsequent research has shown that the Lancasters involved had already returned to base by the time the Norseman was over the Channel.

The fact that the Norseman was allowed to fly when other (but by no means all) aircraft were grounded has given rise to various far-fetched conspiracy theories, including the suggestion that Miller in fact died in the arms of a prostitute in a Parisian brothel. According to such theories, the story of the missing plane was issued as a cover-up to maintain the wholesomeness of the morale-boosting Miller myth. Other rumours suggested that he had been caught up in black-market activities, or had had a nervous breakdown. The Eighth Air Force casualty report simply listed Miller, Baessell and Morgan among many others as 'Missing in flight, presumed to be lost.'

THE BAND PLAYED ON

Before he'd left for Paris, Miller had pre-recorded many concerts with the BBC, for later broadcast. Although the BBC was informed of Miller's disappearance, the news had not yet been made public, and it had to go on broadcasting the concerts with Miller himself doing the introductions. It was not until 23 December that Miller's wife Helen, living in New Jersey, received a telegram from the US War Department. A press release announcing that Miller was 'reported missing' was issued the next day – Christmas Eve. The BBC broadcast a newsflash to this effect at eight minutes past six in the evening, followed by music from Handel's Messiah.

On the evening of Christmas Day itself, the band – after attending a special Mass for Miller – performed a live radio concert that was linked from Paris to London, and thence to New York and Toronto. They were conducted by Sergeant Jerry Gray, and the numbers included 'Sweet Lorraine', 'Jingle Bells', 'Oranges and Lemons', 'White Christmas' and 'Silent Night'. In those grim days of December 1944, with Paris under curfew as fears of a German breakthrough to the Channel grew stronger, there had been talk of dissolving the band and sending the men to the front line, where reinforcements were desperately needed. But in the end the generals realized that with or without Glenn Miller, the American Band of the AEF could still be what Miller had made it, the next best thing to a letter from home.

The sounds of war are better forgotten. The whine of the 88, the woosh of the flak, the death-belch of the burp-gun are all where they should be, quiet in the calm of approximate peace. But, silent among the faded noises of conflict, lies one sound which will be remembered with affection by Yanks of the ETO. It was a warm sentimental sound that poured out of liberated radios behind the lines, spilled into youth-manned cockpits homing for the bomber and fighter bases; it was a sound that made apple-cheeked warriors feel closer to home. This was the music of Major Glenn Miller's American Band of the AEF.

PAUL DUDLEY, *BOMBLIGHT SERENADE* (1946). SERGEANT DUDLEY WORKED CLOSELY WITH MILLER DURING THE WAR.

Righteous Gentile

Raoul Wallenberg

(1945)

'Here is a man who had the choice of remaining in secure, neutral Sweden when Nazism was ruling Europe. Instead, he left this haven and went to what was then one of the most perilous places in Europe, Hungary. And for what? To save Jews.' These are the words of Gideon Hausner, one-time chairman of Yad Vashem, the Holocaust memorial in Jerusalem, where those 'righteous gentiles' who helped to save Jews during the Nazi era are commemorated by an avenue of carob trees. Hausner knew what he was talking about: in 1961 he had been in charge of the prosecution of Adolf Eichmann, one of the main architects of the 'Final Solution'.

The man he was describing was Raoul Wallenberg, a Swedish businessman and diplomat in Budapest who, as the Nazis began to round up Hungarian Jews for deportation to the death camps, issued thousands of them with Swedish passports, so ensuring their survival. On 17 January 1945, after the Red Army had entered Budapest, Wallenberg was put under Soviet 'protection'. Nothing more was heard of him for 12 years, and his actual fate remains uncertain.

A MARRIAGE OF CONVENIENCE

Since 1920 Hungary had been ruled by a regent, Admiral Miklós Horthy, who the previous year had overthrown the short-lived communist government of Béla Kun. During the 1930s Hungary had been befriended by Nazi Germany, and in 1941, after the German invasion of the Soviet Union, the two countries had become formal allies. However, Horthy determined on an independent course, not only resisting German attempts to dominate the country's oil industry, but also – despite introducing a series of anti-Semitic laws – turning down Nazi requests to hand over Hungary's 800,000-strong Jewish population, and even offering refuge to Jews from elsewhere in Europe.

By March 1944 the Nazi regime had lost patience. While Horthy was kept a virtual captive in Austria, where he had gone for talks, German forces occupied Hungary, and replaced the unsympathetic premier, Miklós Kallay, with the pro-German Döme Sztojay. Immediately deportations of Hungary's Jewish population began. Not all the Nazis were fanatical Jew-haters, however; they simply took advantage of the situation to feather their own nests. Some in the SS, for example, were quite happy to exchange the lives of rich Jewish-Hungarian industrialists and their families in return for the control of their businesses.

INTERNATIONAL OUTCRY

By early 1944 the fate to which the Nazis had condemned the Jews of Europe was becoming known around the world. In the same year President Franklin D. Roosevelt set up the War Refugee Board (WRB), which was tasked with saving all those minorities, especially the Jews, threatened by the Nazis. The WRB urged the neutral countries of Europe to do whatever they could to this end.

Secretary of State Cordell Hull instructed the US ambassador in Stockholm to urge the Swedish government 'to increase to the largest possible extent the numbers of Swedish diplomatic and consular personnel in Hungary and to distribute them as widely as possible throughout the country. It is hoped, of course,' he continued, 'that such diplomatic and consular representatives will use all means available to them to persuade individuals and officials to desist from further barbarisms.'

> *Whoever saves a single soul, it is as if he had saved the whole world.*
>
> TALMUDIC INSCRIPTION ON THE MEDAL PRESENTED TO THOSE WHOM THE STATE OF ISRAEL HAS DECLARED TO BE A 'RIGHTEOUS GENTILE' FOR THEIR ACTIONS IN TRYING TO SAVE JEWS DURING THE NAZI ERA

Hull's urgings fell on fertile ground. The Swedish government, perhaps regretful that it had, earlier in the war, conceded to German demands for military transit rights across its territory, cooperated with the WRB and a committee of leading Swedish Jews in searching for someone to lead the rescue mission to Budapest. The first name to emerge was that of Count Folke Bernadotte, nephew of King Gustavus V, and later a UN envoy in Palestine (where, ironically, in 1948 he was assassinated by Jewish terrorists). However, the Hungarian government vetoed the choice. Then one of the Swedish Jews on the committee suggested his young business partner, Raoul Wallenberg.

COMETH THE HOUR, COMETH THE MAN

Raoul Wallenberg was the scion of a distinguished and well-connected Swedish family of bankers, diplomats and Lutheran clerics. Wallenberg's father, a naval officer, had died of cancer three months before his son's birth in August 1912. His mother subsequently remarried, and the young Wallenberg's upbringing and education were overseen by his grandfather, Gustav Wallenberg, a senior diplomat, who instilled in him a liberal, internationalist outlook. By the time Wallenberg had finished school and military service, he could speak French, English, Russian and German. He then went to study architecture in the USA, although his grandfather intended that he should eventually embark on a career in commerce or banking – a wish with which he eventually complied.

After a spell with a Swedish firm in South Africa, in 1935 Wallenberg went to Palestine to work for a Jewish banker, Erwin Freund, a friend of his grandfather. In Haifa he met a number of Jews who had fled from persecution in Nazi Germany, an experience that seems to have had a profound effect on him – not least because he was aware that on his mother's side he was descended from a Jew called Benedicks, who in the 18th century had settled in Sweden and converted to Christianity.

Wallenberg returned from Palestine in 1936, and his grandfather died the following year, after which the young man seems to have drifted somewhat purposelessly. His American architectural diploma did not qualify him to practise in Sweden, and banking did not suit him. It was not until after the outbreak of war in 1939 that his family found him a place in the Central European Trading Company, a food import-export business owned by a Jewish refugee, Koloman Lauer. Wallenberg, as a neutral Swede, could travel round Nazi-occupied Europe, selling smoked salmon and other Swedish delicacies, and buying pickled cucumbers and similar *Mitteleuropäische* specialities. He thus acquired considerable skill at dealing with Nazi officialdom.

But it was an unsatisfactory existence, and Wallenberg gave the impression to his friends that he was anxious to be doing something more worthwhile with his life. They later remembered how he became intensely animated while talking about the plight of European Jewry. After seeing a showing at the British embassy in Stockholm of the film *Pimpernel Smith*, in which an unassuming professor rescues victims of Nazi persecution, Wallenberg confided to his half-sister that was the kind of thing he wanted to do.

> *Of seemingly boundless energy and vitality, he has great imaginative powers and ... a clear and original mind.*
>
> DESCRIPTION OF RAOUL WALLENBERG BY ALBERT FLORÉN, ONE OF THE PARTNERS OF THE FIRM FOR WHOM WALLENBERG WORKED IN SOUTH AFRICA IN THE EARLY 1930s

The Girls He Left Behind

By the time Wallenberg left Sweden for Budapest he was 31 years old, and, in addition to his sense of mission, he seems to have had a strong desire to settle down with the right woman. His social circle comprised the carefree, gilded youth of Stockholm society, not all of whom could comprehend what was happening elsewhere in Europe. One evening, after taking the young actress Viveca Lindfors out dancing, he began to tell her about the plight of the Jews. 'I was rather frightened by the intensity with which he spoke and the subject he spoke about,' she later recalled. 'I remember thinking, he's just telling me all these things because he wants to get sympathy so that I will end up in his arms. That's horrible to think of now ...'

In May 1944, Wallenberg proposed to another young woman, the 18-year-old Jeanette von Heidenstam. She turned him down. 'Some time later he phoned me to say he was going to Budapest on a mission for the government,' Jeanette told Wallenberg's biographer, the late John Bierman. 'He didn't say what kind of mission it was, though I remember him saying it might be very dangerous.'

THE ROAD TO BUDAPEST

Not everybody in Stockholm agreed with Koloman Lauer's suggestion that his partner in the Central European Trading Company was the right sort for the mission to Budapest. Surely Wallenberg was too young, and lacked diplomatic experience? But after talking with Wallenberg through one long white night in June 1944, Ivar Olsen, the WRB representative in Sweden, became convinced that he was their man. An experienced diplomat would more likely be constrained by conventions and protocols, while Wallenberg insisted that he should be free to use any methods he saw fit, and that he should have the power to bypass the Swedish ambassador and normal diplomatic channels in dealing with the governments of both Sweden and Hungary. The Swedish government accepted Wallenberg's conditions, and he was appointed first secretary to the legation in Budapest.

Wallenberg left Stockholm on 6 July, travelling via Berlin, where he stayed overnight in an air-raid shelter while British bombers growled overhead. The next day he boarded a train for Budapest. The carriages were crammed with German soldiers returning to the Eastern Front from leave, and he had to sit on his rucksack in the corridor. In his pocket he carried a small revolver: 'To give myself courage,' he said.

WALLENBERG'S MISSION

By the time Wallenberg arrived in Budapest, over half of Hungary's Jewish population had been deported, most of them to Auschwitz. International pressure had brought about a temporary halt in the process, and the envoys of several neutral countries – Switzerland, the Vatican and others – had already begun the process of issuing protective documents. Nevertheless, hundreds of thousands of Hungarian Jews still faced the threat of annihilation, and Wallenberg lost no time. He used the considerable financial resources available to him to establish a network of influence and to organize possible escape routes, working in tandem with many Jewish volunteers at the Swedish legation, and negotiating with the Hungarian government on the numbers of protective passports the Swedes could issue. He also actively intervened as the deportations recommenced, taking photographs and confronting the authorities at railway stations as Jews were rounded up and packed onto trains.

Meanwhile, the Red Army was closing in on Hungary's Axis neighbours. On 24 August, Romania surrendered to the Soviets, and on 16 September they entered Sofia, capital of Bulgaria. In October, after Horthy had tried to negotiate a separate peace with the Allies, Ferenc Szálasi, leader of the Arrow Cross, the Hungarian fascists, took power in Budapest. The new government continued to

> *A person like me, who is both a Wallenberg and half-Jewish, can never be defeated.*
>
> RAOUL WALLENBERG SPEAKING IN 1930, AS RECALLED BY HIS FRIEND INGEMAR HEDENIUS IN 1980. WALLENBERG WAS EXAGGERATING; HIS ONLY JEWISH BLOOD DERIVED FROM HIS GREAT-GREAT-GRANDFATHER ON HIS MOTHER'S SIDE, WHO HAD CONVERTED TO LUTHERANISM.

respect the agreements reached with the Swedes and other neutral legations, but in early December, as Soviet armies under Marshal Malinovsky began to encircle Budapest, Szálasi and his government fled the capital. Arrow Cross thugs occupied the Swedish legation, and Wallenberg – a hate figure for the Hungarian fascists – was forced to go into hiding. The city was in chaos, and Arrow Cross mobs attacked and murdered Jews formerly under Swedish protection.

The Soviets began their attack on Budapest on 24 December. The German garrison was ordered by Hitler to defend the city to the last man, but their counteroffensives were like trying to fell an elephant with a peashooter. The defenders – both German and Hungarian – fought street by street, house by house, their rations reduced to six ounces of bread a day, supplemented by the meat of slaughtered horses. At one point the two sides fought for days to take control of the city's cemetery, the graves opened wide by the constant shelling. On 11 February some 16,000 German and Hungarian troops were killed during a last desperate retreat. The next day the city surrendered unconditionally to the Red Army. By this time Wallenberg had not been seen by his friends and colleagues for nearly a month.

A COLD WAR WINTER'S MORNING

A fallen city is a place of rumour, panic and desolation. More than 40,000 civilians had perished during what was one of the bloodiest sieges of the Second World War, and the survivors faced rape, starvation, disease and arbitrary execution. Budapest, the jewel of the Danube, had been reduced to rubble, and all the bridges linking the two halves of the city had been blown by the retreating Germans.

When the city surrendered, some 120,000 of its Jewish inhabitants were still alive – the largest Jewish community remaining in Europe. It had been a close shave: in the second week of January, even as the Soviets closed in on the main Jewish ghetto, the SS were about to carry out Eichmann's plan to massacre the 70,000 Jews still living there. From his hiding place, Wallenberg sent a message via a Hungarian intermediary to the SS commander, General August Schmidthuber. The gist of it was that if the mass executions went ahead, Wallenberg would ensure that after the war Schmidthuber would be hanged as a war criminal. Schmidthuber cancelled the operation.

As the city fell about his ears, Wallenberg and his Hungarian associates began to plan for postwar reconstruction, using funds supplied by the WRB and the American-Jewish Joint Distribution Committee. The idea was to set up a cooperative, self-help effort, independent of government control. But in the short term, emergency food and medical supplies were needed from the Soviets. To this end, Wallenberg moved cautiously through the shattered city towards the advancing Red Army, making contact with a forward unit on 13 January. He explained his mission first to a major, and then to a general, who gave him a permit to travel to the city of Debrecen, 120 miles to the east. This was the location of Marshal Malinovksy's headquarters, and of the pro-Soviet provisional Hungarian government. As he drove off with his Red Army escort on the morning of 17 January, Wallenberg told Dr Ernö Petö, one of his close associates, 'I'm going to Malinovsky's … whether as a guest or prisoner I do not know yet.' His colleagues said he expected to be back within eight days. They never saw him again.

LOST IN THE GULAG

In retrospect, knowing what we now know of Stalin's determination to grasp all of eastern Europe in his steely embrace, Wallenberg's plans for an independent reconstruction programme funded by the Americans in Soviet-occupied Hungary appears naïve, to say the least. In the atmosphere of intense paranoia that accompanied all Soviet contacts with the West in the closing phases of the Second World War, it was almost inevitable that the Russians would think of Wallenberg as a spy. They may not have been entirely mistaken, as Wallenberg's appointment was approved not only by the WRB, a US government body, but also by the OSS, the predecessor of the CIA. But there is no evidence that Wallenberg was actively involved in intelligence work during his time in Budapest.

Eight days after Wallenberg drove off with his Russian escort there was still no news of him. The first that anyone heard was on 8 March 1945, when Soviet-controlled Hungarian radio announced that Wallenberg and his driver had been killed by fascists on the way to Debrecen. The Swedish government seems to have accepted the truth of this story, and when the Swedish ambassador to Moscow met Molotov and Stalin in 1946, he declined the suggestion that the Swedes might hand over some Russian defectors in exchange for their diplomat, in the belief that Wallenberg was already dead. It later emerged that Stalin intended holding a show trial in Moscow in 1953, with the intention of convicting two Hungarian Jewish leaders of Wallenberg's murder, as part of a campaign against 'cosmopolitan Zionists'. The trial was cancelled following Stalin's death.

Over the years, a number of German prisoners of war released from Soviet captivity told of encounters with a man who claimed to be a Swedish diplomat, held prisoner because of 'a great error'. One German claimed that in late January and early February 1945 he had shared a cell with Wallenberg in the NKVD's notorious Lubyanka Prison in Moscow. In 1957, during the 'thaw' that followed Stalin's death, the Soviets released a memo dated 17 July 1947 from the head of the prison infirmary at the Lubyanka to the minister of state security. This reported that Wallenberg had died suddenly in his cell, 'probably as a result of a heart attack'.

WHISPERS FROM THE PAST

Since the end of the Cold War and the collapse of the Soviet Union, more information has emerged regarding Wallenberg's possible fate, but none of the evidence is so far conclusive. One hearsay report indicates that Wallenberg was shot in 1947, while a former senior Soviet intelligence officer claimed that Wallenberg was a victim of the unit that in the 1940s used poisons for political assassinations. However, other reports indicate that Wallenberg may still have been alive in the 1950s – or even as recently as 1987 – held in one part or another of the vast Gulag of prison camps stretching across Siberia. The Soviet authorities returned Wallenberg's few personal possessions, including his passport and cigarette case, to his family in 1989. In 2000 the Russian government that succeeded the Soviet regime stated that Wallenberg had been a victim of 'political repression'. No further details have been forthcoming.

Perhaps the last words should be left to John Bierman, who in his book *Righteous Gentile: The Story of Raoul Wallenberg* (1981) first brought the story of Wallenberg to international attention. Bierman's words are inscribed on the statue to Wallenberg outside the Swedish embassy in Great Cumberland Gate, central London: 'The 20th century spawned two of history's vilest tyrannies. Raoul Wallenberg outwitted the first but was swallowed up by the second. His triumph over Nazi genocide reminds us that the courageous and committed individual can prevail against even the cruellest state machine. The fate of the six million Jews he was unable to rescue reminds us of the evil to which racist ideas can drive whole nations. Finally, his imprisonment reminds us not only of Soviet brutality but also of the ignorance and indifference which led the free world to abandon him. We must never forget these lessons.'

My Enemy's Enemy

Subhas Chandra Bose

(1945)

We are all familiar with the names of Gandhi and Nehru, but a third figure, famous in India but little known in the West, stands out in the struggle for Indian independence. This man remains a focus of controversy even in his own country, some regarding him as a Quisling, others awarding him the honorific title *Netaji* ('respected leader'). This man was Subhas Chandra Bose, the Indian nationalist who during the Second World War allied himself and his followers with the Germans and Japanese against Britain and the USA.

Where Gandhi and Nehru advocated non-violent resistance to British rule, Bose called for armed insurrection. In Japanese-occupied Singapore in 1943 he formed an Indian government in exile, and began to re-organize the Indian National Army, formed the previous year from Indian prisoners of war with the express aim of fighting the British. What happened to Bose at the end of the war remains unclear. He was said to have died in an air crash in Taiwan, but since then some doubt has been cast on this version of his fate.

THE STRUGGLE FOR INDEPENDENCE

Born in 1897 to a wealthy Bengali family in Orissa, Bose studied at the University of Cambridge, and joined the Indian Civil Service in 1920. The following year he resigned to work for the Indian National Congress, which was pressing the British to grant independence. By the end of the 1920s he and Nehru had emerged as leaders of a new generation of youth and student activists, adding a socialist perspective to Indian nationalism. Over the next two decades, Bose was imprisoned a total of 11 times by the British, and between 1933 and 1936 was in exile in Europe, where he pressed the cause of Indian independence, and met a number of political leaders. He rejected the Nazi model of nationalism, which he condemned as 'not only narrow and selfish but arrogant'. Back in India, he was elected president of Congress in both 1938 and 1939, but, because he advocated industrialization along Soviet lines, came into conflict with Gandhi, and was compelled to resign. He formed a new party, the All India Forward Bloc, developing a conviction that a free India would need an authoritarian socialist government.

For the present, I can offer you nothing except hunger, thirst, privation, forced marches and death. But if you follow me in life and in death ... I shall lead you to victory and freedom.

SUBHAS CHANDRA BOSE, SPEECH TO THE INDIAN NATIONAL ARMY, SINGAPORE, 5 JULY 1943

With the outbreak of the Second World War, Bose stepped up the pressure on the British, organizing protests against the British viceroy's declaration of war on India's behalf, which he had done without consulting Congress. He also attacked the leadership of Congress for adopting a compromising 'wait-and-see' approach, rather than taking the opportunity to launch all-out action against British imperialism. Under constant surveillance, and facing more charges against him, Bose determined to continue the fight from abroad.

THE LONG ROAD TO TOKYO

On 26 January 1941, with the assistance of German agents, Bose escaped from virtual house arrest in Calcutta and made his way to Peshawar in the North West Frontier Province (now part of Pakistan). From here he crossed into Afghanistan, where he grew his beard to blend in with the natives and disguised the fact that he could not speak the local language by pretending to be deaf and dumb. Crossing Afghanistan via Kabul, he was met at the USSR border by agents of the NKVD, the Soviet secret police. It has been suggested that the British government ordered two agents of its Special Operations Executive in Turkey to assassinate Bose while he was still in Afghanistan, but, if this was the case, the plot failed.

Bose adopted the identity of an Italian nobleman, Count Orlando Mazzotta. In Moscow, he had hoped that he would find support for his anti-imperialist cause, but the response was lukewarm. He received a more sympathetic reception from the German ambassador, who arranged for him to be flown to Germany via Rome.

In Berlin, Bose set up Azad Hind Radio to broadcast his message, and established the Indian Legion from Indian prisoners of war captured in North Africa. Members of the legion, which was later attached to the Waffen SS, swore allegiance both to Hitler and to Bose. Naïvely, Bose had hoped that after the German invasion of the Soviet Union in June 1941 the Indian Legion would spearhead an invasion of British India from the north. In 1943, disillusioned by Hitler's lack of interest, Bose decided to try his luck in Japan. After a 90-day voyage by U-boat and Japanese submarine, he arrived in Singapore on 2 July, from where he continued on to Tokyo. On 4 July, taking up leadership of the Indian Independence Movement in East Asia, he announced:

All organizations whether inside India or outside must now transform themselves into a disciplined fighting organization under one leadership. The aim and purpose ... should be to take up arms against British imperialism.

THE INDIAN NATIONAL ARMY

The Indian National Army (INA) had been formed in 1942 by Mohan Singh, an officer in the Indian Army. Instead of retreating with the British down the Malay Peninsula, Singh had decided to seek support from the Japanese for his idea of forming an anti-British army out of Indian prisoners of war. Singh and other Indian officers emphasized that they would not go into action against the British except with the authority of the Indian National Congress, and that they saw the INA as a bulwark against any Japanese attempt to conquer India for themselves. Needless to say, the Japanese had a different agenda, and Mohan Singh was arrested.

When Bose arrived in Tokyo, he was assured by Prime Minister Tojo that Japan had no territorial designs on India. Returning to Singapore, on 21 October 1943 Bose established the Provisional Government of Free India,

India's war of independence has begun ... Father of our Nation! In this holy war of India's liberation, we ask for your blessing and good wishes.

SUBHAS CHANDRA BOSE, ADDRESSING GANDHI IN A BROADCAST ON AZAD HIND RADIO, 6 JULY 1944

which was recognized by all the Axis powers, and which declared war on Britain and the USA. He also set about re-organizing the INA, with bases in both Singapore and Rangoon, recruiting civilians as well as prisoners of war – and even establishing a women's regiment.

But again Bose's allies failed to share his vision. The Japanese army treated the INA as inferiors, using them for menial tasks. Only one INA battalion served in the Imphal offensive, which took the Japanese over the frontier from Burma into India in the spring of 1944. After that the Japanese – and the INA – were forced to retreat until the final surrender in August 1945. Some of the INA men repatriated to India were tried for treason – to widespread protests from their fellow countrymen.

BOSE VANISHES

It was reported that Bose died in Taiwan on 18 August 1945 when his plane crashed at or near what is now Taipei domestic airport as he tried to flee from Southeast Asia. Some say he did not die immediately, but was taken, badly burnt, to a Japanese hospital on the island. However, his body was never recovered. Some have suggested he actually survived, making his way via Manchuria to the Soviet Union. There is a report that an Indian had met him in a prison camp in Omsk, in Siberia.

After independence, the Indian government instituted a number of inquiries into the fate of Subhas Chandra Bose. A commission under Mr Justice M.K. Mukherjee, a retired Supreme Court judge, investigated the case in 1999–2005. Mukherjee obtained information from the Taiwan government that it had no record of the plane crash in the Taipei area between 14 August and 20 September 1945, an assertion supported by a statement from the US State Department. The Taiwan government also said there was no documentation from the relevant crematorium that it had ever processed anyone called Subhas Chandra Bose or Ichiro Okuda (the *nom de guerre* given to Bose by the Japanese government). The Mukherjee Commission submitted its report to the Indian government on 8 November 2005. It was rejected.

There is no doubt that a surviving Bose would have been a terrible embarrassment for the British: they would have felt obliged to try him for treason, and this could have proved an incendiary act given the breadth of his support. The reappearance of Bose in India would also have been politically difficult for Gandhi, Nehru and Congress. The possibility that he might have died in a Siberian prison camp would have been damaging to the usually good relations between the Soviet Union and post-independence India. One can only conclude that his death in an air crash would have been the most convenient outcome for many.

began his third, fatal attempt. A government report released in 2006 under the Freedom of Information Act reveals that when Crabb failed to return, his handlers decided against mounting a search, in case the Soviets became suspicious. The SIS man who had accompanied Crabb to the Sally Port removed Crabb's luggage from the hotel, together with the page in the register bearing their names.

Ten days later, on 29 April, the Admiralty released a statement saying that Crabb had disappeared underwater during trials of secret new equipment in Stokes Bay, beyond the mouth of Portsmouth harbour. On 4 May the Soviets issued a protest claiming that at at 7.35 a.m. on 19 April a lookout on a Soviet destroyer escorting the *Ordzhonikidze* had spotted a frogman in the water near the cruiser.

> It would not be in the public interest to disclose the circumstances in which Commander Crabb is presumed to have met his death. While it is the practice for ministers to accept responsibility, I think it is necessary in the special circumstances of this case to make it clear that what was done was done without the authority or knowledge of Her Majesty's ministers. Appropriate disciplinary steps are being taken.
>
> SIR ANTHONY EDEN, BRITISH PRIME MINISTER, STATEMENT TO THE HOUSE OF COMMONS, 9 MAY 1957

The British prime minister, Anthony Eden, was put in an embarrassing situation. He had issued instructions to his intelligence services not to undertake any operations against his Soviet guests, and demanded the resignation of Sir John Sinclair, head of MI6. As the identity of 'C' was not then public knowledge, Eden would only tell the House of Commons that 'the appropriate disciplinary steps' were being taken. The Cabinet papers relating to the case are not due to be released until 2057.

KILLED OR KIDNAPPED?

All kinds of theories emerged in the press regarding what had happened to the missing war hero. The most popular was that the Soviets had captured Crabb and taken him back to the Soviet Union. Others went further, suggesting that MI6 had instructed Crabb to get himself caught, so he could work as a double agent. It has also been alleged that MI5, the internal security service, received information that Crabb was about to defect to the Soviet Union, and had him killed. Most recently it has been mooted that Crabb was acting as a decoy for a team of divers from Naval Intelligence who were attempting to plant listening devices on the hull of the *Ordzhonikidze*. According to this account, the mission went badly wrong, and Crabb and one of the other divers were killed.

Without a head or hands, the body found in Chichester harbour on 9 June 1957 was, with the technology then available, almost impossible to identify. Neither Crabb's ex-wife nor his subsequent girlfriend recognized any features, although Crabb's former diving partner, Sydney Knowles, testified that the corpse had a similar scar to Crabb on the left knee. The inquest jury returned an open verdict, and the coroner said he was satisfied the corpse belonged to Crabb. In 2006 Knowles claimed he had been ordered to make a positive identification, and that he had always doubted the body was that of his friend. Ten years after the inquest a skull was dug out of the sand at Chichester harbour, which a pathologist judged to be the same age as the torso found in 1957. There were several teeth, but there were no identifying marks to link them to Crabb.

In 1994 Nicholas Elliott, the officer responsible for planning Crabb's mission, published his memoirs. Crabb, he wrote, 'almost certainly died from respiratory trouble, being a heavy smoker and not in the best of health (he was then 47), or conceivably because some fault had developed in his equipment'. Elliott denied that Crabb had lost his life 'as a result of any action by the Russians'.

In the autumn of 2007 a retired Soviet seaman called Eduard Koltsov appeared on Russian television with an extraordinary claim. He said that on 19 April 1956 he had been ordered into the water to investigate suspicious activity around the *Ordzhonikidze*. 'I saw the silhouette of the diver,' he said. 'He was fiddling around with something near the right side of the ship and the storage bay where we kept our ammunition. I swam closer. I saw he was attaching a mine.' Koltsov then produced a knife in front of the TV cameras, and told his interviewer that he had used it to kill Crabb. He said he had received a Red Star medal as a result.

> They abandoned him. They left him to his fate, which to me is absolutely horrendous after all that he had done for his country. It was a bungled operation, planned without sufficient thought, because those in charge failed to apply their minds to the consequences should it go badly wrong.
>
> LOMOND HANDLEY, A RELATIVE OF LIONEL CRABB, AFTER READING THE 1956 GOVERNMENT REPORT ON THE MISSION, WHICH WAS RELEASED UNDER THE FREEDOM OF INFORMATION ACT IN 2006

This account has been received with widespread scepticism. It seems unlikely that MI6 would want to destabilize the London summit by blowing up the Soviet cruiser; Crabb's purpose was almost certainly espionage, not sabotage. But in the context of the worsening relations between Britain and President Putin's Russia that prevailed in 2007, following the assassination in London of the Russian dissident Alexander Litvinenko, it would have suited the Russian government's purposes to depict Britain as the aggressor in the mysterious events of half a century before.

A Victim of the Undertow

Harold Holt

(1967)

Harold Holt's short spell as prime minister of Australia ended on 17 December 1967 when he went for a swim and never came back. An extensive search yielded no results, and at 10 p.m. the following day the governor-general of Australia declared Holt's premiership to be at an end.

Speculation was rife. Was it an accident, or had Holt taken his own life? Wilder rumours also circulated, some relating to Australia's involvement in the Vietnam War, which Holt had supported. When an inquest was eventually held, the coroner declared that Holt had accidentally drowned – but even so, not everyone believed the verdict.

YOUNG HAROLD

Holt's father had chucked in schoolmastering for the life of a travelling theatrical manager. At school and university Holt himself developed a taste for theatricals, as well as excelling as a sportsman – somewhat at the expense of his academic studies. By the 1930s Holt Senior had moved into cinema and radio, and in 1935 young Holt became secretary of the Cinematograph Exhibitors' Association. The same year, having acquired a taste for politics of a conservative bent, he entered the federal parliament, and in 1939 became Australia's youngest government minister. Holt proceeded to serve under Prime Minister Robert Menzies all the way through his long years in power; among his portfolios were labour, national service and immigration. In the latter post he was a staunch advocate of the White Australia policy, giving preference to immigrants from Britain.

Holt always cut a dashing figure – something that he was more than aware of – and his charm, easy-going nature, good looks and fine physique brought him great popularity. Often accompanied by his wife Zara, he cultivated a taste for foreign trips, enjoying the life of an international *homme du monde*. Holt played hard – but he also worked hard, and conscientiously. In 1956 he was elected deputy leader of the parliamentary Liberal Party, and two years later he became treasurer (i.e. finance minister). When Menzies – the 'Great White Chief' – retired from the premiership in January 1966, 'Young Harold' was the obvious choice as his successor.

THE ACTION-MAN PREMIER

Holt, although now 57 and silver-haired, had moved with the times, adopting an open, informal manner to suit the Swinging Sixties. He saw himself as a man of action in the James Bond mould, and was particularly proud of his prowess in swimming, snorkelling and spear-fishing. Cultivating his youthful image, he had himself photographed in a wetsuit in the company of his three glamorous, bikini-clad daughters-in-law. It was like a publicity still from *Thunderball*.

In his brief spell as prime minister, Holt determined to bring Australia closer to its Asian neighbours. This led him to relax the White Australia policy, and to increase his country's military commitment to the Vietnam War. On a visit to Washington DC in July 1966 to see his friend, President Lyndon B. Johnson, he coined the slogan 'All the Way with LBJ' – a sentiment that did not go down too well at home, although in October his party won the federal elections with an increased majority.

Despite this success, the year that followed was not an easy one for Holt, with dissenting voices in the governing coalition, corruption scandals, electoral set-backs, a robust new leader of the opposition, and mounting protests against the Vietnam War. Holt was said to be tired but in good spirits when on Friday 15 December 1967, unaccompanied by Zara, he left for a weekend break at the family home in Portsea, near Melbourne.

NOT WAVING BUT DROWNING

That Sunday Holt, together with a lady friend called Marjorie Gillespie (just 'one of the queue' according to his wife) and three others, watched the English round-the-world yachtsman Alec Rose pass through Port Phillip Heads in *Lively Lady*. They then drove to Cheviot Beach, one of Holt's favourite swimming places, despite its reputation for strong currents and dangerous rip tides. The surf was running high and wild that day, but Holt, undeterred, changed into his swimming trunks. His companions pleaded with him to stay on shore, but, apparently keen to show off, he dived in. They watched nervously as he struck out through the waves. Then, very quickly, swelling seas obscured him from view.

A large-scale rescue operation swung into action, but hopes of finding Holt alive soon evaporated, and the searchers realized they were looking for a body. But no body was ever found. The search was officially abandoned on 5 January 1968.

The absence of a body meant, under the law of the state of Victoria, there could be no inquest. The law was eventually changed, and the inquest that was held in 2005, almost forty years after Holt's disappearance, concluded that he had been swept out to sea by the undertow and drowned. Although a strong swimmer, Holt was far from fit at the time of his last swim, and was suffering from a painful shoulder injury. Twice already that year he had had to be helped out of difficulties in the water, and some suspected that a collapse he had suffered in parliament earlier in 1967 was due to a heart condition.

> ### Doing a Harry
> In Australian rhyming slang 'to do a Harry [i.e. Harold Holt]' means 'to bolt', i.e. to vanish suddenly and without explanation.

Despite the coroner's verdict, some have persisted in thinking that Holt committed suicide, suggesting that his political difficulties in the year leading up to his death had made him depressed. More outlandishly, others claimed that he had been abducted by Chinese or Soviet agents and whisked aboard a submarine. One journalist has even suggested that Holt was in fact a Chinese agent himself, and that he had arranged a rendezvous with his controller off Cheviot Beach. Another conspiracy theory has it that the CIA had got wind that Holt was about to pull Australian forces out of Vietnam, and had him assassinated. There is scarcely a shred of evidence for any of these intriguing theories, and on the balance of probabilities it seems that Holt was just one more Australian who overestimated his strength in the enticing warmth of the summer ocean.

The Brute of Belgravia

Lord Lucan

(1974)

John Bingham, 7th Earl of Lucan, was born in 1934 with a silver spoon in his mouth – and a sneer on his lips. He was the great-great-grandson of the 3rd Earl of Lucan, commander of the British cavalry in the Crimean War, and held by some to be responsible for the bloody blunder that was the Charge of the Light Brigade. Young Bingham followed a typical upper-class career, idling his way through Eton and the Guards to a 'job' in merchant banking. Unlike his parents, he never understood that privilege brings responsibilities, and by his fortieth year his prodigal life had declined into debt and despair.

No one would now care tuppence what happened to this gambler, playboy and ne'er-do-well if he had not possessed a title – and had he not bludgeoned to death his children's nanny, apparently having mistaken her for his wife. The question of what happened to Lucan after the murder has given the tabloid press more column inches than virtually any other story over the last thirty years.

THE LIFE OF A LOAFER

As a boy, while Britain suffered the privations and dangers of the Second World War, Bingham was sent to live in lavish circumstances on the upstate New York estate of a wealthy American socialite and amateur ornithologist called Marcia Brady Tucker. Returning home in 1945 he found the austerity the country was then experiencing not to his taste. Matters were made worse for this sulky, temperamental child by the fact that his parents – despite their aristocratic titles – shunned luxury, and instead espoused progressive, socialist principles (although not to the extent of sending him to a state school). In contrast, young Bingham enjoyed the possession of money, and the things that money could buy, and adopted a reactionary, anti-democratic stance: later in life he moved in a circle of extreme right-wingers, some of whom liked to brag about mounting a coup against the elected Labour government. He was also, according to his wife, known to listen to recordings of Hitler's Nuremberg speeches, and possessed a well-thumbed translation of *Mein Kampf*.

Bingham was too much the *flâneur* to actually achieve anything in the political field – or any other field, for that matter. Flourishing a splendid Guards moustache and enjoying fast cars, powerboats and bobsleigh racing, he was once considered for the part of James Bond. But his greatest delight was the gaming table, a taste he first developed at Eton, and continued throughout his national service as a second lieutenant in the Coldstream Guards. By around 1960 he had made enough money at the tables – his friends knew him as 'Lucky Lucan' – to resign his position at the merchant bank and live the life of a professional gambler. His house was in the exclusive London district of Belgravia, and his favourite daily haunt – from lunchtime to the small hours of the morning – was the Clermont, John Aspinall's gaming club in Berkeley Square, Mayfair. Aspinall kept Bingham supplied with free food and drink, referring to him as 'the good furniture' because his aristocratic pedigree gave the somewhat louche premises what some might have considered to be 'class'.

> *He was very right wing and never watered it down in front of liberals. He would talk about hanging and flogging and niggers to get a reaction.*
>
> CHARLES BENSON, A *DAILY EXPRESS* JOURNALIST AND FORMER FRIEND OF LUCAN, QUOTED IN *THE OBSERVER*, 9 JANUARY 2005

AN UNFORTUNATE MATCH

In November 1963 Bingham married Veronica Duncan, the daughter of an army officer who had married Veronica's mother when she was 19 and working as the bookkeeper of a Bournemouth hotel. The 6th Earl of Lucan died in January 1964 and Bingham inherited his father's title together with a quarter of a million pounds. The marriage was not a happy one, Veronica soon finding Lucan's lifestyle incompatible with domestic felicity, and as the years passed her emotional poise became more and more delicately balanced.

The difficulties in Lucan's matrimonial arrangements began to take their toll on his performance at the tables. When in 1972 Aspinall sold the Clermont to Hugh Hefner of Playboy, the new owner was less willing to protect Lucan from the consequences of his fecklessness. After the sale, it was said that while Aspinall came away with £350,000, Lucan was presented with an envelope full of his own bounced cheques.

After Lord and Lady Lucan separated in 1973, Lady Lucan was awarded custody of the three children. This caused Lucan considerable distress. He becoming obsessed with recovering his children, started to drink heavily, and took to spying on the family home at 46 Lower Belgrave Street.

BLOOD IN THE BASEMENT

The evening of 7 November 1974 was proving a slow one for Derek Whitehouse (44), landlord of the Plumbers Arms at 14 Lower Belgrave Street. Then, at about 9.45 p.m., a distraught figure entered his establishment. 'The pub was quiet when she burst through the door,' he later told the press. 'She was covered in blood. She kept screaming, "My children, my children." I asked her who she was and she said Lady Lucan. But I could not get much sense out of her and she was in such a state of shock. Her head injuries were quite severe. She had been hit four or five times.'

Mr Whitehouse telephoned the police. At 46 Lower Belgrave Street detectives found a pool of blood on the floor of the darkened basement kitchen. More blood was spattered across the walls, and in a sack on the floor was the body of Sandra Rivett (29), nanny to the Lucan children. Her friends posthumously described her as a 'vivacious redhead' who 'always liked a laugh'. She had clearly been battered to death with the length of lead piping the police found in the hallway. Upstairs, the three Lucan children – Lady Frances (10), Lord Bingham (7) and Lady Camilla (4) – were found huddled together, sobbing.

Lady Lucan (37) told the police that her estranged husband had killed Sandra Rivett, and then turned his attentions to her. On 12 November the police issued a warrant for Lucan's arrest. By this time the bird had flown – but not before stopping by at the house of a friend, Susan Maxwell-Scott, to whom Lucan spun an unlikely tale. He claimed that he had been passing 46 Lower Belgrave Street when he noticed, through the window, an unknown assailant attacking his wife. He let himself in with his key, but skidded in a pool of blood, thus allowing the assailant to make good his escape. Just as Lucan was gathering together some towels to clear up the mess, Lady Lucan fled hysterically from the house. Finding himself in a compromising circumstance, he decided, in the argot of the underworld, to leg it.

WHATEVER HAPPENED TO LUCKY?

In June 1975 an inquest jury named Lucan as the murderer of Sandra Rivett. But no murder trial could take place because the whereabouts of the suspect was unknown. In December of the previous year Australian police had thought for a while that they had their man, but the person they collared turned out to be John Stonehouse, the former British government minister who had faked his own suicide (as recounted below).

Members of Lucan's fast set, such as John Aspinall and Sir James Goldsmith, stated that they were convinced that Lucan, having murdered the wrong woman, had done the decent thing and taken his own life – perhaps by jumping over the rail of a cross-Channel ferry (his car had been found abandoned at the Channel port of Newhaven four days after the murder), or by scuppering

The Man Who Wasn't Lord Lucan

John Stonehouse, the man Australian police mistook for Lucan in 1974, had entered Parliament as a Labour MP in 1957. He held a number of posts in Harold Wilson's government of 1964–70, after which he became involved in a variety of money-making schemes that turned out to be beyond the borders of legality.

Realizing the net was closing in, on 21 November 1974 he faked his own suicide by leaving a pile of clothes on a beach in Miami. He was presumed dead, and obituaries appeared in the newspapers. However, five weeks later police in Melbourne, Australia, arrested a man they thought was Lord Lucan. It turned out to be Stonehouse, who, using the passport of a deceased constituent, had fled to the Antipodes with Mrs Sheila Buckley, his secretary at the House of Commons.

Stonehouse was deported to the UK, where he faced charges of fraud, theft, forgery, conspiracy to defraud, causing a false police investigation and wasting police time. He was sentenced to seven years, but, following a series of heart attacks, served only three and a half. His first marriage had been dissolved in 1978, and in 1981 he married his mistress, Mrs Buckley, the daughter of a master butcher. Seven years later his heart failed him for good.

his powerboat out at sea. Against this was the popular theory – given some credence by a number of police officers – that it was the likes of Aspinall and Goldsmith who had arranged his escape from England. Another claim – put forward by a former employee of John Aspinall – was that Lucan had taken refuge in Aspinall's private zoo, where a tiger had unwittingly become the instrument of justice and mauled the 7th Earl to death.

JUNGLE BARRY, CAMILLA THE GOAT AND THE GHOST OF CASTLEBAR

The tabloid press became obsessed with Lucan's vanishing act – an obsession fed over the years by reported sightings from all over the world. The 7th Earl has variously been spotted hiking up the volcanic cone of Mount Etna in Sicily, changing in the locker room of a gym at the University of British Columbia, working as a waiter in a restaurant in San Francisco, playing cards in Botswana, and indulging in countless other activities in countless other locations, often simultaneously. In 1998 the *Connaught Telegraph* reported that staff in government buildings in Castlebar in County Mayo, Ireland – the original seat of the earls of Lucan – had seen his moustachioed ghost wandering the corridors.

As the 20th century gave way to the new millennium, Duncan MacLaughlin, formerly of Scotland Yard, claimed that a man who had died in Goa in 1996 was Sandra Rivett's murderer, albeit hiding behind a heavy beard and the nickname 'Jungle Barry'. But when MacLaughlin published his claim in 2003, the British singer and comedian Mike Harding recognized the photograph of 'Jungle Barry' as his old mate Barry Halpin, a performer on the Liverpool folk scene in the 1960s, who had thought that India would be 'more spiritual' than Merseyside.

In 2007 locals in the New Zealand town of Moreton became convinced that their neighbour, a man called Roger Woodgate, was the fugitive 7th Earl, on account of his upper-class English accent and military bearing. At the time, Woodgate was living in an old Land Rover in the company of a cat, a possum called Redfern, and Camilla the Goat. It turns out that Woodgate is ten years younger than Lucan, and five inches shorter. He told reporters that another former Scotland Yard detective, Sydney Ball, had paid him a visit: 'He told me that I was not Lord Lucan,' Woodgate said. 'I said, "I know that."'

Woodgate was right: he isn't Lord Lucan. And neither, it seems, is anybody else. In 1999 the High Court in London concluded that Lucan was dead, as far as probate is concerned. However, that same year the Lord Chancellor muddied the waters by ruling that Lucan wasn't quite dead enough for his son to inherit the earldom and take his seat in the House of Lords.

Street-Fighting Man

JIMMY HOFFA

(1975)

Industrial relations in the USA isn't a game for faint-hearts. Both unions and employers play hard ball, and no one ever played harder than James Riddle Hoffa, generous-spirited, hard-fisted, hot-tempered leader of the International Brotherhood of Teamsters. Using his union's industrial muscle, and with some extra sinew supplied by organized crime, Jimmy Hoffa took on the bosses and built up one of the most powerful labour organizations in the country.

Hoffa's success in negotiating better deals made him enormously popular with his members. 'You got a problem,' he would tell them, 'Call me. Just pick up the phone.' But those who wield such power in America are readily corrupted – and as readily make deadly enemies. The government suspected Hoffa was using his position to nuzzle his snout into the trough, and eventually – in 1964 – succeeded in putting him away on a number of charges. After his release in 1971 it was Hoffa's link with the Mafia that was to be his undoing. When one day in 1975 he failed to return from a meeting with a known mobster, it was widely assumed he was on some construction site, mixed in with the concrete.

RAZOR STROPS AND CASTOR OIL

For months the doctor had been adamant that the swelling in Ola Hoffa's belly was a tumour. So it was a relief when, on St Valentine's Day 1913, out popped little Jimmy. He was the third of four children. Hoffa's father, John Cleveland Hoffa, worked as an itinerant coal driller, and was often away. Hoffa remembered him fondly. 'When he was home,' he said, 'it was like the Fourth of July every day.' He died when Jimmy was only seven.

With the main breadwinner gone, the family was forced to depend on Ola's work as a laundress. Jimmy's two sisters were put to work ironing, while Jimmy and his brother did the deliveries. The boys also provided some extras for the table, shooting rabbits and stealing fruit. Jimmy was devoted to his mother, recalling her firm belief that 'Duty and Discipline were spelled with capital Ds'. Her favoured method of keeping the boys in order involved a razor strop and a dose of castor oil.

By 1924 the family had moved from small-town Indiana to Detroit, then the booming centre of the US automobile industry. Ola ended up on a production line polishing radiator caps. Jimmy neglected his schoolbooks in favour of bagging groceries, cleaning basements and loading trucks – and using his fists to keep a step ahead of the game.

FLEXING MUSCLES

At the age of 14 Hoffa dropped out of school and took a job in the stockroom of a department store, earning $12 for a 60-hour week. Then Wall Street crashed. The store laid off staff, and those who remained had to work twice as hard. Hoffa's dreams of making his way up into management were blown away. He decided to try his luck elsewhere.

A friend advised him that the only secure jobs were in the food business. Everybody has to eat, he said. So, lying about his age, Hoffa – small in stature but built like a gorilla – took a job unloading railroad cars for the Kroger Grocery and Baking Company. The pay was 32 cents an hour, and the shifts lasted from 4.30 in the afternoon until 4.30 the next morning. But the men were only paid for those hours when there was unloading to do. There was no union representation, and the foreman, 'a real sadist … a little tin Jesus' according to Hoffa, could hire and fire men whenever the fancy took him.

I don't read books. I read union contracts.

JIMMY HOFFA

Covertly, Hoffa began to organize. In 1931, after two fellow workers had been dismissed for taking a meal break, he chose his moment. Just as a batch of fresh strawberries arrived by rail from Florida, Hoffa called the men out. Rather than waste this valuable, perishable produce, the management agreed to negotiate. Hoffa won a 40 per cent rise in the hourly rate, a guarantee of at least half a shift's worth of pay per day, and union recognition. He also won recognition from the AFL – the American Federation of Labor.

FIGHTING FIRE WITH FIRE

On the strength of his success, Hoffa landed a job as a full-time organizer with the Detroit branch of the International Brotherhood of Teamsters, a union whose membership had been in decline. Hoffa received no salary. The only remuneration was a small percentage of the dues paid by any new members he could recruit. It was a rough world: in those days unions were faced with bosses such as Henry Ford who thought nothing of employing thousands of violent strikebreakers, and were not above having their toughs beat up any union man brave enough to turn up with a sheaf of application forms.

Hoffa was brave enough, and took some beatings. He absorbed the union he'd formed at Krogers into the Teamsters, and brought in hundreds of dockworkers and truck drivers. He had a winning sales pitch: one recruit recalled that he had an answer for everything – 'and he never let up'. Hoffa, seeing that the police 'would beat your brains out for even talking union', came to a hard conclusion. 'There was only one way to survive,' he maintained. 'Fight back.'

Violence became the norm – not just against strikebreakers, but also against officials of rival unions. As time went on, Hoffa and his fellow Teamsters seemed to some more like gangsters running a protection racket. In 1946 Hoffa was investigated on suspicion of extortion. He had been demanding that a number of small grocers buy permits from his union in order to be allowed to operate their own trucks.

He stood right close up to you. His face was, well, open. He was the sincerest little guy I've ever seen. He gave me confidence. Up to then I'd been scared to join a union but Jimmy made me feel that it was just the right thing to do.

WILLIAM CROW, ONE OF HOFFA'S EARLIEST RECRUITS, QUOTED IN ARTHUR A. SLOANE, *HOFFA* (1991)

TOUGH AT THE TOP

Hoffa was not the kind of man who would let anyone stand in his way, and by 1957, having faced out more than one Congressional inquiry, he had tussled himself to the top of the Teamsters, after his predecessor had been jailed for bribery. One of Hoffa's first actions was to reject the ethics code drawn up by the AFL-CIO (as it now was). The federation promptly expelled Hoffa and his union.

Hoffa worked tirelessly for his members, and in 1964 negotiated a nationwide contract that covered virtually all truck drivers. He also set about recruiting airline, railroad and other transport

You will only get what you are big enough to take. JIMMY HOFFA

workers, which set alarm bells ringing in government and big business. They were worried that the union was amassing the power to hold them to ransom. Rumours circulated that Hoffa was creaming off union funds in cahoots with organized crime, who were known to control a number of other unions. As the allegations piled up, the Department of Justice, under Attorney General Robert F. Kennedy, began to investigate. The AFL-CIO, supporters of the Democrat administration and no friends of Hoffa, cooperated.

Eventually, in 1967, Hoffa was convicted of jury-tampering, embezzlement and mail fraud. He was sent down for 13 years. But he had friends – or would-be friends – in high places. In 1971 his sentence was commuted by President Richard Nixon, who hoped that the Teamsters would back the Republican candidate – himself – in the 1972 presidential election. On 23 December 1971 Hoffa walked out of the federal penitentiary at Lewisburg, Pennsylvania, a free man.

IF YOU DINE WITH THE DEVIL ...

Hoffa had held on to the presidency of the Teamsters all the time he was in jail. But Nixon had stipulated, as a condition of his release, that he had to keep away from union activity until the time when his full 13-year sentence would have expired, in March 1980. Hoffa fought the restriction through the courts, and behind the scenes set to work to re-establish his position in the union. Not everyone was happy to see him back in the ring.

Among those who would have preferred it if Hoffa had kept himself to himself was Anthony Provenzano ('Tony Pro'), union vice-president and boss of Teamsters Local 560 in Union City, New Jersey. Provenzano was also the capo of the Genovese crime family, one of five that made up the New York Cosa Nostra. In 1961 he had had Anthony Castellito, Local 560's secretary-treasurer, murdered. It was said that Castellito's body had been disposed of in a tree-shredder.

Hoffa had given Provenzano the nod to help himself to union funds – as he had to other mobsters who controlled Teamsters locals. In return, he got their support. Like Hoffa, Provenzano had been caught by the Feds with his hand in the till, and spent time in Lewisburg when Hoffa was incarcerated there. But the two fell out badly, reportedly because Hoffa failed to come up with a Teamsters loan Provenzano wanted in order to open a new restaurant. It was said they had a bare-knuckle fight, in which Hoffa smashed a bottle over Provenzano's head. In return, Provenzano is said to have threatened Hoffa's grandchildren, yelling 'I'll tear your heart out.'

After Provenzano was released from jail, Hoffa bitterly opposed his efforts to seize back control of Local 560. For his part, Provenzano did all he could to stop Hoffa taking back the top job.

It is not clear why Hoffa should have arranged to meet Provenzano and another mobster, Anthony Giacalone ('Tony Jack'), on 30 July 1975 in the parking lot of the Machus Red Fox, a classy restaurant in Bloomfield Township, Michigan, on the outskirts of Detroit. Perhaps he thought they could kiss and make up, maybe agree a division of the spoils. The choice of venue was presumably Hoffa's. He was a regular, and the place had even hosted the wedding reception for Hoffa's son, James P.

At 7 a.m. the following morning Hoffa's wife, Josephine, phoned her son in a panic. Hoffa had been due back after his lunchtime appointment the previous day by 4 p.m. He always let her know where he was, and if he was going to be delayed. But she'd heard nothing. He'd left the house at 1 p.m. the previous day to meet 'somebody', and about 2.30 p.m. had phoned her from the Red Fox parking lot to demand 'Where the hell is Tony Giacalone? I'm being stood up.' About 3.30 p.m. he'd phoned Louis Linteau, a close friend, again to complain that he'd been stood up. At 8 a.m. on the 31st, Linteau called in the local police. They found Hoffa's car in the parking lot, unlocked. They forced open the trunk, but there was no body inside. Witnesses remembered seeing two men stop by to chat with Hoffa and shake his hand. But no one seemed to know anything else.

COLD TRAILS AND RED HERRINGS

Provenzano and Giacalone denied having met Hoffa at the Machus Red Fox. Both had watertight alibis. 'Jimmy was, or is, my friend,' Tony Pro told reporters, 'I don't know where Jimmy went.' He then castigated the pressmen who'd taken up position in front of his luxury house in Florida: 'You're embarrassing me in front of everyone in the neighbourhood. You guys out on the lawn make me look like a mobster. I'm not. I'm just a truck driver.'

The FBI, who were called in on 3 August, didn't manage any better than the local police or the newsmen. They couldn't get anything to stick on Provenzano, Giacalone or any of their numerous associates – but not for want of persistence over very many years. Although everybody had a pretty good idea that he'd been murdered, it took until 1982 for Hoffa to be legally 'presumed dead'. And it took till 2001 for the FBI, using new DNA forensics, to match a hair taken from Hoffa's brush with a strand found in the car of his Teamster friend and associate Charles O'Brien. O'Brien flatly denied Hoffa had been in his car, and no indictments followed.

Two years later police dug up a backyard in Hampton Township, Michigan, on a tip-off that a briefcase containing a syringe used to sedate Hoffa would be found there. It wasn't. In 2004 Charles Brandt, a former deputy attorney general of Delaware, published a book recounting how Frank Sheeran, another of Hoffa's Teamster associates, had unburdened himself to the author before his death in 2003. Sheeran said he had been ordered by Pennsylvania mob boss Russell 'The Old Man' Bufalino to lure Hoffa to a house in northwestern Detroit. There Sheeran had shot him twice, and left. Brandt said the body had then been cremated. In 2006 two more self-confessed Mafia hitmen crawled out of the woodwork to claim responsibility, but doubts have been cast on these confessions. In May of that year the FBI, acting on another tip-off, mounted a major excavation at Hidden Dreams Farm, Milford Township, Michigan, hoping to find Hoffa's remains. They even removed a whole barn so they could take a look underneath. They found nothing.

The law caught up with Tony Provenzano in 1978, when he was convicted of the murder of Anthony Castellito 17 years before. Provenzano died of a heart attack on 12 December 1988, aged 71.

Business at the Machus Red Fox Restaurant flourished for a while after the events of 30 July 1975, diners coming in droves out of ghoulish curiosity. They liked to ask the manager if he'd seen Hoffa recently. 'No,' he used to tell them, 'but I wouldn't eat the Hoffa burger.'

The Watergate Connection

A year after Hoffa's disappearance Tony Provenzano was photographed playing golf with Richard Nixon, by then a disgraced ex-president. In 1977 *Time* magazine reported that sources in the Department of Justice and the FBI believed that Provenzano, together with Hoffa's successor as Teamsters president, Frank Fitzsimmons, had raised $1 million in cash for Nixon in return for banning Hoffa from union activities. *Time* also reported that it was this money that Nixon had proposed to use to satisfy the demands of the Watergate burglars for hush money. 'What I mean is you could get a million dollars,' he told White House Counsel John Dean on 21 March 1973, 'and you could get it in cash. I know where it could be gotten ... We could get the money. There is no problem in that.'

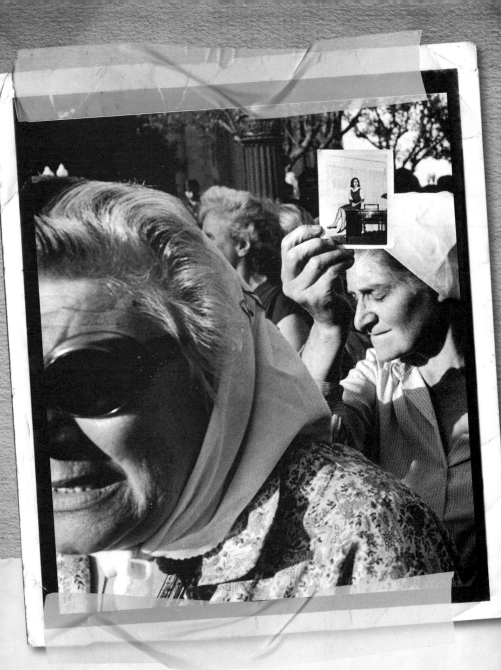

Los Desaparecidos

THE VICTIMS OF
ARGENTINA'S DIRTY WAR
(1976–83)

'They are neither dead nor alive. They disappeared.' These infamous words were spoken at a press conference by General Jorge Videla, a leading member of the military junta that held power in Argentina from 1976 to 1983. He was referring to the fate of tens of thousands of leftwing activists and other political dissidents whom representatives of the regime had kidnapped, drugged and then dropped out of aircraft – still alive – into the sea. With no bodies, the junta felt able to deny that the dissidents had been killed.

In hundreds of cases, the women seized by the regime were pregnant. They were allowed to give birth in captivity, before they were tortured and taken to what the military euphemistically called 'the final destination'. The babies were then given out for adoption to military families, the authorities arguing that 'subversive parents will raise subversive children'.

THE BEGINNINGS OF THE DIRTY WAR

The old populist demagogue, Juan Perón, had died in July 1974, and was succeeded as president of Argentina by his third wife, Isabel. Under her authoritarian but inept rule Argentina declined into violence, both from Marxist guerrillas and from right-wing 'death squads'. The former mounted attacks on military bases and police stations, while the latter were responsible for hundreds of assassinations of trade unionists and others. Isabel Perón targeted the left, authorizing the military and the police to 'annihilate' the subversives, but it seems these extraordinary powers were not sufficient to satisfy the generals. On 24 March 1976 General Videla – who had been appointed commander-in-chief the previous year – seized power, establishing a military junta consisting of himself (representing the army), Admiral Emilio Massera (for the navy) and General Orlando Agosti (for the air force), together with six other officers. Two days later Videla assumed the presidency. Isabel Perón was put under house arrest before being exiled to Spain.

As many people as necessary must die in Argentina so that the country will again be secure. GENERAL JORGE VIDELA, IN 1975, SUPPORTING THE ACTIVITIES OF THE RIGHT-WING DEATH SQUADS

Under the so-called National Reorganization Process, the normal institutions of democracy were dismantled: the junta assumed complete legislative powers, the government was packed with military officers, the judiciary abolished, labour unions banned and civil liberties suspended. Human rights abuses became commonplace, with trade unionists, students and other activists being the main victims. The generals embarked on what they themselves called the 'Dirty War'.

SYSTEMATIC REPRESSION

The military government set about its task systematically, deploying counter-insurgency techniques acquired from American and French instructors. At the same time, the guerrillas stepped up their campaign of violence, making several attempts on the life of General Videla himself. In 1976 one of the generals stated:

We are going to have to kill 50,000 people: 25,000 subversives, 20,000 sympathizers, and we will make 5000 mistakes.

As it turned out, the tens of thousands of men and women who were 'disappeared' between 1976 and 1983 included Cuban diplomats, French nuns, and a even a group of young students who had demanded free bus passes.

In secret detention centres such as the Naval Mechanics School, those who had been rounded up were subjected to horrific tortures, sometimes attended by physicians and psychiatrists acting for the junta. In one case at least, a priest betrayed the confidences of the detainees he was meant to be comforting: when Father Christian Federico von Wernich was put on trial in 2007 for crimes against humanity, the prosecution accused him of complicity in seven murders, 42 kidnappings and 31 cases of torture. He was convicted, and sentenced to life imprisonment.

Torture was only a prelude to 'the final destination', the *vuelos de la muerte* – the death flights. In 1996 a former Argentinian naval officer called Adolfo Scilingo described how victims were obliged to 'dance for joy, because they were going to be transferred to the south'. They were told they needed a vaccination, but were in fact injected with a powerful sedative, before being stripped, loaded onto trucks and taken to an airfield. There they were put aboard a plane or helicopter. Once over the Río de la Plata, or the open Atlantic, the doors were opened and the comatose victim, weighed down by a block of cement, was dispatched to oblivion. In 2005 Scilingo, then resident in Spain, was convicted by a Spanish court of crimes against humanity.

Not all of those who disappeared were taken to 'the final destination'. Those who died under torture, for example, were simply incinerated, until there was nothing left of them but dust.

THE SEARCH FOR TRUTH AND JUSTICE

On 30 April 1977 the mothers and grandmothers of some of the missing assembled in the Plaza de Mayo in the centre of Buenos Aires, in front of the presidential palace, demanding information on the fate of their loved ones. Three of the original 14 women who gathered in the Plaza de Mayo were themselves 'disappeared', and their remains subsequently found. Undeterred, the 'Mothers of the Plaza de Mayo', as they became known around the world, grew into a highly visible pressure group, holding regular vigils in the square. Even after the fall of the junta in 1983, following the disastrous Falklands War, the vigils continued, demanding truth and justice.

In December 1983 the newly elected democratic government of Argentina set up the National Commission on the Disappearance of Persons. This compiled detailed records of the 'disappearance' of some 9000 people, although it is now thought that a total of 30,000 were clandestinely murdered. In his preface to the commission's report, Ernesto Sábato wrote:

From the moment of their abduction, the victims lost all rights. Deprived of all communication with the outside world, held in unknown places, subjected to barbaric tortures, kept ignorant of their immediate or ultimate fate, they risked being either thrown into a river or the sea, weighted down with blocks of cement, or burned to ashes. They were not mere objects, however, and still possessed all the human attributes: they could feel pain, could remember a mother, child or spouse, could feel infinite shame at being raped in public.

A number of generals, including Videla, were put on trial, convicted of human rights abuses, and sentenced to long prison terms. However, in 1990 President Carlos Menem pardoned Videla and others, although in effect the general was thereafter confined to his home, such was the hatred of the public. On one occasion someone painted giant arrows on the street pointing towards his house, accompanied by the slogan: '30,000 disappeared – assassin on the loose'. In 2004 the government turned the Naval Mechanics School into a 'museum of memory', and the following year the

Argentine congress declared that the amnesty announced in 1990 was void. The trials of those believed responsible for kidnapping, torture and murder under the junta recommenced. However, progress has been slow, with only a handful of nearly 900 suspects having so far been convicted.

THE LOST CHILDREN

In 1998 General Videla was sent back to prison for involvement in the kidnapping of the children of some of the disappeared, who were then handed out to military families to raise. Now, a quarter of a century or more since the Dirty War, scores of young people are finding out that they are not who they thought they were. One young man has said that he felt 'like a cat raised in a family of dogs', and puzzled why he was even at the age of 14 taller than his 'father'. Then he discovered that as a baby he had been taken from his mother and handed over to a general's maid.

In all, some 500 children are believed to have been born in detention to mothers who were then killed. The Mothers and Grandmothers of the Plaza de Mayo, with the aid of new DNA techniques, have helped nearly a hundred of them to find out who their real parents were. It can be a traumatic experience. When a judge investigating a case informed one young woman of the truth, she found it difficult to come to terms with: 'A person is twenty years old, and for twenty years she was called something else. Her uncles are not her uncles. Her grandparents are not her grandparents. And they are all people she doesn't know. It's very hard.'

One young man has severed relations entirely with his adoptive mother, even though he describes her as a good and lovable person: 'I can't understand a lie that lasted for 25 years,' he says. This young man likes to go off to the mountains, where he stares up at the sky in an effort to find himself. His aunt has told him that his real mother, before being taken on her last, fateful journey, also loved the mountains, and, like her son, would spend hours looking up at the sky – thinking who knows what thoughts about the joys and terrors the future might bring.

I kissed and hugged his bones. I was filled with happiness and horror.

BERTA SCHUBAROFF, DESCRIBING HER FEELINGS ON DISCOVERING THE GRAVE OF HER SON, ONE OF THE DISAPPEARED

INDEX

INDEX

ILLUSTRATIONS

Author's Acknowledgements

In writing this book I have drawn upon a wide range of sources. In particular I would like to acknowledge the following books and authors:

Max Arthur (ed.), *Forgotten Voices of the Great War* (2002)
Sabine Baring-Gould, *Historical Oddities* (1889)
Francis Beckett, *Stalin's British Victims* (2004)
John Bierman, *Righteous Gentile: The story of Raoul Wallenberg, missing hero of the Holocaust* (1981)
Marcus Binney, *The Women Who Lived for Danger: The women agents of SOE in the Second World War* (2002)
Estela Bravo (director), *Who Am I?* (documentary film, 2008)
Randall Brink, *Lost Star: The Search for Amelia Earhart* (1994)
Geoffrey Butcher, *Next to a Letter from Home: Major Glenn Miller's Wartime Band* (1986)
Curtis Cate, *Antoine de Saint-Exupéry, His Life and Times* (1970)
Anthony Cheetham, *The Life and Times of Richard III* (1972)
Norman Cohn, *The Pursuit of the Millennium: Revolutionary Millenarians and Mystical Anarchists of the Middle Ages* (1970)
Mike Dash, 'The Disappearance of Benjamin Bathurst', *Fortean Times* (summer 1990)
Renee Erdos, 'Leichhardt, Friedrich Wilhelm Ludwig (1813–1848)', *Australian Dictionary of Biography*, online edition
Fergus Fleming, *Barrow's Boys* (1998)
M.R.D. Foot, *SOE: The Special Operations Executive 1940–1946* (1999)
Gillian Gill, *Agatha Christie: The woman and her mysteries* (1990)
Midge Gillies, *Amy Johnson, Queen of the Air* (2003)
Peter and Leni Gillman, *The Wildest Dream: George Mallory* (2000)
I.R. Hancock, 'Holt, Harold', *Australian Dictionary of Biography*, online edition
Ragnhild Hatton, *George I: Elector and King* (1978)
Roslynn D. Haynes, *Seeking the Centre: The Australian Desert in Literature, Art and Film* (1998)
Mary S. Lovell, *The Sound of Wings: The Biography of Amelia Earhart* (1989)
David Marples, *Motherland: Russia in the Twentieth Century* (2002)
Colin Matthew (ed.), *Oxford Dictionary of National Biography* (2004), online edition
Janet Morgan, *Agatha Christie: A Biography* (1984)
Roy Morris, Jr., *Ambrose Bierce: Alone in Bad Company* (1995)
J.H. Plumb, *The First Four Georges* (1956)
Stephen Pope, *The Cassell Dictionary of the Napoleonic Wars* (1999)
Roy Porter (ed.), *The Hutchinson Dictionary of Scientific Biography* (2nd ed., 1994)
Richard Rumbold and Lady Margaret Stewart, *The Winged Life: A Portrait of Antoine de Saint-Exupéry, Poet and Airman* (1953)
Steven Runciman, *A History of the Crusades* (1951), Vol. III
R.A. Skelton, 'Cabot, John', *Dictionary of Canadian Biography Online* (2000)
Arthur A. Sloane, *Hoffa* (1991)
Howard Somervell, *After Everest* (1936)
Elizabeth-Anne Wheal and Stephen Pope, *The Macmillan Dictionary of the Second World War* (2nd ed., 1995)

In addition, I would like to thank the following: Richard Milbank, my publisher at Quercus, for suggesting this book to me, and for his enduring support; Emma Heyworth-Dunn, managing editor at Quercus, for seeing the book through to press with quiet efficiency; Maria Gopaul of Hornsey Library, for her ever cheerful readiness to ransack the darker corners of the reserve collection on my behalf; and Victoria Huxley and Geoffrey Smith of Windrush Publishing Services for editing and typesetting the book with consummate professionalism.

Picture Credits

The publishers would like to thank the following for permission to reproduce illustrations:
akg-images p.12, akg-images/Erich Lessing p.26, akg-images/ullstein bild p. 102; Auckland City Libraries p.54; Bibliothèque Nationale, France p.129; Bibliothèque Nationale/ The Bridgeman Picture Library p.23; © British Library Board. All rights reserved Sloane 1622 f. 70 p.36; Charles Tait Photographic p.75; Corbis pp 20,32,82,105,137,159,163,168; Getty Images pp 8,16, 49,71,87,148,152; Mary Evans Picture Library pp 42,46,68,79,98,118,142; National Archives of Australia: A1200,L44772 p. 62; National Archives UK (HS9/836/5) 123; National Library of Australia 156; People's History Museum p.112; © Royal Geographical Society p. 91.

Quercus Publishing Plc
21 Bloomsbury Square
London
WC1A 2NS

First published in 2008

Copyright © Ian Crofton 2008

The moral right of Ian Crofton to be identified as the author of this work has been asserted in accordance with the Copyright, Design and Patents Act, 1988.

A catalogue record of this book is available from the British Library

Printed case edition: ISBN 13: 978 1 84724 271 6

Paperback edition: ISBN 13: 978 1 84724 702 5

Printed and bound in China